THE BEST OF PARKINSON

THE BEST OF
PARKINSON

PAVILION
MICHAEL JOSEPH

First published in Great Britain in 1982
by Pavilion Books Limited
196 Shaftesbury Avenue, London WC2H 8JL
in association with Michael Joseph Limited
44 Bedford Square, London WC1B 3DU

The publishers acknowledge with thanks the co-operation
of the BBC and all those whose conversations
appear in this book.

Royalties from the sale of this book are donated to
the Police Dependants' Trust.

Designed by Lawrence Edwards
Photography by Godfrey Argent
  BBC Publicity, David Edwards and Sten Rosenlund
Editorial Consultant: Eve Lucas

Parkinson, Michael *1935–*
    The best of Parkinson.
    1. Parkinson (Television program)
    I. Title
    791.45'72   PN1992.8.P4

    ISBN 0-907516-14-9

Photoset by Rowland Phototypesetting Limited
Bury St. Edmunds, Suffolk
Printed by Hollen Street Press Limited, Slough, Berkshire
and bound by Butler & Tanner Limited, Frome, Somerset

CONTENTS

ODE TO PARKY

*by Sir Les Patterson, Australian Cultural Attaché
to the Court of St James*

There's a bloke who's keenly watched and widely read
Who always hits the nail on the head
He kicked off modestly in the UK
And he's a world celebrity today.

If he gets nervous well, it's never showed
His face is like a mile of rugged road,
His crows feet are the dried-up beds of smiles
And his best friends are aware that he's got piles
– Of charm, pazazz and British spunk and phlegm.
Of TV interviewers he's the gem.
He could interview a Zulu or Iraqi and make it interesting
His name is Parky.

This bloke can conjure laughter and applause
In the wake of Ratbags, Poofs and Crashing Bores.
And if he's pushed for spicey dialogue
He'll ask you if you've ever nudged the grog.

Australian critics are all chippy guys
They tried to chop old Parky down to size.
Some even said: 'Go back where you come from
– We won't be taught charisma by a Pom.'
But he knows the average Aussie journalist
Is following orders, jealous or half pissed!

He smiles, he does his job, he doesn't care
When you're the top where do you go from there?
So raise your glass of lager, rum or saki
Whether you be Hun or Nip or Darkie
And drink the health of my old cobber – PARKY!

(SIR LES PATTERSON IS A DIVISION OF THE BARRY HUMPHRIES GROUP)

INTRODUCTION

I was thirteen years old when I did my very first interview. His name was Norman Bone and he made glass decorations for Christmas trees. In a community such as I grew up in where everyone worked at the local pit, I deemed Mr Bone exotic enough to warrant an article in my school magazine. It was entitled 'My Visit to a Glass Factory' and in it Mr Bone spoke of the artistic and financial merits of designing glass baubles. I was on my way. Or so I thought.

Intoxicated by seeing my name in print I planned that my next interview would be with someone very famous. In my world that could only mean someone who played for Barnsley Football Club. In those days, footballers were accessible from the point of view that they weren't isolated from the rest of us because of wealth. They lived on the same council estates as their fans, drank in the same pubs, played in the same billiards halls. They had their respected place in the community (and were respected so long as Barnsley did well), but they were not out of reach of the rest of us.

Thus it took only a little nerve on my part to approach one of the players about my planned interview. I was coming home from school and he sat on the same bus. The unspoken law in such a situation was that no one sat next to him unless the bus was so full that you were forced to occupy the adjacent seat. This was one of the perks of being a famous footballer.

On this occasion, the bus was only half full so my victim was assured of a private journey until, having convinced myself that Humphrey Bogart – then my favourite journalist and the model for my future career – would not funk such an opportunity, I daringly moved into the seat next to him. He looked at me in surprise. 'Excuse me,' I blurted out, 'but could I interview you?' 'No', he said, quite affably. It was my first encounter with the interviewer's nightmare, the unco-operative victim.

Then, as now, I sat there frozen with terror. The difference is that nowadays, bearing the scars of many similar encounters, I have learned the trick of talking to brick walls. Thirty-five years ago on that bus in Barnsley I wondered if that nice Mr Bone might give me a job blowing Christmas decorations or if I might even go down the pit like most of my mates planned.

The footballer read my thoughts. 'Tha' doesn't want to be a reporter, lad, prying into people's affairs. Get thissen down t'pit and watch Barnsley every Saturday,' he said. He went back to reading his paper and I sat beside him in utter and abject misery not daring to move back to my seat because I would have to face the disapproval of my fellow passengers for breaking the rules about the footballer's privacy. He got off before I did and as he left he said, 'Now think on lad. Get thissen a decent job.'

I told my father about it when I got home. It must be explained that my old man had only two ambitions in life. One was that I should never follow him down the mine and the other that I should play cricket for Yorkshire. One I achieved for him easily, the other I failed handsomely. On this occasion he was horrified that anyone should undermine his authority by suggesting that I work at the pit. Typically he soothed my disappointment and dispelled my doubts with his ability to pinpoint the absurdity of the situation. 'Why take any notice of him,' he said. 'He can't even play football.'

Much later, much, much later, just before he died and I was making a name for myself doing what the famous footballer had advised me not to do, he used the same technique to make sure I wasn't getting too big for my boots. 'You've done well, son, and I'm proud of you,' he said 'but you've got to admit it's not like playing for Yorkshire, is it?'

So that was how it started. I bought myself a bike, a drop-handled Raleigh with a Sturmey Archer three-speed, a pair of metal bike clips, and a trench coat like Bogey wore in all his pictures. I was sixteen years old, working for a local newspaper and cycling twenty-five miles a day around a cluster of pit villages interviewing anyone who would stand still for two minutes.

The gap between the glamorous Hollywood image of a newspaperman's life and my own could hardly have been greater and might well have defeated a more sensitive soul. I was oblivious to the discomforts of the job. Indeed, the more I cycled about my area, chronicling the births and deaths of the community, reporting the functions at the local chapels, detailing the doings of the Mothers' Union, the more I became convinced that I *was* Humphrey Bogart.

In homage to my hero, I topped my uniform of trench coat and bicycle clips with a pearl grey, snap brim fedora and further adorned it with a label in the hat band marked 'Press'. I solved the inevitable problem of cycling into a wind while wearing such headgear by making a chinstrap out of knicker elastic, a measure which appeared incongruous but was, in fact, generally speaking, a practical solution.

The only drawback occurred when speeding downhill into a fierce wind whereupon I was in danger of being lifted from my seat as the hat billowed backwards, the elastic threatening to yank my head from my shoulders. On such occasions, Bogey's fedora must have looked like the arresting parachute on a space shuttle.

Thus attired, from sixteen to nineteen, acned, brilliantined, tireless in limb and imagination, I belted through my pit villages embracing everyone with my foolish ambition. I bought a typewriter, a battered portable Corona, and every evening would translate the contents of my bulging notebook onto copy paper.

When I had finished I would sometimes read out aloud my efforts to my parents. My mother, an avid reader and a woman of great natural style, would nod approvingly at some particularly fine phrase. My father, who liked the court reports best, would supplement the telling of the misadventures of some well-known, ne'er-do-well with his own assessment which would be either: 'Not surprised about him. Never could play cricket.' Or, 'Fancy that, I mean he's a good opening bat, that fella.'

The next day I'd present my work to the senior journalist whose job it was to supervise my work. His name was Stan Bristow and I could not have had a finer teacher. He was a proper journalist, methodical, meticulous and, above all, patient with the vagaries of my prose style which varied according to the particular author I was reading at the time. Some weeks I would present him with, say, a report of a wedding written in the style of Hemingway: 'It was a good wedding. You could say that about it. It was a very good wedding.' On other occasions he would have to point out that a review of a local drama group's production of *An Inspector Calls* in the style of Dorothy Parker might be unacceptable in the columns of the *Yorkshire*

Times. Thus: '*An Inspector Calls* is a production which begs the question, why did he bother? Come to that, why did we?' which seemed to me all that needed to be said and sufficiently witty to get me an immediate invite to the Algonquin Round Table, was gently blue pencilled and replaced with a proper review.

About this time I thought I would specialise in showbiz interviews, which, given the area I worked in, would make me the most underemployed journalist in the world. No matter, instead of interviewing Bob Hope, Bing Crosby, Fred Astaire, Gene Kelly, and all that lot who, as far as we know, had no plans to visit Barnsley, I decided to make stars of the more exotic club acts.

My first victims were a couple called Denis and Sylvana, or some such. He was a dark, slim man who wore make-up all the time, she was blonde, prettily plump but perpetually sad. Together they belted out the popular songs of the day to audiences whose attitude to an entertainer was: 'I won't bother you if you don't bother me.' I don't know what attracted me to them but I do remember that at the time I believed they were the most glamorous, fascinating people I had ever met.

Not only did I gave them a rave write-up on their début before two hundred drunks at a local Working Men's Club, but I invited them home for Sunday lunch. Denis's make-up was a definite obstacle to free flowing conversation, particularly with my father, who although not a censorious being, had never been confronted by a man wearing mascara and rouge with his mouth full of Yorkshire Pudding.

Sylvana said nothing at all. She just sat and ate with mournful concentration. The next and last time I saw them I was in the Army with my head shaved like a toilet brush. They came to entertain at the camp where I did my basic training. It seemed to me that Denis was wearing more make-up and that Sylvana was by now a terminal melancholic.

I waited backstage for them. In this case the stage door was the back exit from the canteen where they had been performing. I took my cap off to give them a better chance of recognising me. In any case the army haircut was worth a laugh. He came out first alongside a man with orange hair and lacquered nails. They flounced past me. Farewell Denis and goodbye. She came out a few minutes later, looking beautifully morose. I stepped towards her and without looking at me she pushed a card into my hand. 'Thank you' she said as she went past and towards the waiting car. I looked at her gift. It was a signed photograph of the two of them. It was glossy and flash. She looked happy, he looked normal – well almost. I gave up the world of showbiz that very night.

I re-entered it twelve years ago and a long way from that cluster of pit villages in both distance and time when the BBC invited me to try out a few talk shows to see what the response might be. It seemed all right. It lasted nearly four hundred shows and the one thousand strong guest list reads like an A–Z of the world's most famous men and women. Denis and Sylvana never made it. But a few others did and this book is a memory of some of them.

A talk show is an unnatural act between consenting adults in public. The interview is 'unnatural' because the interviewee is expected to have an intimate chat with the host while surrounded by a million pounds worth of technology, with a microphone pointing at every orifice, watched by five hundred people in the studio and untold millions at home. And yet, surprisingly, it sometimes works. In that setting I have seen Bronowski, Arlott, Muggeridge, Miller, Welles, Ustinov and a few less well-known people bind an audience in a web of words and ideas, to the point where every single person believed that the conversation was directed at them alone.

I have always believed that the ideal talk show is like a successful dinner party where the viewer pulls up a chair and looks over my right shoulder at someone they've always wanted to meet. And the interviewer, as the perfect host at a dinner party, has but one task – to bring out the best in his guests and not treat them like a captive audience for a display of his own wit and opinions.

The fascination of this exercise is that no matter how carefully you choose the guests, no matter how zealous your research and preparation, there is no guarantee that the evening will be a success. Sometimes it's a simple matter of a group of people just not liking each other, on other occasions drink and other mind-numbing substances have had a definite effect on the proceedings.

On the other hand, there have been times, many, many times, when I felt it a privilege to be sitting next to someone who had made a significant contribution to his chosen field. The real joy was that the experience could cover everything from talking to James Cagney about making gangster films to hearing Bronowski's philosophy of life, from discovering what makes people laugh with some of the world's greatest comedians to debating the meaning of power with Dr Kissinger. And the greatest joy of all was listening a lot and learning much from people who had lived a full life and had reached a conclusion about its mystery.

To sit, for example, in the presence of Dame Edith Evans was to be enriched by the energy, intelligence and humour of one unique soul. She taught me more about the proper conduct of the public figure than anyone. She would arrive at the show resplendent in fur coat, new dress by Norman Hartnell and a large Rolls Royce. Immediately she would button-hole anyone within reach and complain about the parlous state of the old age pensioner.

The third occasion this happened I felt confident enough to challenge her. I said that her argument would carry a lot more force were she not so obviously glamorous and successful. I should have known better. 'What do you mean?' she asked in that regal voice. 'Well,' I said, 'you can't really stand as an advocate for old age pensioners when you arrive in a fur coat and a new frock by Mr Hartnell.' She looked at me with chilling disdain. I should have read the warning signs but I pressed on. 'What is more,' I said,' 'you can't complain about the pension when you drive up in a Rolls.' 'My dear boy,' she retorted, 'would you suggest that I arrive in a Mini?' Of course not. She was a star and she knew that the public wanted her to fulfil their expectations of style and glamour. She remained a star to her dying day because she understood her obligation. When she was very ill, her friend and biographer, Bryan Forbes, prepared his young daughter for the inevitable bad news. The child said: 'But she won't die will she? She's not the type.'

The same can be said of some of the people who are quoted in the following pages. The author's royalties are for charity because what follows is the result of a collaboration over the past eleven years between successive production teams led by first Richard Drewett and then John Fisher. I only hope that they enjoyed the experience as much as I did.

Michael Parkinson.

Sydney, 1982

BETTE MIDLER

Well, you have singers and you have Turkish baths, right? So you have to put them together. But this was a very special Turkish bath. This wasn't just your every-day run-of-the-mill Turkish bath.

This was before there was a big gay thing in the States. They were all hiding their light in the club, as it were, and I was, you know, destitute. I didn't have any money. I had quit this show that I was doing and I was trying very hard to build my act and to learn all the things that you're supposed to learn as a performer. My teacher called me up and said: 'I have a man, who has a gay health club and he has an idea, and his idea is to put entertainment in this club and make it something more than a health club, make it a night club proposition too,' and so I said, 'Oh, yes. I'll take the job,' because I didn't care at that point that it wasn't the cogent, noble work that I am offering these days. I tried everything. I wore everything I owned. I remember taking the pillow-cases off my sofa and wrapping them around my head. I stole music from people. I stole arrangements. I stole clothes, I mean, literally. I would go into an old friend's house and look in their piano and see if they had anything that I could use. That's the kind of act that it was, but fortunately it was presented with enough *élan*, enough spirit and enough good nature that it went over. Besides it was so bizarre to have this buxom blonde woman trying so hard to please these men, who were totally naked. Well, they were naked but they all, out of the generosity of their feelings for me, wore a little towel, out of deference . . .

MP: And what did they do, when you were singing.

BM: Well, they listened of course, what did you think they were doing?

MP: I'd no idea.

BM: Oh, occasionally they would, but I wouldn't pay any attention. I felt, well, if it makes them happy . . . isn't it nice that I can inspire such romance and passion in people and all that sort of rot. I never had any clothes, when I was a kid. Mother used to make all my clothes, and my mother was like the greatest seamstress in the world. We were three girls, and she took great pride in dressing us all alike, so, even though you wore out your particular dress, your sister's dress was going to come down to you next year, so you were always wearing the same clothes. Finally, I discovered girlie maga-zines, you know, and, in the front of those magazines they had ads for something called 'Frederick of Hollywood', which I thought were the greatest. Actually, this dress is a sort of a rip-off of one of Freddie's creations. It's the most embarrassing thing I've ever had in my life and really it just makes me feel like such an old chippie to wear it.

MP: You were born in Hawaii?

BM: Yes.

MP: But I mean you're obviously not Hawaiian.

BM: Yes. You're right.

MP: Can you do the hula-hula?

BM: Of course, I can do the hula-hula. Can You?

MP: No.

BM: Well, my girls and I often do a number in the show . . . well, do you want a serious hula or do you want the kind of awful hula?

MP: Whichever way the mood takes you . . . an awful hula-hula, a tacky hula-hula.

BM: Oh, this is a truly tacky hula-hula, but it's so rude to the Hawaiians, who are really the most beautiful people on earth, they are, and they're having a hard time, but, even so, they have a great sense of humour and I am sure they'd . . . oh, well, where am I going? I'll sort of sing the song and the girls can do the hula. We know all kinds of tropical numbers – tropical numbers are my line.

MP: Really?

BM: Oh, yes.

MP: And what else?

BM: Well, I know 'Fiesta in Rio' and 'I had the Clap'. I know that one. Oh, it's terribly tacky. I sang it at the Palladium not too long ago and, of course, it was worth the money that they paid. I'll sing it for you for nothing.

MP: You couldn't do it on American television, could you?

BM: No, oh no. You can hardly do anything on American television.

MP: That's right. I mean, you can't say 'toilet' can you? You have to say 'ladies room' or something or other.

BM: That's right. I don't know. I never tried to use the word 'toilet' on TV.

MP: Extraordinary.

BM: 'Tits' I tried but 'toilet' I didn't.

MP: Did you get away with 'tits'?

BM: No. I said . . . at the time NBC had a programme called 'The Great Event'. I used to say . . . I said, 'Talk about your great event', and that was wrong. 'Talk about your great event', but I don't know, you can't use that kind of language on TV, although Australia, I think, is even more liberal than here. I've seen real naked people running through deserts and streets in Australia. I was really shocked.

MP: I'm sure you were.

BM: I was shocked. I was shocked.

MP: Shocked to the core, were you?

BM: To the core, my dear. I mean, underneath all this drag, I'm really just a librarian, you know.

MP: Talking about other jobs, librarians apart, you once worked, didn't you, when you were in Hawaii, in a pineapple canning factory?

BM: A pineapple cannery, yes.

MP: What did you do?

BM: I was the chief chunker. Are you trying to laugh or trying not to laugh?

MP: I'm just trying to be a serious interviewer. You destroy my act. But what did you do as chief chunker?

BM: Well, I chunked pineapple. You know, they have, like you're chipped and you're chunked, you're sliced and you're chunked and I was the chief chunker.

MP: Was it very boring?

BM: It was extremely boring. I used to come home smelling like a compote.

MP: Did you find any of these jobs rewarding in any sense or did you find them all just very boring?

BM: When I was doing that kind of work, I was very young and I didn't really realise that there were other kinds of jobs besides singing and dancing and showing one's belly button. I'm a lot older now. I have a different perspective on other people. Sometimes I say to myself: what the hell have you been doing for the last twelve years? Sometimes I catch myself in the middle of one of those scandalous, outrageous monologues and I'll say: who is it that lives in here? Who is this that took over my body? Do you ever find that?

MP: No.

BM: Well, you're just peculiar.

MP: No, I'm just very boring.

BM: Don't you ever think of yourself as a small child and wonder how you grew up into this?

MP: If you're making a living as a journalist and an interviewer which is what I do, you don't have that kind of fantasy life. You don't create something.

BM: Oh, I thought you were in showbiz. I didn't know you were a journalist. How dreary. Oh, I thought you were one of those song and dance men like Bruce Forsyth. They play that cheesy intro music for you.

MP: Actually I could get lucky, if I was like Bruce Forsyth, you might lie down in the interview.

BM: You don't have to be Bruce Forsyth for me to do that, dear. It's impossible not to adore the English. I mean, being here is like being on a vast set. It's like being on the set of *Pride and Prejudice* . . . like everyone's an extra in *Pride and Prejudice*.

MP: Do you like English accents?

BM: I adore English accents.

MP: What about English men? Do you like English men?

BM: I like English men. I haven't met that many of them. I adored Alan Bates. I like working with him. He was quite an interesting fellow. Do you remember him in that movie, *Women in Love*?

MP: I do. The nude scene. Do you remember that?

BM: Of course, no I remember the fig sucking scene.

MP: You do?

BM: Yes.

MP: Did he suck the fig?

BM: Yes, he did. Literally changed my life.

BM: I adore the Queen. I love royalty, any kind of royalty. Oh, I was so sick they didn't come to my show, not a single one of them, unless they came in disguise, which I doubt. Oh, I was really mortified that they didn't show. Really, I thought at least I'd meet Chuck.

MP: Chuck?

BM: Charlie, Prince Charles. So, you know, they said a cat could marry a commoner.

MP: That's true.

BM: But no one quite as common as my own self. Oh, I adore him. He is rich. He's not fooling. Oh, I love that whole family. I do. They are so white. They are the white people. Don't they make you feel like the Third World sort of? I just think they are amazing.

1979

BILLY CONNOLLY

I was completely ignorant of the ways of the world when I was wee, especially sex. I used to ask guys in my class – you could only ask them so far – 'How do you do it?' I think, in fact, for some mysterious reason I knew how to do it, although nobody had told me, but it was how you *started* that I wanted to know! From the dancehall to the house and how do you get her from the living-room into the bedroom, or do you just do it in the living room? I knew everything you did but I didn't know what order it came in. I remember there was a park near to where I lived which was where I had my first ever experience of kissing. There was a line of seven of us and I was sitting waiting for my turn with this girl who was just sitting there waiting for us. When it came to my turn I asked the guy in front of me if he could do it again as I hadn't got the hang of it.

Later on in life, I used to read a friend's copy of *Forum* when I stayed there and he would give me a big pile of them when I was going to bed – on my own! It used to make me think I was awful dull. These guys going about in wet suits, firemen's helmets, whipping each other with leather rosaries. I thought I had better start taking my pyjamas off or something. There is no rule book, you see – nobody tells you if you are doing it OK.

I thoroughly enjoyed my teenage years. I always wanted to be a teddy boy, but my parents wouldn't let me get the gear. I was an apprentice in a shipyard at the time and I found an old working jacket which had belonged to someone much bigger than me. It came halfway down my legs, but I didn't care – as long as I could look down and see my jacket it was all right. We used to go dancing a lot, but my trouble was I could never turn corners. I used to pay to go in and ten minutes later I had danced right out onto the street again! I had a pair of winkle-pickers, basketweave with a cuban heel, and I had to pad the front of them with newspaper they were so long. They were black and I used to wear white socks. Eventually the basketweave gave way and you could see my white socks underneath so I used to polish my socks. We used to get paper collars in a packet of six and they were murder to get on. I wasted the other five trying to get one on. I could never afford a tie and

'I was once the
chief chunker in a
pineapple cannery.
I used to
come home smelling
like a compote'
Bette Midler

'The person
I admire for quitting
when he was
at the top is
James Cagney'
Robert Redford

hankie to match so I cut the bottom off my tie and used that. I was quite a fiend for style.

I do get a lot of flak from people in Scotland, but it is my own fault really – I've got such a big mouth. I do get out of line sometimes and shoot my mouth off concerning stuff I don't know very much about. But I like it, and I don't care. I do think that journalists like to knock you down a bit over here, whereas in the States, they like their stars, and they will fight to keep you up there. I have no thoughts of leaving Scotland and it made me very cross when I was reported as having said that I was going to live in America. I am not a Scottish nationalist; I think in this day and age people should be reaching out and touching each other a bit, not splitting away.

When I do a concert, it is always the women that laugh first and most. I think this is due to their position – in a sexual sense. I think they have a different attitude to sex and I'm glad they do, but they are very honest about sex. Whereas the guys are trying to be gentlemen and they are frightened to laugh before the wife does. I have played to a couple of audiences who haven't laughed at all – namely a crowd of drunk Scots in Brisbane. They even booed me on. They displayed all the tenderness of a dinosaur with its haemorrhoids on fire! 'You're rubbish Connolly, get off.' There was one guy that got up on stage and took my guitar off me and started swinging it above his head. He put my guitar out of tune and gave it back to me and then he starts chanting: 'We want our money back' into the microphone, and everybody joined in. I told him that he and I should go into the business together – we could be a pantomime horse; I would be the front, he could be himself.

I set out to be a cross between Lennie Bruce and Robert the Bruce and arrived at where I am, wherever that may be. My heavy thing is the body and its functions and malfunctions – the absurdity of the thing. Like farting, or flatulence as it is called, and how people react to toilets. Like these ones where you all line up to have a pee, and if you're really lucky, you get the VD notice right in front of you so you don't need to look at anyone – you can read that. You're frightened to look round in case somebody is smiling at you. These are things that embarrass everybody – myself included, and you can chase the witch by talking about them. Another thing, racism is something I like talking about, but I very rarely do it because there are greater exponents of it than me. I heard a great racism-in-reverse joke: There were two black doctors in this hospital in Africa and they were walking along a corridor and one said to the other, 'Did you tell that white guy in ward seven that he was going to die?' 'Yes' the other one says. 'You bastard . . . I wanted to tell him.'

I hate jogging and joggers and I hate joggers more than jogging itself. So I invented a 'fitting' for a jogger – it's a wee strap with buckles at both ends with a wee attachment and you put a bit round your willie and you tighten it up – not so as it's uncomfortable though, and you tie the other bit around your leg and then you go jogging . . . What's the use of being fit if you're going blind? So if you ever see a jogger lying against a wall, out of breath, leave him alone, he's having a good time! I'm never going to try and get fit unless I can find an interesting way to do it.

I go fishing – that is my relaxation. I never catch any fish, but that doesn't matter. I love it and I think it's because when I'm fishing I think about fishing only, to the exclusion of absolutely everything. And most comedians are completely paranoid about their careers. For instance, when you read the notices, you can have nineteen beauties and one stinker and you really believe the stinker. So when I'm fishing I think about nothing and my paranoia goes away.

I have this joke about Ivan the Terrible. There is this circus that comes to Glasgow and they had a wrestler as the main attraction, Ivan the Terrible from Russia. He had two famous holds, the half pretzel and the full pretzel; the half pretzel broke your back and the full pretzel killed you. It got to the stage where nobody would fight him anymore. Anyway, the circus arrived in Glasgow and everybody knew it had come because there was elephant shit all over the High Street. The police were putting messages out saying, 'An elephant has shit in the High Street. Drivers are asked to treat it as a roundabout.' One night, the ringmaster comes out, 'Ladies and Gentlemen, all the way from Russia: Ivan the Terrible. I want a volunteer from the audience.' Nothing. 'Five hundred pounds . . .' 'I'll do it', and this guy with a newspaper sticking out of his pocket, four foot nothing, six feet between the eyes, comes down. Then this hairy thing comes out, the ground was shaking and the fight began. The little guy dived at Ivan's mass of hair and disappeared inside. Then this hairy arm came over and the crowd gasped – it was going to be the half pretzel for sure. Then another hairy arm came over and the crowd gasped again – it was going to be the full pretzel. They fell in a hairy ball on the floor and all of a sudden, wham, Ivan flew off, hit the pole in the centre of the tent, slid down unconscious. The place went bananas. The ringmaster got the wee fellow and asked him what his name was . . . 'Shuggy'. 'Well, hello Mr Shuggy. Could you tell the audience how you managed that?' 'Well' he says, 'I was nutting his belly button there and thought I wasn't doing too badly until I saw this arm come over and I thought it was going to be the half pretzel. Then boof, the other arm came over and there I was, lying on the floor waiting for the lights to go out and all of a sudden, right in front of my face, I see this huge willie. There's this willie staring me right in the face, so I knew what to do . . . I sank my teeth right into it. And you know something, it's amazing the surge of strength you get when you bite your own willie!'

1976, 1979 and 1981

MIKE HARDING

I was brought up in a terraced house in Manchester. My mother still denies that we used to run next door for crockery when people came round because all our teacups had gollywogs on. The first time I went to a posh kid's house, I couldn't understand why his eiderdown didn't have pockets and sleeves. The area was a Coronation Street, and my mother still lives in the same house. All my childhood and adolescence was spent in the company of amazing characters. The people that ran the chip shop halfway down the street, Doris and Eddie, would run a bus trip to Blackpool every August Bank Holiday and the whole street would go. At every pub on the road the grownups always decided they wanted to pee, but they were just going in for a drink. I was so full of crisps and lemonade from sitting outside the pubs that the record for throwing up was seven before we got to Blackpool.

I was educated in an all-age school – the kids were from five to fifteen. It was a working-class neighbourhood but there was a great mixture of kids there. You'd go home one night and be sitting there having your tea and your mother would look at your hair, wash your head, pick all the leapers out, and put that dermi stuff all over your head. Then the 'nit nurse' would come round – 'Nitty Nora the Bug Explorer' – and she would look at your hands to see if you'd eaten them and then she would test you for rickets with a brick hammer.

After that I went to a huge school in Manchester and the first time I went there, the big kids said, 'Come here and we'll take you where you can hear the sea', and I said: 'You can't hear the sea in Manchester.' They took me in the toilets, and they said, 'Listen down there, that big white telephone' and they pushed my head down it – all down it, cap gone. Three months ago I was in Blackpool and I saw a seagull wearing my school cap!

I didn't realise that I could make people laugh until I was about two, or thereabouts. I was born with a very deep sort of voice and I used to go into our corner shop for the penny tray and there would be loads of people in there and this deep voice at the back would go: 'Can I see the penny tray please?' and people would laugh and get things for me. I thought here is a formula: laughter equals money, and so I carried on. At school I used to get out of fights by making people laugh and I became the class clown. I remember my grandad told me the first joke I ever told. It's still my favourite story. It's about a fellow in Oldham who staggers into a pub one night and asks the landlord for a drink, 'One for me, one for you, and one all round.' The landlord thanks him and says, 'That's £4.96.' The fella says, 'I'll tell you what, chalk it up on the slate and I'll pay at the end of the night and let's have another one all round.' By this time, word has got around and the pubs are emptying all over the place and they are all coming into this pub and there's a lot of elbow bending going on and this fella is still at it – 'One for me, one for you and drinks all round.' At the end of the night the landlord says: 'That's £483.91,' and this fella says: 'Well, it's been a cracking night, but I'll tell you what, I haven't got any money – it was a joke.' So the landlord picked him up and threw him in the revolving door and every time he came round he hit him with his dog. He threw him out on the street, hit him with a crate of Guinness, got on the 59 bus and drove backwards and forwards over this bloke and left him massacred. Then he threw him in the town hall square where all these punk rockers were doing a Morris dance.

Six months later the landlord is cleaning the glasses in the pub and this mass of bandages on roller-skates comes in. All the landlord can see is one eye and a moustache and he says, 'Oh, hello, it's you again is it? I suppose it's one for you, one for me and drinks all round.' The bloke says, 'Not bloody likely – one for me and drinks all round but none for you – you get nasty when you've been boozing you do.'

1980

MAX BOYCE

The way I dress happened quite accidentally. A long time ago I was appearing in a rugby club. It's very hard in a club and I always maintain that if you can go well in the first thirty seconds, you can keep their attention for the next thirty minutes. So I thought, 'What can I do to get them on my side?' I remembered that it was a Saturday and the club had been playing in a semi-final of the West Wales Cup, and I happened to notice that they'd won, so I thought I would sing a few verses relating to their win. Anyway, they were all drinking and reading their papers and when I started to sing about their win they all sat up and said, 'Not a bad act, this.' They asked me to do it again, and one of the lads came down the front and threw his scarf with the club's colours to me, and I put it on and there was a great roar from the crowd. Then someone threw on a bobble cap and so I put it on, and there was another roar. I thought this was great – so wherever I went I found out the colours and went on stage with their scarf and bobble cap, and I found out how they had got on that Saturday, and sang a little song about it and it went down a storm. It was a tremendous success but it happened by accident.

I didn't conquer Australia really, all I did was make about thirty thousand Welshmen homesick! I was on one programme called 'Fat Cat and Friends'. I'd never heard of this programme and I didn't even know what 'Fat Cat' was. So I turned up – it was half past six in the morning – at the studio, and said, 'Where's Fat Cat?' 'Oh, he's over there.' And there was this eight foot furry cat, with big alley-bumper eyes and whiskers. I didn't know what to do really and so I said, 'Can I have a chat with Fat Cat so that I know what to talk about?' And the producer said, 'Well, Max, there is a problem. You see, Fat Cat comes in earlier than anyone else and once he puts the costume on, he won't speak to anyone, because he really thinks he is a cat.'

I thought this chap was having me on, so I went up to Fat Cat and said, 'Look, my name's Max Boyce and I'm on the programme and I thought we could discuss it and what common ground we can talk about,' and he went 'purr', and he was purring and playing with his whiskers; he really wouldn't talk to me. Well, time was going on and the programme was coming on the air and I'd never seen the programme. I don't lose my temper often, I'm a gentle lad, and I said, 'Listen old pal, I admire your professional attitude and all that, but listen', I said, 'I know you're not a cat, and you *must* know you're not a cat.' All of a sudden he went 'eearghh' and went for me. He wouldn't speak to me, so I went to see the producer and I said, 'This is ridiculous, I've never seen the programme and I don't even know what to talk about', and he said 'Don't worry, Percy is on the programme with you as well.' 'Oh', I said, 'great', I said, 'Will Percy speak to me?' and he said, 'Yes, Percy will speak to you – he's in dressing room 2.' So I went to dressing room 2, and there was Percy – a nine-foot penguin . . .

Going down the pits was the last thing I wanted, but I had to leave school at fifteen because there was no one earning money in the house (my father had been killed in the pits). I wanted an apprenticeship. The first year was in college and so I went on the first day with pens, pencils and compasses . . . and a piece of coal in my pocket – for luck. I went straight underground in my suit and I came home and I was black and I knocked on the door and my mother answered the door. I had a helmet and boots – and she said 'Yes?' and then she said 'What have they done to my boy?' If she'd known that I was underground every day, she would have had me out straight away.

All my songs, all my characters are to do with rugby trips – from the crowd. I make a mental note and perhaps colour them large and they become songs – it varies tremendously. I get tremendous inspiration from people on the terraces. For example, someone kicked the ball and the opposition caught it and this old fellow said 'Worry him, worry him' and a Welsh voice said: 'Tell him his mother's ill.'

The game I play best is cricket. I was playing in a charity match and I wasn't very well-known about four years ago and all these famous people were playing – Phil Bennett, Gareth Edwards – and they had taken their side round on a big board and right at the bottom it said 'Boyce' and a little kid with pink, round national health glasses and a cap turned to his father and said, 'Who's this Boyce then, Dad?' And his father, full of cricketing knowledge said, 'Oh, he's the West Indian and Essex quick bowler' – mistaking me for Keith Boyce. As it happened I was called upon to bowl: the first ball – four, second ball – four. They scored twenty-eight runs in the over and I walked back to the boundary's edge and the little lad was waiting with this autograph book and he looked at me and said, 'Been barred, have you?'

1978 and 1979

ROWAN ATKINSON

There's no real showbiz heritage in my family at all – it's strange, except my grandfather used to own cinemas and theatres in the north of England. So there was no particular reason why I should have turned out the way I have, except I remember when I was about eleven or twelve standing up and doing some strange things in the school changing-room that used to drag people down and have them laughing at me. Then the adolescent self-consciousness set in and I never dared stand in front of my friends and make them laugh again. I've never done it to this day.

As far as I'm aware I've never consciously learnt from anyone or copied anyone as it were; it's all just drifted into the subconscious and mainly, I suppose, from Peter Sellers in terms of film. I think John Cleese is still the funniest man in Britain (there's flattery for you) and he undoubtedly influenced me a fantastic amount from the age of twelve or thirteen – and of course all through his career from 'Sorry I'll read that again' – a radio show in the 1960s – and 'Monty Python' and all that.

It's the 'very ordinariness' of life that I enjoy watching. I've never consciously copied anyone. Characterisations you've seen might have been based on people that I might have seen ten years ago, but I can't remember for the life of me who they are, their mannerisms and things. It sounds like an old cliché derived from a cliché – you know – 'truth is stranger than fiction' – and actually it's just the way the person sitting opposite you on the train behaves.

I think my parents are very happy about my job. It did stop my career as an electrical engineer which is what I did for six years at university. They had strange images of what people in show business were like and I think my mother in particular had images of flashy men with moustaches and bow-ties who slip you money – and I've met remarkably few people like that. In fact, the people on *Not the Nine O'Clock News* are just like me – just fairly normal guys who've come from similar backgrounds.

The Royal Command Show was fun. It was strange because it was a whole new world for me – it was the world of variety, which until then I didn't know very much about. The great thing about it was meeting a small section of the Royal Family in the form of the Queen Mother and Prince Charles. Prince Charles was great. He was very enthused by me. He came over and said: 'Ah, now you're the chap from *Not the Nine O'Clock News* aren't you?' and I said, 'Yes . . . er, yes.' And he said, 'It's really annoying actually because for some reason I never seem to be in on a Monday night. I've hardly seen any of this series, but when I do, I really like it – as long as you don't get at me too much.'

1981

JOHN CLEESE

In spite of all this whacky madcap humour I do, I actually do it by numbers, so I'm really almost most over-disciplined. I'm uptight as a performer, much too uptight.

Visual humour, gestures, get across much faster. Gestures are faster than a sentence and oddly enough, when people at home think back to great moments that really made them laugh, they are visual. They are quicker, that's why. With visual humour, what's more, you can hit someone three or four times very quickly.

Basil Fawlty was discovered; we were filming in 1971 and we all moved into a hotel called The Gleneagles down in Torquay (which is now run by disappointingly charming and efficient proprietors – we went there recently and to my disappointment, this perfect hotelier gave us a wonderful time). The only real difference between him and Basil was that he was small and had a very large hen-pecking wife, and obviously you can't find anyone bigger than me, but otherwise he was just as bad-tempered. I went up to the desk on the first day and said, 'Excuse me' and he was one of those people who just doesn't look up. And I wondered whether he had heard me and then he said 'Yes . . .' I said, 'Could you possibly call me a taxi?' 'What!' – 'Could you call me a taxi?' – 'Call you a taxi? – huh, yes, well.' It was wonderful – all the other clients moved out of the hotel into the Imperial. I stayed on. He also rebuked one of the others for his table manners (the chap was American). He said 'You don't eat like that!' He had real madness in him, apart from rudeness, because one day Eric Idle left his briefcase by the door while we were waiting to be picked up and he forgot the briefcase and came back, and Eric said to the guy, 'I left a briefcase by the door,' and he said 'What? – Oh yes, it's behind the wall outside.' Eric asked, 'Why is it behind the wall?' – 'I thought there might be a bomb in it.' And Eric said 'A bomb?' (this was pre-IRA) and he said, 'Well we've had a lot of staff problems recently.'

I think I started acting humorously because I was an only child and I think when I first went to my prep school at eight or nine I wasn't popular – in fact I got bullied a lot as I was an enormous height but so skinny and thin that you wouldn't believe it. I remember the PT instructor referring to me as six foot of chewed string. I was very awkward and ungainly and I wasn't easy socially and I think I found I could get popular if I made people laugh. My father was marvellous – he had a wicked sense of humour and I think that's where I got it from.

I was subversive and did things lacking in courage to make people laugh. I wasn't an overtly naughty boy – I used to sit at the back of the class and make a comment and then not own up. But gradually my courage grew and I found I could get away with quite a lot. I remember being late for chapel one morning at Clifton College and being challenged at the first lesson. A school marshall came in and said 'Why are you late?' and I was going to say 'I'm sorry, marshall' and then I thought: oh hell, I go through that awful rubbish every morning for quarter of an hour and I don't want to be there. So I said, 'I'm very sorry, marshall, I was walking to school absolutely on time and I was walking underneath that big block of police flats in Redland Road and someone leant out of the window, I don't know who it was, and threw a pan of hot fat all over me and I had to go back and change my suit – that's why I was so late.' And he looked at me for about twenty seconds and said, 'You don't expect me to believe that do you?' and I said 'It's true', and there was nothing he could do, short of walking along the school route and asking everybody if they had thrown a pan of hot fat over someone . . .

My mother didn't enjoy the 'Python' series. She liked the radio show and she likes *Fawlty Towers* but never *Monty Python* which I can understand. 'Python' is totally silly unless you see the abstract idea floating around the back of it, but if you don't get the abstract idea, then it is totally silly, futile. It tends to follow with education. The number of cab drivers I've had who've sat down with their sons and daughters in front of the television enjoying it while the wife says she doesn't understand it. Younger women enjoy it, but older women don't have the education to understand the abstract thought behind it which gives it meaning.

We were wondering how we were going to get someone to publicise *Life of Brian* and we thought we'd get our mothers to do our advertisements. I went down to Weston super Mare with a tape recorder – I'd written a script – and mother is eighty – so she put her glasses on and read the script and it showed that she should have been in show business all along because she said 'Don't you think it would be better if I did . . .?' The marvellous thing was that it was chosen as the best radio advertisement of the year and she had to come to London to receive her award from Lord Snowdon in front of twelve hundred people.

1980

DUDLEY MOORE

I am a discovery for the Americans, even though I have been around for around twenty years. I felt I was a star in 1959–1960, especially when I was at the airport. I was at the airport and John Gielgud was there, and when I told him I was going to Portofino he said I must see Lilli Palmer, so he gave me a note. I was curious in the plane so I opened it up and it said: 'Darling Lilli, this is to introduce the young pianist from *Beyond the Fringe* – Stanley Moon.' I was a little embarrassed and so I didn't go. Years later when I was trying to get rid of an apartment he came to the door and said, 'I'm so sorry about the awful mistake I made.' And then literally years later I was sitting in a restaurant with a friend – I was in some corner with a bird – and there was Sir John. I got a note which said: 'Dear Stanley Moon! It's so nice to see you again.' I thought that's nice, he's remembered it. And I went over and was just about to tap him on the shoulder, when a waiter gave me a note which was from my agent who was sitting in another corner. Well, I nearly disgraced myself laughing.

I have always been talking about 'finding myself' and I think I have in the last couple of years. I've reached a plateau of basically feeling OK with myself. A series of analysts and I think everyone takes time to get out of the quagmire of the past, and I feel I have my head above the bog as it were. I feel good now. I never thought I would stop saying that I'm looking for myself, but I have now.

The film *Ten* happened to come along when I felt basically good and relaxed; it was really a mirror image of the way I was feeling; I had a good time – maybe that's why it worked. I've become a known face in America. America doesn't seem that different from here. I tend to lead the same sort of life wherever I am. I have my music and that is a tremendous interest to me – that and friends is all I require in a city. I don't require tradition or architecture or culture. I do require music and films.

There is something in me which stops me being more active musically – I'm afraid of it. I would like to sing – but I can't do it; except under a pile of sacks . . . or sex.

1980

DUSTIN HOFFMAN

I was born in Los Angeles but I was not at all influenced by 'Hollywood up the road' when I was a kid. I seemed to be unaware that it was a movie capital. I didn't think about acting until I got into college and my first fantasy was to be a sex symbol film star. The first thing I did Off Broadway when I went to New York after college was to play a Nazi German – hunchbacked, homosexual with a bad limp. I got an agent out of that and then he made sure I didn't work for a year and then a year later I was in another play by the

27

same author and that started off my luck. Soon after that I was asked to screentest for *The Graduate*. There were three directors and the first two wanted me dismissed, but the producer liked me so he dismissed the first two directors. The third director had never directed before and he was so frightened of it being a disaster that he said he would do it if his name was a fake name on the credits. We had a lot in common and we liked each other and he is one of the best directors I ever had – Alan Arkin. I wasn't right for the part – Benjamin was even physically described as someone quite different from me – being blond and beautiful I thought I was all wrong!

They didn't think *The Graduate* would be the huge success it was. They thought it would have an art-house, small cult following and nobody seemed to know what was going to happen with it until about four weeks after it had opened. I don't know the reason it was such a hit, if there is one. I think there are a lot of excellent things about the film – the music as much as anything. I've now done nine films, but every time I see *The Graduate* my own respect for it increases and I suddenly understand what an excellently made film it is. It has a wonderfully cinematic rhythm to it and I think that it will last, if for no other reason, from that point of view.

Of course, the character I played struck a chord in all men. Everyone seemed to think he was a virgin, but I never thought of him as that, but that it was the first time he was making love to a woman who was old enough to be his mother, and who was his mother's friend. Some of the best things in the film came out of improvisation and it was Mike Nichol's point of view that you should always be as close to yourself in the most personal way to convey not only truth but humour. Real humour perhaps is the purest truth when it works. In one scene I am trying just to get a room key and I have still never been to a hotel – I usually go behind a tree! But when we were rehearsing Mike said that I had to find in my life what was the most painful thing for me to do that had a sexual connotation, in a public way. From some reason that I have never understood, because I was always considered rather 'dirty' when I was at school, I could never go to a chemist and order male prophylactics, as opposed to female prophylactics which I could always get. Although I had not had a sexual experience when I was at high school, I thought I should be ready, if and when it came, and so I thought I should stock up. I would always plan on a day when I felt brave and I would walk into the drugstore and see who was behind the counter. This was very important – if it was a woman I would walk right out again – I wanted someone young – a kind of 'big brother' image. I would ask for some Kleenex, some razor blades and I would get to that word and I couldn't do it. So when we rehearsed this scene I based it on my drugstore experience, because in acting, as in life, you are thinking about many different things and your mind has to be elsewhere for it to be interesting. It is the job of the actor and the director to make the choice of where the mind is, concentrate on that and let the words come out as they would.

My next film was *Midnight Cowboy*, a very different sort of film. I had turned down lots of scripts that were carbon copies of *The Graduate* and about ten months later I read this book, *The Midnight Cowboy*, and loved the character of Enrico. When you are playing the part of someone who is not having an easy time of it, it depresses you the same as it would if the person was somebody you knew in real life. In one sense it was not that difficult to do, meaning that it was not as much of a stretch for me to do that role as people might think. It was a character that I felt to be a very basic part of me and when I read it I had that immediate connection with him. I had for many years had this feeling about myself – that I looked like that – not literally, but in an inner way I felt I did. I felt a combination of unattractive and anonymous and I felt that the way to play that part was to forget about what he was and to think about what he wanted. I feel that we are all partly Ratso and partly J.F. Kennedy if you like – a most successful, attractive person. It always strikes me when you see meths drinkers and imagine those people as children – they were all beautiful then, and it is simply an inexplicable phenomenon which makes me sit here and that other person is out there on the street. Much of it has very little to do with what you are, and that is an emotion I have always felt and will always feel.

When I got the part of Lennie in the film about Lennie Bruce, I had never met him or seen him work. I then spent about six months talking to about fifty or sixty people, including his ex-wife, daughter and mother. From the research I did, and I must say that I am not an authority on this man, I feel that he would have had his self-destructive problems no matter what he was – he was a man who used drugs, needed drugs as an addict. From what I understand, that was a part of him and was not tied into persecutions he suffered. It was the most difficult part I have had to play. It worried me primarily because it had been a real person and he had only been dead eight years, and there were people who loved him still living.

There has never been a particular role that I have wanted to play – there are certain things I would like to do rather than a particular role. I would love to make a love story about people who are elderly when I'm older because I think we have a tendency to think of people who reach a certain point in age as being different from human beings and I don't think that's true. I go along with my friend who says that we really are only four years old, or five all the way through our life and it is only because we look in the mirror and see the ageing taking place that we then have to act older. If we were eighty years old but still looked like five, we would behave like that. I want to do a really sexy movie about two elderly people who make love like nobody else!

1975

ROBERT DE NIRO

The most recent film I've made is *Raging Bull*, the true story of Jake Lamotta the former middle-weight champion known as the 'Bronx Bull'. I first read the book about seven years ago and the power, emotion and jealousy really got to me. He was very basic, like an animal and there was something very interesting about him.

Of course, it is very difficult playing the part of someone who is still alive, but Lamotta is just happy that the movie is being received well. He is the first one to admit that he was a destructive, brutal man, not very sympathetic at all. He is much mellower now. He told me the other day that I had made him a champ again, so I just hope his life gets better and he gets back on his feet, because he was really down and out. I had not been interested in boxing before I did the film – I learnt to fight when I was doing *New York, New York* about five years ago and then about a year before we started shooting *Raging Bull* I began to train with Lamotta. I want to keep training but I'm not interested in fighting – just watching special fights.

As the film progressed and I had to portray Lamotta going to seed, going downhill, ending up fat and slug-like, I actually got fat myself rather than pad up. I gained 60lbs. There was no way I could do it with artificial padding and I was curious to see if it could be done. We suspended shooting for a few months for me to put on weight as quickly as I could, which I did by eating a lot. It actually became a bit of a chore after a while, especially as I had always eaten like a monk before – just a little of the right things, like raw fish.

Some actors work cerebrally, some physically when they are trying to get a part right. I like to work physically a lot of the time; putting on certain clothes can give you the feeling of another character, as can the way you move. When I played a cab driver, I spent some time as a cabbie and for *New York, New York* I learned to play the saxophone. The most important thing for me was to learn the fingering because I didn't want it to look like I didn't know what I was doing, I wanted it to be natural.

I don't like being recognised in certain situations, I like a certain amount of privacy. Some of the trappings of fame and success are a drag, but basically I enjoy it. I have no complaints.

1981

ROBERT REDFORD

When I first started as an actor I was an actor for hire and I had no options as to what roles to play. I certainly didn't cast myself as hero.

The story behind Paul Newman's joke on me was that we had made a few films together and we used to play jokes on each other. He is obsessed with racing and he would get so boring talking about racing that sometimes I couldn't take it. So on his fiftieth birthday (we had homes in Connecticut that weren't so far from each other) I found an old wreck of a 1964 Porsche that had been completely demolished, and so I had the thing wrapped up and delivered to his back door as his birthday present. I waited to hear. He didn't say anything. About three weeks later I came to my house and in the foyer of the house was this huge package and I opened it and it was this gigantic block of metal that had been melted down from an old wrecked car. So I didn't mention it to him. I couldn't get it out of the house either so I just let it sit there for weeks on end and finally he couldn't take anymore and he said, 'Say, have you been to the house? Anything different there?' I said 'No, except that the basement is leaking.' And he said 'Nothing else?' It drove him crazy. I then went to the people who had delivered the thing. I made the arrangements to have it taken out of the house and to have it melted down further and I hired a sculptor to do a piece of garden sculpture and have it delivered back to his garden. As far as I know it's still there.

I wasn't a good student which seemed a good reason to drop out of school. I was also not ready to be educated, at least not in the formal academic manner. I felt that I learned more from travelling than from sitting in a classroom. There was no real stimulation in my background and education because it was a lower middle-class upbringing.

Once, while I was down and out in France when I was young, I was hitchhiking to the south and it was so cold and I had no way to get warm; I had no place to go and I had very little money and I was running back and forth in the street waiting for a ride which didn't come. It was the middle of the night and the town had closed up. Finally I got tired of running and I started to get worried that I wasn't going to be able to get warm, and across the street was this mound of manure. So I went over there and just planted myself in it and just stayed there for a while until dawn came and I could go into a pastry shop . . . needless to say it was tough to get a piece of pastry. The time in Paris was rough but I really felt I was learning for the first time.

I've always been interested in the West of the States. I don't know how it initially started unless it was the desire to get out of Los Angeles. I've always been attracted by space and something about the remaining heritage that my country has seems to be primarily focused there in the West. It's diminishing rapidly. I got interested in it because I was comfortable there – I like to ride, climb and be outdoors. I felt comfortable playing in *Butch Cassidy* and had more fun making that film that any other I've made. I developed this interest throughout the years until finally one day I heard about something called the Outlaw Trail which runs from Canada to Mexico. I decided to explore the trail myself before it was too late.

There's no question that in the films I have done, either produced or acted in – roles that I have been able to select – that there has been some tone or some hint of something autobiographical. At least in those areas of issues that concern me.

I am very keen to go more into directing. I directed my first film *Ordinary People* and it was very fulfilling – far more than I expected and acting isn't going to last forever. I think it's time to move on, I don't know where to, or how radical it will be, but I don't think I will act. Very few people I know have the disposition to quit when the time is right. The person I admire for quitting when he was at the top is Jimmy Cagney, he is the only person who I think did what is right. I think he is one of the greatest talents that our country has produced. In fact I modelled the character I played in *The Sting* after Jimmy Cagney. He used his talent widely and fully and let it speak for him. This is what I believe in doing for myself – I think the best spokesman for you is your work.

The best reaction I've had from someone in the street (mainly because it reminded me of when I was young and it really set me straight) was in Beverly Hills. I was walking across the street and I went to step off the kerb and this car comes rolling by, full of young teenagers and they spot me and the car slows down and I thought: oh, here it comes, and they were clawing to get the window down and finally they get the window down as the car rolls by and one yells 'Robert Redford' and I said 'Hey' and he said 'You are such an asshole.'

1980

JAMES CAGNEY

It was a middle-class neighbourhood where I was born – middle-class, and every now and then they spotted a family who had produced a tough one. I wasn't a tough one, I had a mother who stopped all that nonsense. I was fairly handy with my fists – that's not hard. Everybody was a street fighter. In order to get along you had to fight your way through. I recall one fight: three fights, one after the other. Third one, the boy and I went in again, and the result was interesting – because I hit him on the bridge of the nose with my right hand – and broke my hand. He was tough as tough. He was just a very nice guy, but he was tough as could be.

The guys were tough there and they learned how to take care of themselves. The girls could do it too. My girl, Maud, was a left-handed girl, and she could punch her way through a brick wall. She was really something to cope with.

My first job was in vaudeville. It was – are you ready – as a female impersonator. That was an act that had five fellows and five girls and I jumped into the act on a Monday and I was with them for about three months. It was just another way of making $35 a week.

Vaudeville taught me everything. You see anything that came along, you grabbed it. It didn't matter what it was – a straight act, a sketch or a musical act – whatever, you did it all. Dancing was something you got right from the sidewalks. Everybody would dance. I don't know if I was just naturally gifted. But if it's there to do, I try to do it. Tap dancing? It's easy. It was nothing really – a lot of hard work, I may say, but it was still easy. I wanted to make a movie with Fred Astaire. Years ago Freddie and I had a kind of common agreement where he said 'let's do one' and I said 'fine', so we got it all set and nothing ever happened.

Hollywood – I went there to get a job that paid living-room money – that was it, the sole idea involved. It wasn't so terribly different. Being in vaudeville, you were used to anything. Whatever came along, you grabbed it and did it. That was all. I used to write poetry: just little things that don't amount to anything. As the idea came along I'd just put it down in writing. You see, Bogart had a nervous habit of picking his nose – he was a very nervous guy. I was driving north on Ventura Boulevard and he was driving south. So this thing, I didn't write it, I just said it:

'In this silly town of ours, one sees odd preens and poses,
But movie stars in fancy cars shouldn't pick their famous noses.'

I find the tough guy in movies easy to play – it's a matter of turning back the clock, that's all, to my early days. The scripts for those films were just working scripts, the people who wrote them were workaday writers and they just made them up as they went along, and we improvised. I invented a lot of phrases – I didn't expect the writers to know those at all. There was a difference between Bogie and me. He came from a very nice family – they were entirely different from my family. He just used his head as a tough guy – he had to work at it.

Jack Warner described me as being the 'Professional Againster'. He was paying me $400 a week and they were paying other actors 125–150 thousand dollars. So I just left the studio. Six months I was out. I stayed on up at the farm, my second love. They tried to get somebody to fill the shoes then finally they came to me with an offer and I went back. Those are chances you take.

I didn't have much choice of scripts really. There was always that script ready and if you liked it you'd do it, if you didn't, you'd discard it. The part of Bottom in *A Midsummer Night's Dream* came out of the blue. But it was just another job, and that's my attitude to every part I'm offered.

I never took any acting lessons. Why should one take lessons in a perfectly natural thing to do? *One, Two, Three* was the last film I made before I retired. I just called it a day then, for twenty years. I farmed. I raise horses and cows – white-faced cattle. I was never tempted by the parts offered me. I was determined to be a farmer – no strain. But the doctor said, 'Get this man moving' and he did – I'm a diabetic. I did *Ragtime*, directed by Milos Foreman. And no strain again, no strain. He was just wonderful. And the film got up on the words and that's it. You say your words and that's it. I enjoyed it thoroughly.

1981

FRED ASTAIRE

I started at the age of four and a half, and if you add it up I have been performing professionally for seventy-one years. I wasn't forced into it, I went with my sister Adele to New York. I don't think anyone thought I was going to do anything. I just went because my sister was going to dance at school, stage school, and I went along too and the first thing you know I was in it . . .

I was glad when my sister did retire because she didn't want to work any more; it wasn't easy to get her to rehearse. I'd say we ought to try that step over again and she'd say why, so she'd come out – I'd warm up a little bit and she'd do a few little nothing exercises and she wanted to retire, and it was fine. Then when I did get on and do something myself everybody missed her very much because she was a very, very successful girl, a very good comedienne, she was wonderful. We got along great. She's marvellous today, I see her all the time.

I was thirty-four when I went into the movies. It was an area that was unexplored in terms of dance at that time. There were a lot of things that we brought into it – fortunately people said it made it better. Whatever that was, it was nice to know. I always know that I love the movies, I love working in them, and I still do. Sometimes you get an idea from the choreographer (I had a number of different ones) but I had quite a few myself, naturally. I could never sleep past four o'clock in the morning for some reason, and I'd lie there and I'd think up some things. I remember that one of the particular things I got at that hour was the top hat number. My sister had the room next to mine and I was up, and there was an umbrella standing in the corner of my

33

room and I was making a noise, and my mother said: 'What the hell are you doing in there?' So I said, 'Oh, sorry, I got an idea.' She says, 'Well, sleep on it, will you, don't do it now, it's keeping Adele awake.'

Practice makes the dances look easy – that's the secret of the success of almost anything – I mean it looks as if it's no labour, that's why I work so hard on it, I try to get the dances so you don't have to think about what you're doing next – that's the thing that counts.

I don't like wearing full dress suit, though it became my trademark – I hate it. I had so much of it that people thought I was born in it. But it was necessary for the thing that we were doing at that point, and actually I haven't worn it anywhere in a film for quite a long time. I had to wear it to do a couple of shindigs I went to recently, but I just don't like it.

It's difficult to make comparisons between dancing partners because all the girls are so good – I mean each one had something special and so to say which is the best, I really don't know. When it comes to actual dancing there are certain ways and styles and techniques that do show – but I don't want to hurt anybody's feelings. I must say Ginger Rogers was certainly one of the most effective partners I had – everybody knows that. I just want to pay tribute to Ginger because we did so many pictures together and she had it, she was just great. Seriously, we never had a fight, never, never. There were questionable conversations about the material, say: I like it, or I don't like it . . . but I can't fight with people I work with, I just couldn't do it. But the Press liked it that way, so we just laughed about it!

My mother said I should retire when I was thirty-four. She said: 'Well, you started so early, and it's about time.' She was such a wonderful woman, she had these cute ideas, and I said, 'I'm afraid it isn't going to be possible,' and that was all there was of that.

I think everybody gets that feeling I came to: look, I've done all I can do now, I think I want to quit. Actually I did decide to retire and then something happened – it was a couple of years back. Gene Kelly was doing a movie called *Easter Parade*, and he fell out of it because he'd hurt his leg and they got after me and said would I come and take it on, and they'd start over and do it with me. It looked like a good show and so I did it, that's all, so I was back in business again. So then I stayed again for a while, and had ideas again, quit again . . . I think many people do that.

1976

GENE KELLY Fred Astaire's success, I believe, was his elegance, a particular style which was unique. No one could really dance like him and when I wanted to dance I started in the Broadway theatre; a couple of decades later and I wanted to dance like Marlon Brando wanted to act – roll up my sleeves and say 'hey . . !' I would categorise it by saying, let's see if I can put it succinctly, Fred represents the aristocracy when he dances, and I represent the proletariat.

My brother taught me to tap dance, very quickly, and we formed this poor little double act and then we tried to improve on it: we put on roller skates and we were gymnasts – we did a tap dance, and roller skated, and we were foolish enough to do acrobatics, which I would never do today.

People were looking for new ways of relaxation, and MGM gave us a free hand experimenting with things. I danced with a cartoon, I danced with myself and danced with girls – everything – so they did give us room to explore. Also we had a great champion there, Arthur Freed, who would hire people we recommended from the Broadway theatre. The president of the company at that time, Louis B. Mayer (a great man, I guess, when he started this thing) never seemed to be around, but he had a string of racehorses, and he was more interested in the racehorses than the actors.

They said to me, when war broke out, 'You're from Hollywood, you're a photographer', and I said 'No, I'm an actor,' but they said 'You're from Hollywood, you're a photographer,' and so I took the camera. I didn't even have a gun! Nothing! I was scared to death all the time. When I came out of service I said, 'In films you should try to do what you can't do on stage, for example: if it's *Singing in the Rain* on stage, it would flood the orchestra pit.

Sinatra didn't know how to dance – he was very good at rhythm and he had done two pictures at another studio which did not go down very well, so he came and asked me if I would work with him on it, and I told him he would really have to work like a prize-fighter every day, and after about a week he turned a bit recalcitrant because I'd make him do the same thing over and over again. He got quite good and, of course, I did things that were within his range. He became quite adept and a very good partner. He was very good for me and I'm grateful to him because when I worked with someone like Francis Albert, or Judy Garland, they would sing the ballads in the show and I wouldn't have to sing any. Occasionally I would get stuck with a ballad, when the other person wasn't a good ballad singer – that's when I appreciated Francis Albert the most.

Dancing is a form of athletics, you have to have a bit of masochism in you, you have to keep very fit and that means you pretty much have to work every day. If you have a drinking bout some evening, the next day you have to have about three or four hours to work it off and that means hard exercise. That's the best analogy I know – like being a boxer.

Dancers are at their peak at about twenty-two to twenty-three, but during their late twenties they have matured enough to take advantage of this but around thirty their bodies won't answer their brain as much; you have to use all the skills you've learned – you can't jump as high, leap as far, you can't do all the things you could do at eighteen – that also applies to sex. In all other art forms you have a much longer career. Any dancer has to be a perfectionist. If he dances and stumbles across the stage, he is a bum. You have to be highly disciplined.

1975

'Fred
represents the
aristocracy
when he dances,
and I
represent the
proletariat'
Gene Kelly

'I enjoy
dancing. I love
dancing;
from the age of
six I have not
thought of
anything else'
Rudolf Nureyev

'I would love to
do more films, but
you have to be
asked to do them'
Twiggy

DAME MARGOT FONTEYN

All dance has some magic to me. Of course I don't hope to transmit that to everyone the way I feel it, but I thought some years ago that it would be nice to tell people about things in a way that was easy, not in a heavy, boring, chronological, historical way, and this led to my series *The Magic of Dance*.

Fred Astaire is one of my heroes – he is one of everybody's. I would have liked to have been Ginger Rogers. He was a perfectionist, which one should be. When I started dancing at the Sadler's Wells Theatre it was 1934–5 and Astaire was the greatest dancing star known to the greatest number of people in the world. Fred Astaire was, and is, the magic of dance. To me his dancing looks better and better every time I see him.

I think dancing with Rudolf Nureyev was very good for both of us. I thought: how am I going to be seen if I dance with this young, brilliant dancer who is so sensational? He leaps in the air and astounds the audience – how is anyone going to look at me? He also, for some reason, thought: well, she's famous and she's a great ballerina, so how is anyone going to look at me? So we were both feeling that if we were not absolutely at the top of our form when we danced together we wouldn't live up to each other and that is the best way to work. Theatre depends on giving more than you have to give. At a rehearsal you can do your best but when you get out on the stage you have to try to do more than your best so, if you are with another artist who is top in their field, then you are really on your mettle and think: now I'm going to try to live up to this, and this is the way to work. That's what is exciting – it's what theatre is all about. If it's just going to be comfortable and you say: I know how to do this and I'm going to go on and do it and the audience will love it – then this isn't any good. The whole thing about the theatre is that you have to live up to the challenge.

The significance of Nureyev is very great because he made male ballet dancers popular. He was the first ballet dancer in tights, ballet shoes, doing grandes jetées and everything, who became a household name. He affirmed the fact that ballet exists with ballerinas and men – it is at its best when they are both at the top.

I was very lucky in my career because it was very much easier to reach the top then. I had opportunities that no one would be able to have now because there are so many more people dancing. I was there when the British ballet was beginning. That was my good luck. I was in the right place at the right moment.

1979

RUDOLF NUREYEV

During the war my family had to evacuate from Moscow, and of course it was very tough. There was no food, we could only eat once a day – potatoes; boiled potatoes if you were lucky and two hundred and fifty grammes of bread a day. Once I gave that ration to a dog, so I thought the dog should feel grateful and I embraced the dog and it bit me – here, on the lip – marked for life! My father wanted to kill it, only I would not let him.

What we do on stage is an illusion – not facts. We conjure – if you are a natural performer you will know the tricks. I enjoy dancing, I love dancing; from the age of six I have not thought of anything else. I was constantly day-dreaming of being a dancer. My body was very supple and everything I did was on the brink of being a dance, I suppose. I wouldn't boast about my body – there are a lot of flaws, and things could be much better. I started dancing very late – I went to the Kirov School at seventeen – they graduate at sixteen, so I was working too hard and made my muscles fight one another. But you learn to disguise certain things or give the illusion of what you want the public to see – you select, and present the public with what you want the public to see. You emphasise only a particular movement.

I admire Fred Astaire. I did not pay much attention at first but then I realised how much this sort of dance had influenced contemporary dance. Fred Astaire, particularly, liberated dance – the way he dissects music – goes through it, creates his own rhythm. There is a somewhat feeble attempt to dance that way in *Valentino* – I do some kind of 'hoof' dancing.

In my childhood I remember stars like Deanna Durbin, Bette Davis, Garbo, Vivien Leigh, but when I came here and said I would like to see Deanna Durbin there was not much response. In geography lessons at school I would close my ears and open a map and I would be travelling: 'I am going to dance in Milan, I am going to dance in Paris,' so in a way I had danced everywhere before I came to the West.

I objected to bureaucracy in particular in Russia, to being dependent on a number of people – they just control your fate, you know. But thank God for free enterprise – if Covent Garden or the Paris Opera or La Scala don't give me enough performances, I create them elsewhere. The performance exists where you make it. It would be nice to go back to Russia to dance, but I wouldn't risk banging my head. They would probably let me in, but they wouldn't let me out! I chose exile – but I don't regret it. Never.

1976

MISS BLUEBELL

My real name is Margaret Kelly. I got the name 'Bluebell' because as a baby I had no face at all apart from these two big blue eyes, and the doctor suggested that I should be called 'Bluebell' and I have always been called this – it's nothing to do with the theatre at all. I was a very sickly child, and after we moved to Liverpool the doctor advised some form of exercise for me and I was put into ballet school when I was six years old. My family was very poor and we couldn't afford ballet lessons so before and after school I would get up and do a paperound and then I was a caddy at the local golf course, from the age of twelve.

It was fifty years ago that I formed my own troupe, the very first Bluebell Girls. I had always intended to be a principal dancer but the owner of the Folies Bergère asked me if I would like to form my own troupe so I thought I would. I wrote to a lot of people who had been at the ballet school in Liverpool and many of them came to join me. Now I have three troupes in America, one in the Far East, one in Marakesh and of course the home of the Bluebell Girls is the Lido in Paris. Every day of the week I am supervising one of my troupes somewhere – usually at the Lido. I am now seventy years old and I still dance.

Bluebell Girls don't have to be a certain physical type; but the smallest girl I have at the moment is 5ft 9ins and the tallest girl is 6ft 2ins without heels, and with heels on she would be 6ft 4ins and that is why I have so much difficulty finding male dancers!

I married a man who was in the theatre in Paris – he was a Jew and during the war we were in occupied France. First I was arrested as a British subject and then eventually I managed to get out through the Irish Ambassador, and then my husband went to the other side of France and when the forces took the whole thing over he was arrested. A friend of his, who had been important in the Resistance, went over and got my husband out with false papers. He was hidden for two and a a half years just in front of the Préfecture of Police – quite amazing really, in this very small attic. I used to get food for him from the black-market.

It was very difficult. It was continually given out on the radio that anybody who was hiding people would be shot. I was called up for interrogation many times, firstly when my husband escaped. They called me up to the Gestapo to ask me where he was – so I said: 'Well, you should know where he is, you took him.' They had asked me what language I wanted to speak in, so I said my own language, and they brought in a Polish lady who was nervous of the big officer. I can understand German, as I had been in Germany before, so when she translated once or twice I answered too quickly, and he said, 'I have a good idea that you understand our language', and I said, 'I have a feeling you understand mine too.' I was also a fighter. I got very 'British' with them.

When my husband was in hiding I wanted to have a family and I didn't want to waste time, so I had the family then. The last time I was called up I was eight months pregnant, expecting my third child, and I expected at any moment the German officer would say something to me, but I don't think he dared. I looked him right in the eye. I always knew even on the very darkest days that we would be some of the ones to get through – I was always absolutely sure of it.

The Bluebells have come a long way since they started in 1946 – they are even topless now. I usually meet the parents and talk to them first, so I don't think they are worried. I think too that I have built up a reputation over the years, and the parents know that their girls only work in the best places, and the girls are looked after the way one should be when one is a child. I never ask the girls if they would like to go topless, they usually come to me and ask if I don't engage them for that role. One of my girls came to me and said she would like to go into the topless troupe when there was a place, and I said this would be fine and I'd see what I could do for her. So then she said, 'I haven't told my father.' I replied, 'He's bound to see you when he next comes over' – most parents come over and see their daughters when they are in Paris. So the day she got ready to perform she said she would phone home and she phoned her mother. However, her father answered the phone (her mother was not in) so she said: 'Dad, I'm going to go topless in the troupe tonight', and he said, 'Oh, don't tell your mother.'

I have had 8,000 girls over the years in my troupe. Some girls are with me for seven, eight or nine years. My biggest problem is marriage. When I was in Las Vegas last time one of my girls – who was with me out there about eighteen years ago – told me that I had formed the British colony in Las Vegas because nearly all my British (and most of them are British) girls marry out there!

I have never contemplated retirement, I never have time to think about it.

1982

TWIGGY I am enjoying motherhood, but it's hard work – I think all mothers are amazing. My mother loves being a grandma and she loves little girls, she had three herself. When I was born they told her that I was a boy and she told them to take me away!

We are living in America at the moment – it's not for ever, it's temporary really. I've got mixed feelings about it as I miss England terribly and I don't like the weather there very much, and most people do of course. I miss the rain and I miss cloudy days, but we do have a lovely house. My husband, Michael, is an actor in America and he has been working on a film of his own and you really have to be there. I've been recording a new album and I've been lucky enough to get involved with a lady called Donna Summer and she has been coproducing me. I would love to do more films, but you have to be asked to do them! But I don't just want to sit around waiting for the film to come along, I like to be doing things.

I would have loved to have been Ginger Rogers. I met Astaire once when I went to promote *The Boyfriend* in Los Angeles and we went to the MGM studios. They asked me if there was any film star I would like to meet, so I told them I would like to meet Fred Astaire. They told me it would be difficult as he was very shy and kept to himself, but a lady who was there at the time and who had worked at the studios when Fred was there got on the phone to him without anyone knowing and he invited me up to his house for tea. He was absolutely wonderful. I discovered later from his daughter that he was terrified of meeting me! He is the most charming, beautiful man I have ever met.

My image in the 1960s is both a help and a hindrance to my present career. It's more of a hindrance in America because they haven't seen much I've done since then and they remember me as being the model with the short hair and the eyelashes. Those four years, 1966–1970 were wonderful really. Up until then I had just been at school and had never travelled abroad. I went into a completely new life – I travelled the world, got to wear wonderful clothes and it was just like a dream. I think that my family background had a lot to do with the fact that I have managed to keep sane – I mean so many people from that era are dead now! My mum is mad but lovely and my dad is very down to earth, and although they were excited when it all happened, they had never pushed me into it and my dad was always telling me that it could all end tomorrow. I was around people that looked after me. Michael and I are very close and we lead a very ordinary kind of life at home. Michael calls our house our monastery, because we hardly ever go out. We have a few very close friends, English and American because there are lots of English people out there now.

When everyone is telling you that you're wonderful, it can go to your head of course, but other things happen to slap you down. When I went to New York, everyone was going crazy and I got mobbed and I could have got overwhelmed by that. But then on the other hand I was followed around New York by a film crew who were interviewing people as I passed asking them if they knew who I was and what they thought of me. One middle-aged New York couple thought I was 'cute', 'the little English, skinny girl', and added that they thought I would last a couple of weeks! Another time I got into a New York cab and the cab driver told me that I had a pretty face but that I was no Marilyn Monroe.

I do not have to work hard at keeping slim. I'm just like my dad and he hasn't changed weight since he was twenty. In the days when I was very skinny, I did get upset by some of the jokes made about me; I mean every comedian used to crack a Twiggy joke. They were usually flat-chested jokes, but at the same time they were going on about Mick Jagger's lips. At least I can take consolation in the fact that Mick Jagger's lips are still the same, whereas . . .

1980

DOLLY PARTON

I have about two hundred wigs at least – and I wear about a hundred of them at once. When I was at high school I used to spend a lot of time making my hair as big as I could because I was so short and I enjoyed working with the hair because it was something creative. When it went out of style, people in the music business said I ought to change it as people would treat me more seriously if I would look more fashionable. Then I had the idea that I would not only *not* change it, but I would exaggerate it and I started wearing the wigs for the convenience of it and for the gimmick and it worked very well. The main thing is it's for attention and you can't miss me.

In the States we have 'Dolly' lookalike contests . . . I'm very easy to look like – all you need is a big wig and a costume and . . . you know . . . But the majority of the people are men dressed in drag, and they are usually the prettiest ones. I'm especially popular at Halloween and at masquerade parties – it's a cheap and convenient thing to do. You can see me on many street corners . . . in the right part of town. I almost entered a Dolly contest once. I wanted to play myself down, and go under another name. I thought how funny it would be to go in and lose. For fear that I might lose, I didn't. But I really wanted to – one of these days I might.

I'm not very trim. I tried jogging once but I blacked both my eyes. On a more serious note – I am now having to be more conscious of my weight – I weigh 1001 lbs and plenty. I enjoy eating because there is nothing much to do while you're travelling around. I'm on a special diet now, a seafood diet – every time I see food I eat it.

We are a family of six girls and six boys – just farm folk and we didn't have things, we made our living from the land. I was really impressed with pretty things. I really enjoy things. When performing I project better if I have all the glitter and glamour. We were extremely poor – had no electricity, few neighbours – we would wear things that people would send us. But we had a good mummy and daddy and a love of God. We'd sleep three and four in a bed and in the summer, take baths in the river. I had an aunt, fifty miles from where we were born, and she had the first television we had seen and the first flush toilet and I was horrified – nobody wanted to use it because we thought we were going to be swept away.

I developed fast because we worked on the fields. At thirteen years old people thought I was seventeen – I tried to show it off. We weren't allowed to wear make-up on religious grounds and daddy trusted us girls but he didn't trust the men and so we used to use baking flour and matches. We had a red medicine and if you put it on your lips, it looked like lipstick but you couldn't get it off and so you had permanent colouring. You make do with what you've got and use vanilla flavouring for perfume.

I get some fan mail. A lot from soldiers, sailors, prisoners etc. Some want to marry me and I keep all the letters. To be honest I have never had a cranky letter – I think this is because I'm so open and they can see something under the artificiality. I do carry a gun, it makes me feel better when I'm travelling in motels. I try to be safe and wise.

1979

MICHAEL CAINE

I think that cockneys are almost a race, but what they definitely are is a frame of mind which means that you recognise each other by the way you take things – you never take things seriously especially dignity and pomposity and one of the things about them is that they are very sharp. There is a natural quick wit which must be a survival thing. If you are a cockney you are working class, I mean you can't be a cockney lord – although there are some now. Usually you speak very quickly because no one listens to you, you move your hands a lot because you try to attract attention. Have you ever noticed that aristocrats stand with their hands behind their backs and speak very slowly because they know that they have got everyone's attention?

Complete and utter arrogance meant I thought that I could break through being a cockney. I was the most arrogant git I've ever met. I never listened to anybody, I never took any advice and I used to say I was going to be an actor and people used to say: 'Look at you, you look like a thin milk-bottle.' And they all walked into dead-end jobs paying a hundred and fifty pounds a week and I went into rep for two pounds ten shillings, and I just worked at it all the time and took no notice.

I went on stage when I was about eight. I was in the school pantomime, and I went on and I got a great deal of laughs, a big round of applause and I won the prize of five shillings for the best performer which the local MP gave to me. I thought this was wonderful, but then I realised, I looked down – all the laughter had been because my flies had been undone. So what I've done is I've spent an entire career working for applause, laughter and money but just before I go on I always make sure my flies are done up and I also wear a double-breasted coat so that even if they are undone no one will notice.

I think you become an actor because you have to, not because you want to, because it is so hard in the beginning. I wish that I was rich and unknown so then you don't get all the funny stuff in the street. I remember once I was walking along Shaftesbury Avenue when I first met my wife and I was taking her out on the first date and suddenly there was this bloke and he stopped and said, 'You're Michael Caine' and I said, 'I know.' He said, 'I'm your greatest fan. Look, I never expected to see you – it's fantastic. I love you, I think you're smashing. Here listen, where are you going?' I said, 'I'm taking my young lady to dinner.' So he said, 'Can I come?' and I said 'No, I'm – you know – taking her on her own.' He said 'No, I know, but can I come with you? I'm your greatest fan.' So I said, 'Quite frankly, no. I don't mind how big a fan you are and I'm very grateful, but I'm taking my young lady to dinner and we want to be on our own.' He said, 'You conceited git', and suddenly there was this madman; he said 'I've paid money to pay you . . .' and there is this crowd around and I am suddenly a villain, having been stopped by this strange man.

I live in America and the one thing I don't miss is the class distinction. I didn't realise what a burden class distinction is here and when I went to America how free it was. It must be like a black man going to Africa and everyone is black and so no one cares. I think it has been so divisive here. It's affected me in a way so that I even go on about it in the United States, it's a chip on my shoulder which will remain there forever. I got my education in the public library, on the street corners and in backs of cars: it's what is called an 'al fresco' education – that's from *Alfie*.

My priority now is first and foremost my family. I mean if I have to make a picture and my family can't come, then I don't make the picture. My family is extremely important to me and my home is extremely important to me – I don't go out a great deal, though I have bought a restaurant. I find every restaurant in London very small, run by two of the sort of fellows my father thought I would become. One's in the kitchen with a pink apron and the cookbook and the other one is outside with a bow tie. I am a big fellow with a loud voice and I smoke cigars and what happens is everyone can hear what I'm saying on either side, and I light a cigar and everyone goes limp in the smog and they can't see each other and they are just able to breathe and it looks like a swamp. So I went into partnership with a man called Peter Langan and opened somewhere called 'Langan's Brasserie'. A great big noisy place, the ceiling's high and the air conditioning works like hell and the tables are far apart. So when I go in there I can be noisy and shout and bawl. The unfortunate thing about it is that everyone else who is noisy, shouts and bawls comes in there so there is a hell of a racket – like a football stadium!

1982

ROBERT MORLEY

I come of a shy family – there are such things. My family were besieged by shyness and it spoiled their lives to a certain extent. My mother's life was made much less happy than it could have been by her inability to come across to people. She hadn't the courage to go out and meet people. I was a shy child and that is why I escaped from myself and became Robert Morley. I think actors very often get out of their skins – it is a great escape. Shyness is an awful curse – it is far better to be loud and snubbed than shy and not spoken to.

Last year we went to New Zealand with a play *How the Other Half Loves* and my younger son got himself married before I arrived and produced the most beautiful wife. He managed the tour and my wife came out and my daughter used to cook the food behind the scenes, so we had a sort of family junket round New Zealand which I simply loved. Although, I must tell you, not as many people came to see me as we had expected. If you are an elderly actor going to New Zealand you need a return ticket and a guarantee! It is not a good theatre country – why should they go to the theatre when they have the sun and the sea and beautiful scenery? In any case, even if they wanted to go, it is considered very sissy in New Zealand not to do everything yourself – like plumbing, electric work, building etc. and so there isn't a lot of time anyway once the weekend comes to go to the theatre for culture. One of the most touching things about New Zealand is this migration of grand-mothers to see their new grandchildren. The grandmothers of England who go out – they are marvellous people but they didn't come to see me either – I hope because they had already seen me in London!

You would hardly believe I'm in my seventieth year would you? It's been a great year; I've been messing about, and travelling a bit – I've been to the States, South America, Turkey and Canada – where I did my transvestite play – I'll do anything! One met the most fascinating transvestites at the stage door, always married with children, and problems. They are the most patient, charming people who have this curious compulsion to dress up as women. It is a compulsion – not a vice – a gimmick, and it has no particular sexual significance – it's just that some men, when they're harrassed by business and families, want to get out of the role and dress up as women and relax. I wore the most beautiful dresses and simply loved it, although putting on the stockings was a bore.

I still do enjoy touring – I love taking the money. I think there is something of the gypsy in all touring actors – they like to take the money and then get out. I don't know why it gives me such satisfaction, but it does. It sounds terrible, it is terrible, but it is true.

I think this is a bloody marvellous country. In England we are changing our habits, we are becoming different people and I think this is good. It is the great beginning of something entirely new and it means that in years to come you and I will be able to sit in the plane and the women will fuel it – they are going to do the heavy work! One of the unhappy things about the country is the unemployment. What seems to me so strange is that the children are brought up in a way that does not seem to fit them for the work they are going to be asked to do. I think it is very sad that so many school leavers aren't getting work and you would have thought it was within the bounds of British inventiveness to get the ones who are working to do shorter hours, and have the ones who are not working share it. Mr Heath, who never gets enough praise from me, invented the three-day week which admirably suits the British people! If you have two sets of people each doing three days a week, you have a six-day week and you have to tell people not to work so hard. What you have to do now is to slow people down, like the Russians, so that they won't work so hard. If they don't make so much money it doesn't matter if inflation comes down and it is far better that young people should work three days a week than not at all. If you don't give them work and you don't make them feel useful, you are heading for a big disaster, not only in this country. It will be the death of capitalism and the defeat of democracy as we know it.

Maybe my ideas are slightly more humorous than practical, but shouldn't we now adopt the humorous ideas? We have tried all the practical ones, and they haven't worked!

You have to be able to take criticism if you're successful, and I've had my share. An early one was, 'Mr Morley was trying in every sense of the word.'

1976 and 1978

DAVID NIVEN

I had a very unhappy childhood – it wasn't meant to be but my father was slaughtered in 1915 at the Dardanelles in the First World War and we were broke at the time. My mother had to cope with four children and I was packed off at six to a boarding school and it was a foul school. There was a dreadful amount of bullying by the older boys and by the masters. I have never been so frightened in my life as I was then. I was saved by the mad matron. I got a boil and she lopped off the top with some rusty scissors so I had a terrible infection and was put in hospital and then my mother realised what a terrible place it was. Then I was sent to a wonderful school at Ascot from which I was expelled; I had become the school clown because I found the boys liked me if I made them laugh. I split my trousers on the school walk on purpose and walked through Ascot with a bare bottom, that kind of thing. I got expelled finally, because I sent a present to a friend of mine at another school who had pneumonia – at the time I thought it was flu. I sent a large box, with a smaller box in it, with another smaller box and so on until finally a matchbox with dog's mess in it. It was particularly unattractive for the matron who opened it and apparently it flew into a medicine chest and had to be got out with forceps. Dreadful.

I was first invited to the States by Barbara Hutton who was the richest girl in the world. Off I went to New York and I shared a cabin with a man who had a prohibition suit – down each side was a tank, one which he filled with whisky and the other with gin. He was a gorgeous man. On the last night we went to the bar to drink colours – the colours of the national flags of the countries he had been to. It was finally Belgium that got me with the black, red and yellow. Black beer, port, and yellow chartreuse.

I eventually went to Hollywood because I wanted to be an actor and I joined the legion of extras – 22,000 of us after jobs for 800. There was a system then called 'The Meat Market'. When they were casting small parts they would cast them right there on the set. If a director wanted someone to play a horse doctor he would line up twelve young men who looked like horse doctors and give them all a stethoscope and then they all had to say the same line and whoever said it the best got the job.

I have been so lucky in that I have met practically everybody that is anybody at some time or another. During the war when I came back from America to England to join up, I met Winston Churchill, as at that time he was spending the odd weekend in the wing of a house of a friend of mine, as Chequers was liable to be bombed at any moment. I had no home and was invited by my friend to spend my leave there, in his part of the house – so I used to meet Churchill and he loved to talk about the movies. The first day I saw him, I had come in late and still had my uniform on and he got up from the table and walked up to me and said, 'Young man, a most magnificent effort, to give up a most promising career to fight for your King and Country. Mark you, if you had not have done so, it would have been despicable.' He used to love to take me for long walks and I remember that when things were absolutely at their blackest, I asked him if he thought that America would come into the war. He said: 'You mark my words, something cataclysmic will occur,' and six weeks later, Pearl Harbor. The next time I saw him I asked him what on earth made him say this and he said, 'Young man, I study history.'

I never actually worked with Ronald Reagan in Hollywood, but I knew him very well as he lived about two doors up from me. I have, in fact, spoken to him on the phone since he became President – he was very nice and cosy, chatting about the old days, and he said, 'I want you to know, Dave, that lady of yours is doing just great, just great.' I said 'Well, I don't know about that, she's in a very tricky mood at the moment as she keeps hearing little voices in the woods – that's the Swedish blood in her I suppose.' I thought he was talking about my wife but he was talking about Mrs Thatcher!

I think the favourite director I worked with in Hollywood was John Ford, because he was so much fun. I had a birthday once while I was doing a film with him and he brought out a great cake and said: 'Now go out tonight and really tie one on.' So I went out and got drunk – I thought he would be very happy – and I arrived on the set in the morning direct from the bar. He asked me if I was drunk and when I said yes he said, 'Get Mr Zanuck down' (the head of the studio). I was a doomed man. So he arrived with all his henchmen and Ford told him that I was drunk on the set. Zanuck asked to see a take: I was put in a white coat and given a stethoscope in my pocket and a box of dressing. So on cue I put my hand into my pocket to get the stethoscope and pulled out a snake. Then I opened the dressing and it was full of little green turtles. There were roars of laughter – it was all a huge practical joke.

I think that probably nearly everybody becomes an actor because they want to be liked, and I do enjoy being liked, but I don't work hard at it. I suppose I am survivor of a lost time really – thank God. It has been such fun and I've been so lucky to do a job I really love. Of course, the old 'star system' has gone now but there is much more opportunity for people now with television etc. and it is much easier for the young to start now, but much harder to keep going. I try to be the best I can for my age – I ski and swim and all that, but I don't view the future with any great longing and I just hope that I'll be gone before those awful things start dropping, the big ones.

1981

LAUREN BACALL

I didn't really want to be a filmstar. I really wanted to be on the stage, but I wanted my name in lights, I wanted that dream. I don't know where I got it from because no one in my family even came close to being in the theatre. I just had to do it and I would have done almost anything, and I *did* almost anything to be recognised.

I didn't have the physical attributes to be a film-star. I was flat-chested, large of foot and very gawky, and I was always shy about smiling because my teeth were crooked – oh God, I was a mess! I wanted to be a ballerina very briefly and I actually studied dancing for a great many years – since I was two years old until I was fifteen. I was taking lessons from a Russian teacher and my feet always hurt. It didn't matter how much lambswool I put in the toe of the shoe I still couldn't do it; my toes were too long – I would get dizzy doing pirouettes – I was a disaster. One day my mother came to collect me from a lesson and he said, 'Really, Mrs Bacall, I think it would be a good idea if your daughter forgot about toe-dancing, she really doesn't have the feet for it.'

Bogart was a very uncompromising person and it was very difficult for him to maintain his stance. It was very difficult to tell the truth and to be honest in a town which is full of 'hello darling' and icing on the cake. Most people in Hollywood didn't want to hear the truth – if it was negative. Bogie didn't understand that; he was incapable of telling a lie. In New York we would go to a restaurant for dinner and some drunk would walk over and say 'Hey, you think you're tough?' and Bogie would turn around if he had had a couple of drinks and say 'yeah' and start playing the part which had nothing to do with him whatever, just leading him up to the brink. He was terrific on brinkmanship. The moment the guy was ready to punch him Bogie would start to laugh because he knew that fisticuffs were out of the question – he couldn't fight his way out of a paper bag.

I've had the problem of living up to my image all my life. I'm looked at as a woman in total control and command of every situation who doesn't need anyone and who has all the answers, just like all the parts I've played. Well, as we all know, no one is that sure of themselves. If they are, I don't want to meet them. It's very tough to walk into any room privately and have someone decide what you're all about. I'm immediately on the defensive so I have to live up to that.

Men are *not* out, the ring on the finger is out. I don't see any need to get married again, although I can't say I won't. I feel better concentrating on work, friends, whatever happens. I'm very open to everything but I love to work and I really think it is the most important thing in my life. I think using oneself is more important than anything, just being aware and awake and knowing what is going on.

When you start reviewing your life you have to review the shortcomings and I don't like moments of envy that I have, professionally. I don't like, or admire myself, for not having the courage to stand up to Howard Hawks every time he made a crack about the Jews and it took me many years to deal with that. I always felt I was singled out and had additional obstacles to overcome. It became a weight round my neck and I hated the fact that I thought that.

I think to be judged by one's age is totally unfair – why should we be so limited? Everything in America is categorised by your age. Age should not confine us and make us unable to spread our wings. This affects men as well. I would never have plastic surgery. Firstly I'm terrified they'd make a terrible mistake. Secondly I'm terrified of losing my expression. That's what life has done to me.

1979

INGRID BERGMAN

I have a very morbid sense of humour. I am very open and very frank, and sometimes that is stupid. There was no rivalry between me and Garbo. The strange thing was she ended her career just as I began mine. I hope she didn't feel I was chasing her away; she stopped very early – I don't know why. She was at the height of her career – thirty-five and very beautiful; she was probably scared to continue and I was not.

I wrote my biography because my son said to me, 'When you are dead, people will throw themselves on your life story taken from gossip and rumours and we, your children, can't defend you because we don't know the truth.' That made me sit down and think very carefully because I know that after you're dead, they sit down and write a lot of things about you which aren't true.

I felt very upset and guilty when my affair with Rossellini became public knowledge. I thought I had ruined the movies I was in, such as *Joan of Arc*. I don't understand why I was villified. I was told that they loved me so much in America, I had played so many 'good' girls, and I had played nuns and saints and somehow I was put on a pedestal and used as a good example for the parents – I could do nothing wrong. There was no gossip about me in my private life and suddenly this happened, and I had a child. This was before I was divorced or before he was divorced and we didn't do anything to prevent the birth of this baby. We wanted it and that shocked the world.

I had many friends – I had a box with 'good' letters and a box with 'bad' letters and they were about even. People were very kind. Ernest Hemingway did something positive about the scandal – he was very upset about it. He talked to the newspapers and he wrote and talked to me. He helped. But most people were very afraid. Afraid of losing their career; their name. A little Swedish actress – Marta Toren – said she thought it was all right. She said, 'I think she is courageous and I admire her and I am very proud to be Swedish,' and the studio almost fired her for saying that.

I was very shy as a child – I was a lonely child and only wanted to be an actress and it seems very strange to want to be up on a stage and show yourself, when you cannot show yourself in a room. I couldn't talk to people, I was blushing, I just couldn't fit in; but on the stage I was behind a mask, it was another person, it was not my words and I wasn't responsible for what I said. I could be free then, so that was my relief – to be behind someone else. My acting was dictated by my heart – I was very stubborn. I suppose it was my German mother and my Swedish father, the combination of those two must have made me very strong in a way. Your desire and wish is so strong that it carries you to what you want. I wanted to be an actress; and not only that, but to be a very good one.

1980

LILLI PALMER

As a child I grew up in Berlin and I think it was when I was about eleven years old that I was first made to realise that I was Jewish. I had this yearning to become an actress and to play Mary in the Christmas pantomime at school. When I asked to play the role of the Virgin Mary, my teacher said I couldn't because I was Jewish and in spite of the fact that Mary was a Jewess, Christmas had become a Christian symbol. I didn't understand that at all and so I told my father, who was a surgeon, that I had to get baptized at once before Christmas. He told me that I should postpone it until I was twenty-one and then he wouldn't stand in my way. My father wanted me to be a surgeon, but I wanted to be an actress like my mother.

I was made to realise quite forcefully that I had to leave Germany. I was appearing in my very first engagement in repertory and Hitler had just taken over – I was eighteen years old – and there were twenty stormtroopers in the first row to demonstrate as soon as I entered on stage. It was pretty terrifying but as we all danced on together holding hands, we saw that the first two rows were empty. They had found out that my father had earned the Iron Cross in the First World War and that saved me from concentration camp. My father then told me that I had to leave at once so I went to join my sister in Paris. We formed the most dreadful nightclub act that you could imagine – we were like two fat girl guides and we sang in five languages and we never lasted more than about a week. I have never been able to dance and when the script arrived for the film I made with Fred Astaire in Hollywood and there was a scene in which he had to sweep me up in his arms and we had to dance together, I said to the director that I could not dance. He told me that anybody could dance with Astaire and so the first rehearsal came and he swept me in arms of steel and dropped me gracefully, and I landed with both my feet on his nailing him down to the floor! I think I'm the only person who ever nailed Fred Astaire down. We managed the rest of the scene because he picked me up and held me as we were dancing round and my feet never touched the floor.

When I was younger I had a crush on Gary Cooper and when the day was over, I used to imagine him sitting next to me and I would tell him all my troubles. When I went to Hollywood much later with my first husband, Rex Harrison, I was called to come to the Warner Brother studios to make a test opposite Gary Cooper. I thought they were pulling my leg but I got the part and it was like holding a sugar bun in front of a baby. For four months I was lying more or less in his arms and it was simply delightful. He didn't disappoint me at all – he even smelt good. We became great friends and he would come into my dressing room and tell me about *his* life story and I had been telling him mine for years!

I worked with Clark Gable shortly before his death and he was a wonderful professional. Nobody waited for inspiration in Hollywood in the great days – they were on the set at nine o'clock and ten minutes later the first shot was in the can. Clark had a way of frightening you by suddenly taking his teeth out and putting them in again. They were made for him by a famous dentist in Hollywood called Dr Wallace and I called these things his Wallace Collection!

51

I brought about the meeting between Greta Garbo and the Duke and Duchess of Windsor. The Duke and Duchess used to come a lot to Portofino where Rex and I had a house and the Duke loved to come there because he took his German lesson with me and we made records together of Goethe poems. As we were having dinner one night, Greta sent a note up saying she was there and could she come up. The Duke wanted to meet her and so up she came, dressed in slacks and an old pullover and sat next to the Duchess who was always beautifully attired. These two women looked each other up and down – they knew they were sacred cows of the century – and then the Duchess gave a famous party for Garbo who didn't own an evening dress, so we all went in slacks.

The Duke used to tell me the most extraordinary things. For instance, something that absolutely flawed me was when he told me that his misfortune was that when he was nineteen he discovered that the love of his life was America, not England. His bad luck was that he married an American who insisted on living in Paris. I asked him if he ever had a longing for England and replied that he had not since his mother had died.

I've now been writing over the last twenty years and like most things in my life, it came to me by chance. An American producer asked me to write my autobiography, hoping I suppose for some dirt from my marriage. As an inducement, he sent me a cheque for $5,000 and I went out and bought myself a mink coat that very afternoon! He wanted to have a book about the joys of being over forty, so I sat down and wrote and found that I ran out of joys on the third page. I wrote to him and offered him back the mink coat, but he already had one, so we left the idea for a while. Later, when I started making a new career in Germany, a German publisher wanted my autobiography and bought me out of that mink coat contract. He told me that I had to write because I was the only person who had come back to the country of my birth, not even knowing her language anymore. I went back to Germany when I was thirty-eight years old, after my marriage had broken up.

I have now written my first novel *A Time to Embrace* which was much more difficult to write than my autobiography but much more fascinating. After a while you get bored with yourself, but it is fun to create new characters and situations. I started this new career after I was forty and I would describe myself as a late, late developer.

1980

DIRK BOGARDE

I know it's a funny thing, but being in the Army was the happiest time of my life. I went in when I was eighteen and came out when I was twenty. I went in dreading it; my father said that they would be the happiest days of my life, and it was actually almost true. It's strange what happens to a man when he goes into war, a strange growing up, very quickly. I would have stayed as a soldier if there had been a war to fight, but there wasn't, and so I came out. I just enjoyed being a soldier. I liked the camp-fire life, I liked being with the other men, I liked having the responsibility, I liked having the excitement of it, and I liked the fear of it. My background as an actor was completely eliminated.

I became an officer; I went before a terrible board and I had to go into a room with about twenty elderly colonels, all with red tabs and glasses. One was just like Himmler's aunt – writing everything down (that was the psychiatrist). Anyway, the long and short of it was that I was going to fail because I had been an actor – unstable you know. Then it dawned on me that if I told them something I had done perhaps it would help. All I could remember was that I had been in a play at the Wyndham Theatre with Peter Ustinov and we had been some sort of chorus boys. I told them and they looked in absolute ashen shock – I could see Himmler's aunt closing her file – that was it, I was out. Then the general turned round and said 'Your father, some journalist fellow?' 'Yes, he's the art editor on *The Times*.' And somebody chipped in, 'Not your sort of thing, General, *The Times* is rather intellectual. It's not *Men Only*.' I rather quickly said, 'But all the editors know each other, Sir.' And the general said 'Your father knows *Men Only*?' Anyway, I got my commission simply because my poor father provided twenty pin-ups of naked ladies for the Officers' Mess. It's absolutely true, it's how the British Army was founded.

I was taken to the movies by my nanny. Much against my parents' advice she used to take me somewhere called the 'Ionic' in Golders Green. I saw a film and it was so scary that I ate the strip off the side of my cap in my terror, but gave the whole game away because we pretended that we had been to Fullers for walnut cake, and when I was suddenly rather sick my mother said: 'Why is he bring up cardboard and flannel?' I'd eaten my hat. That was my earliest recollection of the cinema.

The first film I made in Hollywood was the life of Franz Liszt, 'a biog'. I had to play Franz – the money was enormous. I had never been there before, I was nearly forty and I thought it was about time I went. The script was unspeakable; lines like 'Hey, do you know my friend, George Sand? That's your friend Chopin, this is Schubert, come on and meet George Sand.' I had to play Liszt's music on the piano and I can't play a Jewish harp. They said I had to play. I asked how much there was to play and they said eighty-five minutes (it was a three hour film). I was given two dummy keyboards, a hotel suite, a rather nice Russian Jewish man called Victor, and a stack of records of all this music. It was fine except I discovered that I had no co-ordination, so what my right hand was doing my left hand could not do. Well, we learnt it in the end after seven months of work. The producer came to me one day and said, 'We've just seen the run-through of the movie, and it's just great, kid, you're going to be a star.' I thought I had been that for some time.

There is and there isn't a different technique for stage acting and films. The most important thing is that you have to think, because I didn't realise that the camera photographs your mind. The lens is my love and it photographs you right inside your mind – you can't think of your laundry list and play a role; you can't do it on technique – actually you can, but it's much more exciting to do it with your mind. It controls your face and your body and the way you move. Every line comes out only if it's in your mind. That's the secret of screen acting.

It also depends on looks. I remember a long time ago, at Pinewood, Alan Ladd was making a film. He wasn't very tall, and he stood on boxes. His 'group' were sitting beside mine in the restaurant, and were sending him up for his size, knocking him all the way through. He came in and they changed their tune, and asked whether he had had a good morning, and whether he had got on the horse. He said 'No, I just did a great look.' A great look is a still regard, but it's not an empty look. It's a look that has thought behind it. I went straight back on the set and thought from now on I'm going to try and do great looks. The rest of my film career was built on this advice from Alan Ladd, and I think it worked. It's a love relationship with the camera.

1980

KIRK DOUGLAS

I think the actor hides behind every character he plays. I have always had a theory that most actors are really shy people, myself included, and I think the most difficult thing is what I'm doing now, to be myself. It's much easier when you've got a character to hide behind.

I sometimes think that if you want to tell the truth, you write a novel and if you want to lie, you write a biography. My story is so typical of so many people in the United States that come from immigrant parents (mine were Russian Jews). You work your way through college, go to dramatic school and you're fortunate to go into the kind of work that you like to do. It's the corny American story. I come from what you might call abject poverty – not having enough to eat, days when we didn't have any food. I don't actually think that there is any reason for anyone in the world to be hungry and poor and I think that hopefully, someday, some of our politicians will certainly work out a way to ensure that nobody is hungry and poor. I was the only boy in a family of six girls; I not only had six sisters and my mother, making seven women, but my father and mother separated at an early age and that left me with the seven women which I think was a very difficult upbringing. I found going to college was really a form of escape. My father was a very powerful man, a peasant, who drank a lot as a form of escape and I have often thought that one of the bravest moments in my life was when I was about ten and we were all sitting round the table drinking tea, I took a spoonful of hot tea and flicked it in his face. Well, he grabbed me, spanked me but I just felt satisfied to have done it and it was almost like an act that saved me.

Kids are the greatest actors of all, they are so natural and they pretend to

54

be whatever they want to be. I think you have to retain a childish quality in you to be an actor – it's a childish profession. I believe that most actors become actors as a form of escape and it's really a continuation of your daydreams.

I had to work my way through college and I had all sorts of jobs; I was a gardener, a waiter and I worked in a carnival during the summer vacations. I was an undefeated wrestler at college and during the summer, one of the fellows in the carnival wrestling team would be the 'Masked Marvel' and I used to take him on and I would make about ten or twelve dollars a night. Then my 'Masked Marvel' friend and I would go out and have a beer. As a kid I had always been attracted to carnivals and I always loved working in one. I think the excitement has always stayed with me and the profession I am in now is quite similar to that.

At that time I was aiming towards a career on the stage and I well remember my début on Broadway! I came in at the end of the second act to sing a telegram and that was all. As a matter of fact, it went steadily downhill after that because my next performance was as an offstage echo! Still, you keep trying and I was fortunate enough to be in several Broadway plays, none of which were successes however. Then a very dear friend of mine, Betty Bacall (who then became Lauren Bacall) was talking to Hal Wallace and told him to look me up when he came to New York, which he did and made me my first offer. I turned it down at the time because I never thought of myself as a movie actor – I still thought I could be a Broadway star. It was only months later, out of desperation, when my wife at the time was pregnant with my son Michael that I wondered if he still wanted me, and I called him. The next day I was on a train to Hollywood to make my first picture.

I started off in movies as a weakling. It was playing the part of 'Champion' that changed it all. My agent thought I was crazy because MGM had offered me a part co-starring with Ava Gardner and Gregory Peck, but I loved the script and I loved the idea of playing a different kind of role. Overnight I became a tough guy.

I remember I was driving to Palm Springs one day and I saw a sailor who was hitching. I used to be in the Navy, and I stopped and he got in the car. He studied me for a while and then said 'Do you know who you are?' I am always intrigued with the reaction of people when they recognise stars and I think that all performers have funny stories to tell about this. Often, people recognise the face, but in their nervousness, they forget the name and Burt Lancaster and I often seem to get confused.

When I first came to Hollywood, everyone was under contract to a studio. Now that is quite rare, but at that time it was quite different. I didn't have a contract then and I have only ever had one contract in my life. I have always been a loner in that sense and I didn't always like it; most people had their own group; they would complain about things, but they 'belonged' to a studio, and at times I felt lonely. It was in 1956 that I formed my own production company.

I enjoy doing my own stunts generally – it's part of being a kid. I've had a broken nose, broken fingers, a broken rib, but I try to be sensible although I can't resist seeing if I can't do the stunt. I know that the intensity of my performance always comes across and I don't know if that makes me a difficult man to work with. It's true that among certain people in Hollywood

I wouldn't win a popularity contest and I think a lot of that is because I work very hard and I've always been independent but I would like to think that things have mellowed over the years. I think the more well-known you become, the more the spotlight is thrown on you and your behaviour becomes exaggerated, and generally speaking, faults are much more interesting than virtues. There is a story that Billy Wilder tells about when they were casting for *The Defiant Ones*, which was a picture about a black man and a white man: they first went to Marlon Brando who said that he would only play the black man; then they went to Robert Mitchum who said that he wasn't going to play in any movie with any black fella; then they went to Kirk Douglas who said that he wanted to play both parts!

I've been nominated for an Oscar three times, but I've never actually won one. Obviously, I would like to win an Oscar, but I can't say that I *should* have one. I was very disappointed not to win when I was nominated for *Lust for Life*, because people had led me to believe that I was going to win. My wife did a very sweet thing; she had a miniature Oscar made up for me from her and my son Peter, in case I didn't win – so that's the only Oscar I've won. I love making movies, being on location – it really stimulates me and if ever it gets monotonous or boring, and I don't have the feeling of a challenge, obstacles to overcome, then I will stop making movies. But I don't foresee that happening for about thirty or forty years!

1979

JAMES STEWART

My father had a hardware store in Western Pennsylvania, near the big industrial city of Pittsburgh. His father established the hardware store, and my father was able to celebrate the 100th anniversary of the hardware store before he died. I think that the reason he kept the hardware store for so long was because he was sure that people were going to catch up with me out in Hollywood and I would have something to go back to. He wasn't too happy about the acting profession as a way to make a living. When I was leaving to seek my fortune on the stage, he said, 'Well I think this is fine. There haven't been any Stewarts in the film business, except one – a third cousin of yours, Ezra, and he ran away and joined the circus. And he's the only Stewart that I know that's ever been to jail. But good luck to you.'

I was asked by some people that ran a stock company up in Massachusetts to come up, not as an actor but as an accordion player, as an entertainer in a tea-room which was next to the theatre where they did summer stock. And I lasted two nights in the tea-room. It was rather embarrassing really, they said that my music destroyed their appetite. Then I was given a job in the property department and I helped paint scenery and I sort of got in, and then I got small parts.

I don't ever remember trying to change my voice. Except perhaps when I played Lindbergh, I tried to raise the voice, because he had a very high voice and he didn't hem and haw the way I do. Also I remember I was in a play in New York. I played an Austrian nobleman: that'll give you a little idea that I needed the work. It was a terrible, sad, tragic play and I somehow felt that I should have some suggestion of an Austrian accent. And there was a woman in New York in those days by the name of Frances Robinson Duff, and she would coach people mostly in voice projection and so on. So I went to Miss Duff. This was tough corn, you know, it was five bucks a throw to go to the lessons, but I felt that this was important and she said, 'Yes, I think we can work on some kind of a suggestion of an accent.' But after three lessons, she called me in and she said, 'I'm going to have to let you go, there's no way I can teach you an Austrian accent. But any time in the future that you feel that you'd like to learn to speak English . . .'

When you were under contract to one of the big studios in those days you worked all the time. You had tiny little parts in big pictures and every once in a while you would get a big part in a tiny little picture. You did tests of all kinds. I was told I was going to test for the part of Shane in *The Good Earth*. I was stripped to the waist, darkened down, and I was to do the test with Paul Muni. The test was a walking shot of maybe fifty feet, and the first thing Paul Muni said was, 'There's a helluva tall Chinaman.' What they did, they dug a trench and Muni walked there and I walked in the trench. I didn't get the part . . . they gave it to a Chinese person.

I remember when I first read the first draft of the script of *Wonderful Life*. And that scene of the little prayer affected me. This is a theory that I've always had – I think that creating moments in movies is the important thing. Nobody knows exactly how it happens. What you should do is to prepare yourself as best you can, to make these moments happen. Because in a movie, it's really not so much the performance, but the moments like this.

I'm the plodder. I'm the inarticulate man that tries. I'm a pretty good example of true human frailty . . . I don't really have all the answers. I have very few of the answers, but for some reason, somehow I make it. I get through. When I'm at the head of the wagon-train, for some reason we get across the water.

1973

HENRY
FONDA
It never occurred to me to be an actor, I didn't have any background in my life, in my family, or in any way. I didn't grow up going to movies and thinking I want to be a movie actor, I went to the movies but it never occurred to me whilst I was at college. I studied journalism at college – thought I was going to be a writer; my grandfather I think sort of encouraged that. Anyway I'm home from college and a very good friend of the family named Dorothy Brando – who later had a son called Marlon – was very active on the board of directors at the little Community Playhouse, an amateur group, and they were suddenly stuck without a juvenile and it wasn't that Do thought that I had talent, I just was the right age. She literally pushed me and I was too shy to say 'don't do this to me!' and that's how it happened.

Finally the season was over and my dad told me it was time I had a proper job. Through an advertisement in the local paper I got a job as a file clerk in a

'I think to be
judged by one's age is
totally unfair . . . why
should we be so
limited?'
Lauren Bacall

'I didn't realise
the camera
photographs your
mind . . . It's
a love relationship
with the camera'
Dirk Bogarde

'I've never been
seduced into
leaving England
. . . I loathe California –
it's the suburbia
of the souls'
Trevor Howard

retail credit company. I got the job in June, and the following September the director came back for the Playhouse second season and called me and said that they were going to do *Merton of the Movies* and I was to play Merton. I didn't know what this was, but I said fine, because I'd had so much fun before, but my father said, 'No way – you've got a very important job, important in the sense that there is a chance for advancement, and you can't do justice to both,' but I was determined I was going to do it, not because I had ambition to be an actor but because I had had so much fun the year before. So I had the only argument I'd ever had with my father. My mother was the diplomat and I didn't have to leave home, which I'd threatened to do because I was twenty-one by then. I stayed at home but my father didn't speak to me for a month – well he didn't get much of a chance because I wasn't home enough. Opening night, the family came of course to see *Merton of the Movies*: two sisters, my mother and father. My sister came back afterwards to the dressing room and said 'We'll wait at home for you.' So eventually I got my make-up off and I leave and go home. Now my father is sitting in his chair reading the paper and he doesn't speak to me so I join my sisters and my mother and they just went on with extravagant praise and just everything, oh marvellous, for about ten minutes, and then my sister started to say something that sounded like it was going to be less than extravagant. 'There was only one point when I thought if only . . .' she got about that far and Dad said 'Shut up he was perfect'. Three years later when I learned you got paid for acting in New York and I decided to go there there was no quarrel at all.

I was managing to avoid the studio system but then *The Grapes of Wrath* come along and I'd read the book and I'd been a great fan of Steinbeck. I'd read everything he's written and then when Zanuck bought it I thought I'd love to play that part and everybody else wanted to play it too – all the young actors around. When he called me I'd done several films for him but as a freelance actor, and he'd been after the contract and I just resisted it, but he held that one out like bait and I confess I was a hungry enough fish; I grabbed it and I took the bait, but I can't say I regret it, because I did get *The Grapes of Wrath*. Who is to know whether he'd given me the part anyway? But *Grapes of Wrath* did happen to me and I'll be forever grateful, but I did some forgettable films right after that.

I've done about eighty-five films actually, and I don't think more than fifteen of them were westerns, but I do have the reputation of being a western actor. Westerns were popular around the world then; Japan loved westerns, and Australia and Italy. Anyway I've done my share and I guess I've been lucky that some of those were the good ones – *Ox-Bow Incident* and *Darling Clementine* and *Jesse James*. There were some good ones and they are remembered. I'm not western, even with my accent I'm from the middle west of the States, but cowboy – forget it! I don't like horses, I don't like riding. They had to pay me a lot of money to get me on a horse. I was scared to death. It's dangerous. You can get killed.

Both Jane and Peter went through what is known as a classic rebellion. When a child decides to go into the father's business, whether he's a banker or in show business, there has to be a kind of rebellion – you don't want to feel that your father made it possible for you, or that you're a success because of your father. So they both went through what is recognised and called classic rebellion, and I like to think that I was smart enough to recognise it for what it was. Also they both did well almost immediately so I didn't have to hold my breath too long and the rebellion didn't last very long, but while it lasted there were some provocative things said. *Time* magazine did a cover story on us only three years ago, and they assigned a reporter to each one of the three of us for two weeks each, and then all of us were together – Jane and Peter and I were together with the reporters. Not one word was taken during those two weeks and used in the story, it was all a rehash of the old stuff, and both of them were as unhappy with it as I was, but that's why it lasts, because it's in the file, and it's part of the legend and we could not be more friendly and happy together. I couldn't be more proud, and really in awe of both of them. Jane is one of the most incredible actresses I've ever seen. But when I saw *Klute*, as an example, I couldn't wait to sit and talk to her and this was not father to daughter, this was actor to actor. 'Where did it come from? How did it happen to you? When did you know?' We were talking actor talk, and then I realised the scene that had knocked me out was improvisation which I couldn't do if I was paid money to do it. I just can't, I have to have the written word and a director to help me along. They got to this scene and the director knew what he wanted but it wasn't written and he talked to Jane about it, and she says: 'Just give me a moment', and this came out in improvisation. And just tore you apart. Anyway, she's not only this incredible actress, but she's the activist that you would know her to be and I'm in nothing but sympathy with her.

I was going to say that my son is the original hyphenate – (producer-director-writer) but I realise that Orson Welles was ahead of him. When Peter was twelve years old in his little boarding school, he wrote, produced, built the scenery, made the wardrobe and played four parts and directed this play. And he's doing it now in films; he is more knowledgeable about films in the few years that he's been involved than I have been in forty years, he knows not only every different kind of lens, but why it's used. He knows all the technical things about making films, he also knows how to release them and distribute them, which I'm not only unknowledgeable about but couldn't care less about. He's brilliant.

1975

TREVOR HOWARD

I have just finished making a movie in the Utah Mountains in which I played an Indian chief. It was very tough and 12,500 feet up in fourteen foot snowdrifts. There was a lot of physical work involved and I'm too old for that sort of thing. However, they said I looked more Indian than the Indians! I was the only non-Indian in the cast and I had to learn the language although, quite frankly, I was saying all my girlfriends' names, streets and towns in a funny accent and nobody seemed to mind because they didn't know what I was talking about.

I actually started in the theatre but have worked more or less predominantly in movies since the War. I enjoy making films and I think that if one is going to work hard at what you most want to do and what you do best, then it's stupid to dissipate it by doing two or three things. Most young actors today don't want to be actors, they want to be directors and I think that is a pity. I feel that if you are going to get recognition as a director without writing the script, without doing the cutting and just being there and for everyone else to do the photography, you are playing a bit of a prostitute. I don't think that's fair. If I wanted to be a director I would have to give up being an actor and I much prefer to be an actor.

Before the War, we didn't have burning ambitions, we used to enjoy life so much. The War, for me, was the waste of some of the best years of my life, and when it was over, I was determined to get this back. When I started my career as a film actor, I also acquired a reputation as being a 'hell-raiser', but I don't understand why! I've been arrested quite a few times, I don't remember how many. I was arrested in Paris, Italy and Vienna because I was enjoying myself. I've worked with one or two other 'hell-raisers' with reputations for boisterous behaviour, one being Robert Mitchum. In fact he is the most relaxed man who doesn't really do anything. He doesn't court trouble, it comes to him and I think that happens to me too. I enjoyed working with him very much on *Ryan's Daughter*, but I didn't enjoy working on the film – nobody did. If you are working with David Lean you have to realise that it will take at least six months, possibly a year before it is finished. I took a holiday in the middle of shooting for five and a half weeks and they didn't even realise that I wasn't there! They were waiting for seagulls and Mitchum to change his clothes or something.

I was in New York with Mitchum promoting *Ryan's Daughter* and David Frost interviewed him. He had been asked beforehand what he wanted to talk about and he had said that he didn't mind what they talked about as long as it wasn't the War. The first question Frost asked was 'What did you do in the War?' He was smoking a pipe at the time, full of marijuana, and he paused for a few seconds and replied that he had been an anus inspector. On being asked to repeat that, he said: 'I inspected people's arseholes'. Well, that was too much for Frost and he asked Mitchum if he ever saw any of them now and Mitchum replied that he didn't recognise any of them by their faces, he just asked them to bend over!

Nowadays I keep getting the offer of eccentric parts to play! I'm going to play a man who decides to live without people, but with birds and I mean the twittering kind. He makes himself a pair of wings because he wants to get up into the galaxies. This man is quite insane in my opinion, but the director didn't think so. I don't find that now I'm getting older that acting gets easier, no it doesn't. I went to RADA and I think this sort of training is very necess-ary. Way, way back when I was a young man we were terribly inhibited and to come down to acting school in London where there are twenty girls to every five boys, you really get rid of a lot of inhibitions! I don't think it taught me how to act and the girls didn't go there to become actresses either.

I have travelled all over, but I have never been seduced into leaving England. I think it's the roots, the chaps and what you get used to that keeps me here. I loathe California – New York is another story but California is the suburbia of the soul. I think I've said enough now. I want to go backstage and talk cricket!

1980

JOHN ARLOTT

I think the greatest change in sport since I first started watching it is that the really mature men, spiritually and mentally, can no longer play. One Sunday league cricket match would kill them – diving and sprawling about. The game is harder.

Politics governs everything we do – the games we play, the way we play them, who we play. Politics control life because politics is the philosophy by which you live, exist and behave. I'd call the Olympic Games off although I do realise how desperately important this is for some men who are at the peak of their careers and the last thing I want to sacrifice is what means the world to them. I don't think the Olympics is fun any more. Not many games are fun these days. But I think that sportsmen are so single minded about these games that they don't appreciate the political or any other aspect. To many people sport is the be all and end all of their life – but the real sense of life is that war and humans are more important than a game of any sort.

I think performers have lost the real perspective of what they do. But if they don't accept the over-importance they are going to fail. They are in a Catch-22 situation – they may want to play for fun but if you want to be the best at any sport you can't afford to play for fun – you have to be single-minded, you have to concentrate on it. So it's the external forces which drive the fun out of a performer's make-up.

This is the age of confrontation. This is the age which won't accept justice or judgement. They don't want to accept the ruling of the umpire, but if we don't accept discipline there is no shape or purpose in what we do. There is a remedy – the players must adjust this. The professional cricket players above all recognise the need for discipline and pattern. Jack Hobbs above all is the example of how a sportsman should be. There was a humility about him that enhanced his greatness. There are great characters about now – what greater character could you ask for at the moment than Ian Botham?

The one-day cricket game was intended to attract a fresh public, which it did. When one has to go out and take a go at a chap who is bowling a blind length and you've got to attack him, this adds a particular element of peril or risk that was never paralleled in the old game. Would it be glib to say that cricket is poetry in motion? A lot of poetic quality, a lot of poetic thought, a lot of poetic imagination and excitement exists in cricket, far more than in any other sport.

I always met Dylan Thomas for cricket in Swansea. He loved watching cricket, especially because the bar was open all day! He also loved to watch it and seize on someone exciting or stimulating – he enjoyed the whole pattern of the thing. He'd suddenly dive on someone and say: 'Tell me all about it.' He was a very full man – Dylan – he was a superb poet and he was also interested in every aspect of life. He worked for me on the radio; he did seventy-five per cent of his broadcasts and poetry programmes himself and I was very fond of him. He was incredibly human, humorous and generous. He could read like an angel, and if you are a poetry producer, you had to like him. Mind you, he needed to read poetry he enjoyed. I remember once putting him in a programme – really because he needed the money – on late Victorian poets. He looked at one of these and said, 'John, I don't want to read that poem because it's unbearably arrogant about women and I can't put up with it, pick me another one.' Always he was alive. He was an original in every way. He gave me two answers as to why he got drunk. He said that 'I drink to feel good,' and he also said, which has always intrigued me, 'I get drunk because every time I get drunk it's different and it's wonderful.'

When I retire I am going to miss the company of cricketers. But what will be wonderful is that I will never have to fight for a drink or for lunch at the Oval and get the left-overs. I will be at home watching it on television, never getting upset by rain or stoppage of play.

1980

GEOFFREY BOYCOTT

I first played cricket in the backstreets at my home in Fitzwilliam. We used to play down the middle of the street using a manhole for the wicket, and it was there I learnt my best shot – the straight drive – which if struck right went all the way down the street. We used to play until it got dark and then carried on playing by gaslight until my mum called me to bed. I suppose I realised that I was above average when I played in the Festival of Britain competition aged about ten and I did fairly well – I took six wickets for ten runs and made forty-five not out. It was then that my uncle started to encourage me to go for private cricket coaching. As a cricketer himself he was exceptionally keen for me to play. We didn't have much money to pay for coaching but the family contributed and I used to go religiously every Saturday morning in winter until I finished grammar school at eighteen.

I played for Yorkshire schoolboys when I was fifteen. I had a rude awakening when I went to the schoolboy trials. I was the best in my area but there were lots of other good players which brought me down to earth. It was very difficult to get into the side.

When I was sixteen I was very single-minded about it. I wanted to play cricket and I wanted to do it well. The driving force was that I wanted to see how good I was. If I failed I could live with it but first I had to know how good a player I was.

I am a professional man. I don't socialise much, I play cricket. I don't think I should be judged on how good a talker I am or how many pints of beer I drink, and I think that's why in the long run people have supported me, because they know I will do my best.

I'm a plain speaking man and a professional and because of that some people think I'm selfish but I'm just a single-minded, determined cricketer.

To me the most priceless commodity is loyalty but there doesn't seem to be much about these days.

1977

BASIL D'OLIVEIRA

It wasn't until I first came to England in 1960 that I realised I was being treated as a second-class citizen. Before that I grew up in the system in Cape Town – you were born into it. You were born in a certain area and you were told you had to live there, you were told where to go to school and what bus to use. You are told where to go and it becomes part of you. You just live in that system and you can't measure it against anything. So there was no specific point when I realised I was a second-class citizen in South Africa, but when I came to England I could put that against what I'd seen in South Africa, and then I knew how it was and it became annoying.

The differences were enormous and they are even today. I mean you had no facilities at school, you had no coaching as such, you had no areas that you could play on, so everything that was given in South Africa was given to the white child and not to the coloured or the black child. And it is the same today and this is one of my big arguments, one of my big grievances. I don't feel any animosity towards South Africa or anything there for what happened to me, but what I do feel very sincerely about is the children. And I think the time has arrived when the South African government should be fair to all the kids. They should have equal facilities, they should have equal schooling, the syllabus should be the same. If they are going to spend six hundred and fifty quid on a white child's schooling and forty on a black child's then I think it is slightly wrong. I want to see that put right. That is what I am really concerned about.

When I got the letter inviting me to come over to England I really thought my chance had come, but I had to find £250 for my air fare. Then I had to look after a wife who was pregnant and possibly pay for digs while I was over here. When I showed my wife the letter she told me I should go, which was all I needed, and she has been like that ever since – it's been marvellous. I still had no money though so I went to see my pal at the Grand Hotel in Cape Town. I'll never forget that; I couldn't go through the entrance because it is a white hotel and he was working up in a bar upstairs. So the only way I could get to him without anybody seeing me was through the back entrance. I did reach him and he insisted that I went, he told me he would raise the money for me and look after my family while I was away. He thought that if I won over here, I would be winning something for the blacks. That is why I have not become involved with politics or any militant groups as such, because I feel my role is always going to be as a shop window and I want it to remain like that. My shop window has got to be the cricket field.

I can't describe my feelings when I was picked to play for England – I just can't put it into words. Just consider that when I came from South Africa, all I wanted to do was to play here and get a coaching certificate so that I could go back home and coach my own people. That was all I thought of. Then I played so well in the leagues that I suddenly wanted to play county cricket. It was just incredible when I was selected for England. I couldn't believe it – at my age and the way I played. I looked at all the great players of county cricket at the time and I didn't think I had a chance of making an England side. To walk into an England dressing-room is the end of the earth for any man, and that's the way I think anybody who is going to play for England should view it. It is the biggest and finest accolade you can get and should be treated as such.

I very much feel that I am an Englishman now. I made up my mind when I came to live in England to get involved, to become more English because that was the only way for me, otherwise I would have had grievances all my life. That is what I have done and I've been very happy doing it and I am very happy where I am living now.

1980

MUHAMMAD ALI

It's a big thing to be, you know, the number one in the world. I mean, Nixon was in power yesterday and now all of a sudden he's running around like a bag of bun in the wilderness. You understand now, Heavyweight Champion, President of the United States, can fall quicker than anybody.

I'm going to tell you something now. You're intelligent. They told me I had to come and do your show. You see, you're not as dumb as you look. When they told me I was going to do your show, I was honoured. People like you, David Frost, David Susskind, I like people to make me think. You'll find out that I'm a witty person and it's kind of hard to talk to a man like me. I need people of wisdom such as myself to make me think, keep me going.

I don't like the way you write about Bugner. To put that man down, that's a shame. The British can't even unite. Look, you've got a good White Hope there, you can build the man up, give him some confidence, and might make him be better than he is. He's representing England, you should stand up for him, he's your champ. He's got more class than George Foreman. I didn't knock out Joe Bugner, he went twelve rounds with Joe Frazier. If you don't think he is talented, then that means I'm nothing. You mean a man can go twelve rounds with me and have no talent? I hit him with everything . . . that was a hell of a fight, me and Joe Bugner. Of the top ten best heavyweights in the world, he's the fourth best.

Have you always been on this television show? You was a little old hostel run-around before you came up here one day. Now look at you. Supposing I told you, supposing I told you you'd never be nothing and you're not as good as David Susskind, and you're not as good as Eamonn Andrews, or you can't make it like Harry Carpenter. Anyone tell you that? Now look at you, you're the number one man around here, but you had to work up. It's people like you that make Joe Bugner train hard, because one day curly-haired, handsome Joe Bugner is going to be champion and you're going to say, 'Joe, would you come on my show?' And Joe will say, 'Didn't I tell you, didn't I tell you, what I used to say?' No, but it's people like you, you're a good man, you speak your piece and I'm sure you wouldn't say what you say if you didn't mean it. But I'll tell you one thing, people like you are good. I admire people like you, because it makes you train, it makes you work to prove you wrong. So Joe Bugner, when you watch this show, you come back, and I want Mike to be the first man you slap when you get your title.

You say I got white friends, I say they're associates. I don't have a single white friend. I don't have one black friend hardly. A friend is one who will not even consider giving his life for you – that's a friend. The one who will not even think about it. A friend is one who is always out to give and keep nothing back – always is out to give and not look for nothing in return.

It's a fact that white people hate black people and you're the biggest hypocrite in the world if you can go on nationwide TV and tell me white people like black people. I'm not saying you dislike them in the way that you want to show it, but white people give black people jobs, black people are dying in hospitals, white people are operating on them. American black people have been there for four hundred years, and white people feed us, they clothe us, we don't make shoestrings, and we don't have our hair combed, we totally rely on the white man and the white man's good to us. The white man's doing a lot to help us and make a way for us, and still it's the same, white men talk about us and don't like us.

I'm not just a boxer, I'm taught by Elijah Mohammed, I'm educated, even Oxford University – your biggest seat of learning – offered me a professorship in philosophy and poetry to come here and teach. I'm not just an ordinary fighter, I can talk all week on millions of subjects and you do not have enough wisdom to corner me on television. You're too small mentally to tackle me on anything that I represent. I'm serious – you and this TV show is nothing to Muhammad Ali and if you've got some more questions, I'll answer them, and I bet you I'll eat you right here on the air. All of you are tricky, that's how your John Hawkins, a white Englishman, tricked us out of Africa and America. You get me on your show and ask me all kinds of tricky questions. How you going to get me on the TV and trap me? Ain't no way. You can't beat me physically nor mentally. You're a white man and your knowledge ain't nothing to a Muslim. You are really a joke. I'm serious, this is a joke.

I didn't miss out on education. I wouldn't learn. I didn't know the value of it. I was a little black boy in Kentucky. I didn't know nothing about I'd be on your show, didn't know nothing about I'd be a world champion. Playing hookey, playing at the girls, just going to recess and eating lunch and joking and not knowing the value of education like many children, during the day. Never thinking that one day I'd have to feed myself. Didn't have no idea of profit and getting out and making money like a lot of children do. And all of a sudden I found myself having trouble reading things, looking at contracts. I got to hire lawyers or watch lawyers. I know the value of education now so I'm going to brainwash my children. My daughter's six years old and she speaks Arabic, English and Spanish.

I have a wisdom that can make me talk to you or an educated man on any subject and if the audience or the people listen, they'll say I won. I study life, I study people, and I'm educated on this, but when it comes to reading and writing, I'm not. I may be illiterate in that, but when it comes to common sense, when it comes to feelings, when it comes to love, compassion, heart for people, then I'm rich. I wrote something once which says, 'Wise man's wealth, his wealth is in his knowledge, for if his wealth was in the bank and not in his knowledge, then he don't possess it, because it's in the bank.' Do you understand? My wealth is in my knowledge.

I could have been a professional man, a lawyer, a poet if I stopped boxing at twelve years old. But then I loved it so well, I forgot all about school. I could have been like Martin Luther King if I'd got a lot of schooling. I would have been an integrator, I wouldn't be a . . . rebel, what do you call it? I wouldn't be speaking from a minority group. I wouldn't be speaking to my people. Real educated people . . . it's hard to change their minds to give up wealth, and they don't believe in a god. A lot of real educated people, they don't believe in a god once they get really educated. It's the poor people who believe in God, and go to church and believe, but a real educated man gets so wrapped up with his books and education and knowledge and he knows why things happen, he don't believe no more in the supernatural. He don't believe no more in spirits or God or this and that, so if I'd gotten real educated without this teaching of black, I'd be just like the type of man Sammy Davis Junior is, or Sidney Poitier, or somebody like that.

I prayed to Allah before my fights, but I prayed only the day before the fight, not every day like a month or two before. I didn't live like I should, I was nightclubbing, I was around people I shouldn't be around, I took it for granted and I was clowning in the ring and I didn't do as I should, I didn't train as I should do. The Press even wrote about how I wasn't living clean. That's when Norton broke my jaw. When I fought Joe Frazier I was a manner of beast, joking and playing and not being serious. I know why I lost those two fights. I whopped him the second time though didn't I?

I've thought about being a movie star, but I couldn't make the movies I want to make. We've got a million black movies being made in America and all of them belittle black people. The wise man who makes them knew what he was doing. He's lulling black slaves to sleep. Black women on television with their titties out, kissing on each other and walking around in nude scenes, in bed with white men. They're low rate black people, always cussing 'son of a bitch' and so on and so on. Every movie they make for black people is to show them down. I don't make movies because they use black people to keep black people down and that's the latest trick they got – making black people think they're stars, putting them into bad movies. They won't put me in no movies, won't put me in none of them, because if I make a movie, it's going to have to be like *Ben Hur*.

A lot of boxers end up with nothing at all. Joe Louis made it, but he had trouble. Those fighters today don't make much money. And then with the upkeep and the way things cost, I'm the only one that's really making money. I'm an honest fighter and the ones that fight me make money. The only reason I really make it is because governments are paying for me. We got Iran wants us to fight, Egypt, Estonia, Russia. Governments are calling for us, not individuals, hustling promoters, so I'm the only fighter really making money today. I don't think I'll be beaten in the next five years, and I'll be thirty-seven then. Sugar Ray Robinson fought till he was forty-two. Archie Moore fought till he was fifty-one. I'm greater than all of them. Thirty-seven is young. Joe Walcott won his title at thirty-seven.

I was a young man a few years ago, now I'm an old man – I'm more seasoned. I stood there and took everything that George had, and I'll be here five more years before there's a threat of me being beaten. If I could build the fighter to defeat me, he'd have to be about my height, a little taller. He'd have to be about one tenth of a second faster than me on his feet, he'd have to be more experienced. And when you add it all up, it ain't nobody just going to come along like that. They've got to build themselves up and I'm going to see them while they're building. Nobody's going to start fighting tomorrow and have these qualities. It takes time and I don't see nobody on the horizon. If I'm not in condition, if I'm not serious, there's quite a few that might win, but if I'm serious and go in with ideas of Allah God in my heart, I'm fighting for a cause. See, I bring God into my fights. I'm not fighting for me. I'm not only show talking just for publicity. Everything I do – there's a purpose involved. I'm not just here for the money. So now you know. Muhammad Ali's starting to fight for freedom of the black people. Now God is involved, now you're fighting a spiritual, holy war, when you face me now.

1974

SAMMY DAVIS JNR

I started on stage when I was three years old, so that's forty-seven years now. I was singing and dancing because in those days the tradition of American show business, vaudeville, was that if you had a son you brought him on. He took the bows at the end of the act. Well, my dad used to bring me out and we were working at a place in Philadelphia and they had an amateur contest and I won it when I was three years old, and the prize was five dollars or something like that.

I never went to school. Not one day of formal education at all, not one day! I'm not proud of that incidentally, but if I had a choice to make being where I am now, and using hindsight, I would probably do it the same way. In those days they disguised me when I got to five years old (I was by then a regular member of the act): they used to put burnt cork on my face. I used to 'black-up' and they passed me off as a forty-four year old midget.

It was rough on the vaudeville circuit, but I don't know if you are tough if you were a kid in show business. The only time it became a job was when I would see kids playing baseball, and I would see kids roller-skating and bicycling and I couldn't do it – my dad and uncle wouldn't let me because I could hurt my legs. They were afraid if I went out and played baseball I'd slide into a base, break my ankle, whatever, so the normal things – the things everyone took for granted – including going to school, became pushed aside and I focused purely on show business. Why does a man get a laugh when he does that? Why does a comic get a laugh when he goes: 'What the hey . . .'? I wanted to know, and show business was totally my life. It consumed me and I wanted to consume show business.

When I was in the Army there was one guy and he turned me around and said: 'Where I come from niggers are never in front of white people.' I said, 'But I've been in this line for a long time. I was at the back before and moved up.' And I turned back around. He said, 'Obviously you don't understand me, nigger, do you?' Well, when he said that, I swung my bag and caught him square on – pow! I knocked him to the ground and when he was lying there he looked up and said: 'I'm on the ground, but you're still a nigger.'

And I realised there had to be something, there had to be another way.

Because violence wasn't it. There had to be another way to communicate with people and I had to find another way to tell him he was wrong. I still find myself getting angry today. People wouldn't call me nigger today, but they would say, 'Well, we know your kind.' Every black performer has to swallow a lot. I think most black people do and those who survive are those who realise that the stupidity of man still exists and we must deal with it. I wanted to use my talent that God had given me. I thought I can do this, and I can do a white man, and I can sing like a white guy – I can, so I must not be any different, and that's what used to shock the audiences in the early days: 'He sounds just like them you know,' and even to this day when I do the impression people will still say: 'You know, you sounded just like Frank Sinatra' and I say, 'Well, I'm an artist and if I'm doing an impersonation you're supposed to sound like the person.' That was the way I fought it and tried to fight it all during the years – with my talent. I got my nose broken three times trying to be violent and this is it. I ain't getting it broken no more, because I am definitely not a fighter.

I was a Catholic until I was sixteen, then I became agnostic and I believed in something but didn't go to a church or a temple or anything. I started reading religions and I became fascinated to know how a religion could make a race of people survive and keep fighting back over hundreds of years and still maintain their dignity. What was the subtext? What was the foundation of the Jewish religion, because it is very, very traditional, and maybe there is something in me that's masochistic – persecuted minorities. I've been a Jew now for twenty years and tomorrow is the beginning of the High Holy Days and I will fast. I am still waiting to see if I can get tickets for the Temple here. The last time I walked in and I had a skull-cap on and it was before the start of services and people smiled, and talk about feeling conspicuous, you know there wasn't another black face in the entire Temple.

When I lost my eye in the accident, I was very fortunate to have a doctor who came to see me and said to me straightout when I was still bandaged: 'Hello, Sammy, we had to remove your eye. Before you panic, there's nothing else wrong with you, you can still sing, you can still dance and just don't worry about it.' The funny thing was that it sort of focused in on me, because I had been doing very well but the money doubled after the accident. It shows you about where people's heads are: 'We've gotta see the guy with the one eye.' I had an artificial eye put in, but I kept on wearing a patch for a year; I got enamoured with the patch until a friend said to me: 'You've got to make a choice, Sam, you're either going to hear: that's the guy who wears the patch, or: that's a good entertainer.' I took that patch off that night and I never wore it again. I think I learned a lot from that.

If ever I said I was going to retire – then after about two years of hanging out sitting there just getting the little stomach (nothing's more embarrassing than a guy who weighs a hundred and ten pounds with a stomach like that) – you know I would be wanting to get back on that stage. There has only been one person that really did it successfully – Maurice Chevalier. He worked when he wanted to work, otherwise stayed in his château enjoying himself. And that's the way it should be.

I think that psychologically I have no desire to go out and prove that I can do everything in the world anymore. I select three or four things and try to do them the best I know how and I think that I am singing better than I have ever sung, because again it's selectivity. Don't try to do everything. Be the best Sammy Davis you can. You can't be Frank and you can't be Stevie Wonder, and you can't be Marvin Gaye – you can't be those people. Be the best Sammy Davis that you know how to be and if your people like you – that don't mean they are going to like you all the time – at least you'll have the satisfaction when you walk off the stage: I gave the best performance I know how to give, and that's my ambition.

1976

WARREN MITCHELL

Having played *King Lear, Death of a Salesman* and Alf Garnett in *Till Death Do Us Part* during the last year, I think they are all very well written. Shakespeare knew a thing or two, Arthur Miller and Johnny Speight write about people that the public recognises – about those family relationships. People told me, when I was going to play *King Lear* that it was impossible, that he is so irrational, so illogical in the way he banishes his daughter and the way he behaves towards his children. Alf actually loved his daughter – she was pretty, she was lovely – and she was his sole link with any kind of affection. I think that Garnett will become a symbol for bigotry, stupidity, thick-headedness. Alf is everything nasty – a pig, a hypochondriac, a coward, a jingoist, a racist, a hypocrite, and yet he is hysterically funny.

I have been an actor for twenty-seven years. I first started performing when I was seven or eight years old – singing and dancing in a dancing academy in Walthamstow and then when I was about nine, I was asked to do high kicks and I thought that was very sissy so I 'retired' from the theatre. Richard Burton was at Oxford with me and we joined the RAF together and I got ideas of becoming an actor through meeting him. I was sad he went to Hollywood. After the war, Scofield and Burton were the two lions, young lions in the English theatre and Burton spoke verse like nobody else could. To me it was criminal that he went off to Hollywood. OK, money is fine, we all need money, but he would have earned enough here.

As a kid, I went with my mother to all the Crazy Gang shows, every Max Miller show, and I have always had this affinity with comedians. I love variety and I think at that time I would have liked to have been an Eddie Cantor and I suppose the showbiz thing has always stuck with me. People told me I was crazy to go on doing Alf because it was ruining me as an actor, but I think it is perverse of people who make a success of a character to turn round and say, 'I'm bored, I don't want to do it anymore, I'm getting typed.' *Till Death Do Us Part* was a great show and it appealed to every kind of intelligence and every kind of taste, except Mary Whitehouse of course. She was our biggest publicist. Every time she protested to the BBC, we got another million viewers.

I met 'Alf' all the time. Like many actors, I spent my early years unemployed and at the Labour Exchange or at Euston where I worked as a porter for a while, there were always these know-alls, so when I first saw the script, I didn't have to reach very far, I just remembered all these know-alls I had met. Anyway, I am very self-opinionated and my children say I'm a bully so I'm well suited to play the part.

When you get into a success there is always dispute about who thought of what. You can be in failures and everybody loves each other but when we were in a success like 'Till Death', it generated so much heat. We all hated each other at times, and loved each other – not often, but occasionally. I suppose it was true that Dandy Nicholls and I did not get on well. She is a brilliant actress but Johnny was obsessed with the character of Alf and he wrote reams for me and Dandy had very little to say. She got very bored, as did the other members of the cast because they had very little to do compared to me. I think that after listening to Alf week after week in rehearsal, Dandy did think of me as Alf and I understand that.

My father has lived for years on the glory of Alf Garnett. He signs his name in hotel registers 'Alf Garnett's father'. He loved being Alf's father. He came to the National Theatre the other night and saw me as Willie Loman in *Death of a Salesman* and now calls himself 'Mr Loman Senior'. He had a heart attack some years ago, the first of many, and as a salesman he was worried about the business. I told him I would take samples round to the customers (he sold china and glass). Well, I took them around about half a dozen customers and I didn't sell one thing. I realised then something that I know now when I'm playing Willie – that the life of a salesman is tough. They go out day in day out having to flog, flog, flog and it's really tough, and full of despair.

I'm going to be playing Shylock in *The Merchant of Venice* for the BBC. I haven't done a lot of Shakespeare and he's got some good stuff and I learnt the lines. I don't know if it helps to be Jewish to play the part. I used to get quite embarrassed at school at being Jewish and hearing about this Jew wanting a pound of flesh and I was made to feel very different from the other kids. I wasn't allowed to go into prayers and at home non-Jews were not welcome – boys were all right but a non-Jewish girl was a threat as I might marry one of them and I was only six. I had a very orthodox grandmother. In the RAF it was 'Fall out the Jews and Roman Catholics' and I didn't like being Jewish, being different. When you're a kid you want to be like all the rest. Only once did I come across any physical anti-semitism and it was nothing much – a bloke rubbed my face in horseshit. I was more or less taught that only Jews could be my friends and be trusted. When I was fifteen, I was finally picked to play for the school first eleven football team and the match happened to be on the Saturday that was Yom Kippur – the holiest day of the year when everybody fasts. I told my father I was going to play football instead of going to the Synagogue and at half-time when the thunderbolt hadn't hit me, I began to suspect that it was all a load of cobblers. Since then I have never been to Synagogue as a worshipper but I feel terribly left out and I envy those people who believe in it – they have a marvellous time – at Passover they all get drunk and they have 'nice' weddings and 'nice' funerals and I miss it very much.

At the time Shakespeare wrote *The Merchant of Venice* there weren't any Jews in England and that's why it's miraculous that Shakespeare could know anything about how it felt to be a member of a persecuted minority. I believe there was one famous Jew at the court of Queen Elizabeth who was finally executed. When people say the play shouldn't be done because it encourages anti-semitism, it's cobblers because I don't believe it's accidental in the play that after the destruction of that man when he is made to change his religion, to become a Christian and his world is at an end, the play switches to Belmont where all these social butterflies are poncing about having a marvellous time, Shakespeare knew what he was doing – the contrast is so enormous. I believe he couldn't write overtly what he wanted to say. There was a public to be pleased, just as there is today. Bloody public. You know I could not believe it – last night, during our performance of *The Caretaker* there was this man in the audience blowing his nose, and all right, coughing is an involuntary thing, but really! It's television that has done it of course, people at home can talk and not pay attention to the television. People just don't realise when they come to the theatre. I would give them all a chest x-ray for a start. I would put all the coughers in a sound-proof booth having had a chest scan before they come in. If they are at all bronchial, I wouldn't let them in the theatre!

I don't know what it was that made me a non-conformist. I would have liked to have been a conformist, would like to be a member of the local Jewish community and go to 'nice' weddings and bar mitzvahs and subscribe to all the well-known charities. I had no idea that I was going to be an actor. I was a rebel as a kid and hated at school – I used to play about and get the maximum number of detentions *and* come top at the same time and that was really infuriating. I guess there is something in the genes. Doesn't it sound rather pretentious to say that I am not like the rest?

1979 and 1980

MEL BROOKS

I am a complete Anglophile – I love England, I love the bricks, I love the sidewalks, I love the stones, I love the tradition, I love the courtesy, I love the tea. The English are so polite, I love them, the little ladies with their tweeds, their little hats, sitting in the parks and when you go by they say, 'How about it?' One thing I don't like about the British is trifle, it's just a little too wet. I'm head over heels in love with British comedy – I always have been. I'm the only American who likes Benny Hill. Seriously though, the Ealing comedies – *Kind Hearts and Coronets*, *The Lavender Hill Mob*, *The Man in the White Suit* – they were all marvellous, and the late, great Peter Sellers. I used one of your best comedians in my latest film *History of the World, Part One*, Spike Milligan, the bird man of the Bastille. He is a pleasure to work with and he is genuinely funny and creative.

I think, in a way, God ordained that I should be a funny man by giving me a very different face and my father passed away, and died by the way, when I was only a baby so I had three older brothers and a mother who was crazy about me. I kind of felt that it was my destiny to be an entertainer, to be funny and make people smile and now I'm making over £100 a week doing it – not bad for a kid from Brooklyn. Brooklyn is a very tough neighbourhood to grow up in. Everybody in Brooklyn was a little on the shady side and when

I was about nine years old I went into the equivalent of Woolworths and I stole a little cap pistol. I was walking out and the man grabbed me, but I was clever – I pulled the gun out and said, 'I'll blow your brains out', and I got away with the gun. You see you've got to be smart and Brooklyn gives you a cleverness that you don't get in Stepney Green. My mother worked hard, she had four sons and she sent us all to school. She's a wonderful woman and she lives in Florida – we keep our Jews in Florida you know – it's like a hothouse.

Actually, when I was a kid I wanted to be a drummer and I wanted to be in music. I became a drummer and one night I was playing the drums and the boss came up to me and said 'Melvyn, the comic is sick, go on the stage because you know the dopey jokes.' So, that's how I became a comic. The jokes went something like this: 'Good evening ladies and gentlemen. I've just flown in from Chicago and boy are my arms tired. I met a girl in Chicago that was so skinny that when I took her to a restaurant, the waiter said: "I'll take your umbrella." I got a room in Chicago that was so small that the mice were hunchback. You closed the door and the doorknob got into bed with you.' I was not thrilled about doing those jokes so I decided to do character comedy.

I think there might be some anger and frustration in my humour. I feel that there are many injustices heaped upon the little man. It's the crushing of the little man, it's the insanity of each and every administration whether it's Nero's Rome or Louis XVI's France, but they all pick on the little guy. This helps energise me in writing a crazy comedy, but I do need that anger, that bitterness and frustration, it's true. Behind all the comedy there's a little bit of anger and Kenneth Tynan captured that. He was brilliant and he wrote a long profile on me and we got along splendidly. He was a great writer and I miss him. I miss his smoking and his coughing and his manner – he was the dearest, brightest man.

I'm doing a show called 'Winos' in America – it's seventeen people with paper bags and bottles of wine and we drink and vomit in doorways. It doesn't sound funny, but it's hysterical, believe me. I'm also doing a musical called 'Elephant Men' and we're going to sing 'Put on a Happy Face'.

1981

PETER USTINOV I very much regret this business of the Olympic Games myself because I think that it is like the Arts – these are relatively clean things still which should not suffer when the grubby hands of something as inefficient as politics, as fundamentally corrupt and pragmatic as politics, gets hold of them. So I think these lifelines have to be kept open. After all, we have lots of forums in UNESCO which take place quite often – we had one the other day about peace which is a very urgent subject when you realise that there are three tons of high explosives in this world for every person living in it. That means that if the Olympics do take place, whoever wins the gold medal as a weightlifter will need the help of all his rivals to lift the ration which is reserved for him. It's a really terrifying prospect. I think it's terribly irresponsible to grab at everything – it used to be 'too little and too late' and it is now 'too much and too late.' It's idiotic to try and counter-attack on every front, no matter how deeply one feels about what's happening. If the Russians are going through a McCarthy period at the moment, one has to play it slightly cool because they are changing all the time, they are trying to find their way and they have enormous problems inside Russia, of that I'm sure and they are also very well informed. That report in *The Times* I thought was absolutely fascinating. One of their correspondents was 'lost' in Russia and was picked up by a Russian Patrol, and all the officer wanted to know was if it was true that Paul McCartney had had trouble in Tokyo. It shows the power of Paul McCartney – it's a different form of diplomacy, but nobody is going to tell me that it's less important.

One of the things I have done over the last two years is to play King Lear in Ontario, and this was the first time I have ever played Shakespeare. I have never understood why, and this is not vanity, just puzzlement, I always found it more moving to read than to perform. I think it's a play about senility and the terrible thing about senility is that it's not constant, that a person who is no longer fully in control has moments where he is completely lucid and he has to live with things that he decided when he wasn't quite all there and he cheats a bit to try and make it normal. I think it's fascinating because I've also noticed that when people are dying they are very often like butterflies impaled in an album – they become the victims of the people that visit them. I came to the conclusion that Lear, at the end, is completely insane, but it's much less trouble to pretend that he's not.

I find that there is an automatic link between the very young and the very old, which is quite normal because they are nearer the mysteries of birth and death than the people in the middle who make all the mistakes. In Russians families such as mine, you are always surrounded by very old relatives, like Peter and the Wolf. They are much kinder and cheat much more and give you things you shouldn't have. *King Lear* is full of the link between first and second childhood. I remember my grandfather vividly, although I only saw him once or twice. He came to visit us one summer and there was a lot of milk becoming yoghourt and full of flies and he said to me, 'Flies are very, very unhealthy', and tried swatting them, but of course, the flies could see him coming. So being very young, about seven, I grabbed the fly swat and started killing flies tremendously fast and suddenly my grandfather said: 'Stop it, give it back.' I said 'Why? – There are still many flies to be killed', and he replied 'Yes, but you're taking pleasure in it now', and I said 'But you said yourself that flies are the carriers of disease and we are all going to be ill' . . . 'Better we should be ill than that you should take pleasure in taking life.' He was a wonderful old man.

I'm not the shape to be immaculate (unlike Hercule Poirot). I was never able to be immaculate. In the Army you had those kit inspections and you were supposed to have square socks and if you're a round person the socks may be square for a moment but before the officer arrived they had resumed their original shape. I always got into trouble for that so I could never be Hercule Poirot for long. I flatter myself that I am able to retain a certain freshness in the role of Poirot in *Evil under the Sun* by being absolutely unable to think from day to day who did it and so I was continually really asking.

I went all round the world promoting the film. I had never been to Manilla before and there was a press conference when we arrived. They asked us whether we had had any threatening letters or threats and I said that I had been moving around so fast that I hadn't received any although there were probably three or four threats in the mail so we all got bodyguards. I got a bodyguard called 'Captain Bong' – very thin lipped, obviously highly professional policeman – he took it tremendously seriously. He was the kind of policeman that if he leant against a wall he assumed the colour of the wall. I felt safe and unsafe at the same time because I felt that he would attract trouble because he needed it. At the first night of the film with the public he sat next to me; I didn't want him to but he insisted and afterwards waiting for the cars I said to him, 'Captain Bong, now tell me the truth, did you guess who the murderer was?' and he said: 'Oh yes, I'm an investigator too, you understand.' I thought it was very strange to take Agatha Christie that seriously.

I'm known in Russia more as a writer than an actor because they have only seen *Spartacus*, I think. This success must be something atavistic; I must write in such a way that they can automatically 'relate' to it as the Americans would say. They weren't going to pay me royalties but I suggested that it would be unkind of them not to. They said that they couldn't at first because I wrote the book in 1971 and they only signed the Berne Convention in 1973. I said that's unfair because Karl Marx said everybody should be paid according to their work, and, I said, on top if it all in a geriatric society why penalise the older writer who started writing earlier? You wouldn't do that to Brezhnev! They came with a lot of money the next morning and I said 'What's this?' and they said: 'We have convinced the Ministry that you're right,' so this monolith has a very tender skin – they're very, very easily upset and hurt by your attitude. So I got my Russian bank book which was a nice surprise at my time of life.

In Russia you have very strange hotels – they always have enormous rooms with a grand piano in it – and always a refrigerator which is usually linked in some way with the television. So that if you turn the television off everything goes sour in the fridge. I kept the television running all the time to prevent the milk from turning. There is a concierge on every floor and you have to give in your key. You do feel that it is rather controlled but occasionally you have incidents like that of a couple of people I know who had been told to look out for being bugged. They got slightly loaded one night in very good company and they said: 'It's a lot of nonsense', and suddenly one of them crossing the floor felt something under the carpet and they got ugly, being slightly drunk, and rolled up the carpet – and there was a sort of black thing and they (not being technically qualified) didn't know what it was. They started undoing it and suddenly there was a terrible crash and the candelabra in the room downstairs had fallen from the ceiling.

1980 and 1982

SIR RALPH RICHARDSON

I am now playing my ninety-first part on the London stage and I still always lose my nerve before going on. But it is necessary for the concentration; you have to dream the part you know, some of it must be true to you, you have to really believe it is happening and it takes a good deal of concentration to do that successfully. It is a difficult job, acting, but it is also very interesting because an actor has eight or nine hundred people put together into an audience and these amalgamate into one person. In the end you are speaking to one creature, and each time it is a different person! I think you can tell within a few minutes the kind of 'person' you are playing to, but I get very nervous indeed before I start.

I am still learning my profession – more expertise and craftsmanship, but you also find there is still a great deal more that you don't know – vistas of what you could learn open up. Acting is a kind of confidence; if you believe in what you are doing, it is very likely that the audience will believe it too. One day my wife and I were sitting on a bank in a field and she saw a stoat, and not far away from the stoat was a baby rabbit. The stoat was after the rabbit, moving very slowly, very carefully, watching it all the time. Then it came to a blade of grass, one tiny little blade of grass which it stood behind and convinced itself was hiding him – and to the rabbit, the blade of grass *did* hide him because he suddenly jumped forward, surprised the rabbit and the rabbit was dead.

Apart from this particular performance, I have a great regard for Charlie Chaplin who is, perhaps, the greatest actor that there has ever been, and certainly the greatest actor there has been in our time. We have had many great actors – Burbage, Garrick, Kean, Irving and modern ones like Olivier and Gielgud, but they have all been great because they have illustrated and illuminated great parts written for them by great poets, particularly Shakespeare. Charlie Chaplin invented a character part for himself. He was a very handsome young man, very determined, very brilliant and sharp with a great strength of mind and he invented this part for himself – covering his face with chalk to look like a clown, putting on a silly moustache, blackening his eyes, fuzzing up his hair and pretending that he was absolutely terrified of the world. The little frightened man is very, very appealing – he was a loving little man with love in his heart all the time, but when attacked he had the cunning of a weasel and the heart of a lion. He also conquered the greatest audience that any actor ever has done because he was shown to millions on film and had millions of hearts loving him and laughing at him.

There was a predecessor of Chaplin's 'Little Tich' from whom he undoubtedly borrowed something. He was a very small man with a wonderful voice and a funny pair of boots, but the audience didn't seem to realise how odd he was because he was so near to reality in his madness. I used to see him on the stage a great deal when I was a boy. They for me are the two great masters. I think it was seeing Chaplin as a boy that gave me the idea of trying to be an actor because I saw what wonderful things you could do; he never spoke, but just by a gesture, a movement, he could make such a tremendous effect.

I prefer these days to perform in plays by contemporary writers rather than classics. I can't afford to contemplate retirement. No, certainly not!

1980

DAME EDITH EVANS

I'm being the most patriotic person. I've put my heating down. And when the bill came in, it was so much less, I was scolded by everybody for having the house cold and I nearly cried. They said, 'We didn't want you to be cold.' I said, 'I'm much too selfish to ever be anything I don't want to be.' I couldn't bear going away. I've got a friend now whose husband is retiring and he's part of a firm in New Zealand, and they have to go out there and retire you see, and she writes me long letters about the ship and it sounds awful. Absolutely terrible. The ship was built for half the quantity and double the number on it, and it sounds like hell to me. I couldn't bear it. Because I like space, and I'm so grateful to God that he's given me space, because I like it. I like a lot of room for everything.

I've only learnt to be ar-ti-cu-late, because I went to marvellous Elsie Fogarty who taught me to speak properly. But I was once told by my Sunday school teacher – I had a Sunday school teacher . . . I was born in that generation, and I wouldn't have been born in any other, I can tell you . . . it was lovely. And she said, 'You know, your mother has a very beautiful speaking voice, Edith.' I said, 'Oh,' and ran all the way home to listen. I didn't know she had a beautiful speaking voice . . . it didn't seem beautiful to me. It was just mother, you see. I like words and I like hearing people use them. Oh the other day I listened to a play . . . I mustn't mention – It was *The Importance of Being Earnest*. I thought perhaps I wouldn't enjoy it. They spoke beautifully, absolutely beautifully. I heard every word – it was beautifully articulated. Oh, I do wish people would speak now. I think a lot of our troubles would be over if we spoke properly.

I love good manners in people and they don't have them today, do they, much. I don't mean to say I want them bowing and scraping, but . . . for example, I don't like people who, the moment the luncheon is finished, just light up their cigarettes without asking. I remember people who strike up the minute the meal is finished. I say, 'Why have I bothered to cook for him if he's going to jolly well spoil all the taste with the nasty cigarette?' My husband used to smoke a pipe and quite often it had no tobacco in it, you know. Just the pipe in his mouth.

The leading man who really almost gave me the greatest pleasure, the man who's very ill now and not doing very much work, was Ronnie Ward. Oh, he was sensitive, marvellously sensitive. I enjoyed him very much. I enjoyed most of them, you know. It's better to enjoy them, isn't it? Better than a love scene with someone you hate the sight of.

I'm like Ivor Novello, he says he was born intoxicated. I was born intoxicated. My mother told a story which is really rather sweet. When I was very tiny, we used to live in Ebury Buildings and I don't know how we got the lodger in, but we did have a lodger. He sounded a charming man, because mother used to have his meal ready for him and I would come in, and he had to eat with his right hand while turning my skipping rope with the other hand. Even in those days, you see, I got the boys to do what I wanted. The other day a man came to lunch in the country, and I put on a dress that I thought was making me look pretty – you know, I'm not a pretty woman, but I do look better sometimes than others. He said, 'We don't want you to be pretty. We want you to be distinguished and charming.' So there you are. Now I'm distinguished and charming.

Glamour – I believe in glamour. I think that glamour is part of any public person, especially acting people. You shouldn't have scrubby clothes and scrubby hair and a mingey car. I saved up the money and bought a Rolls. It's a beauty, too. And I feel nice when it drives up, you know. And they say, 'Oh, somebody's getting out.' You know. If you're earning good wages, it's all right. It's not so good now, because I don't earn many wages. When I was wise I bought some annuities. Always buy an annuity. Always. Because they're the blessed thing when you've stopped being paid wages. I'd like to talk to Mr Wilson, the shocking way people are taxed. I know someone whose pension is a good one. Mind you, he earns it – it's not the government pension, it's something that was paid to him when he retired. He pays £70 tax. Have you heard anything so awful? On your pension . . . that you've already paid tax on. Well I wouldn't be educated enough for politics. That's the worse side. Say all the wrong things. I'm just a Cockney girl.

I've always said that I think I'm a great actress because I speak the truth on stage. I don't speak what I've heard other people say, or the way they say it. I say it the way it seems to come to me, you see. And that's all I can say. Speak the truth. And you act, you do what's good. I think it's the same with painters, or writers. They paint what they see, what they know, and it's marvellous. Well, I speak it the only way I know how to speak it. Whatever it is. I can be directed, oh, slavishly, by someone I trust, but not by somebody I don't trust.

Yes, I would change certain things of myself. If I could just give God a hand, I would like my hair to be long, and I've got a crooked eye, but it doesn't notice as much as it did. When I was a girl, I used to wear my hair all on one side to hide it. Oh yes, yes. If I could petition God personally myself, I should say, 'Would you please give me a lot more courage, mental and physical courage?' Sometimes I'm very frightened, and I would like to have some courage. This thing about wanting to be noticed, I don't like to be noticed, you know. Except when I want to be noticed. If somebody raises his hat when I get out of the car, I bow in return, but I don't like being looked at, because I'm not acting you see. When I'm acting to be looked at, look at me.

1974

'Once I've done
a film it's
finished.
I never look at
it again'
Sir Alec Guinness

SIR ALEC GUINNESS

I never had any ambition to be in the cinema at all, I don't think even when I was a drama student a long time later. I went into an advertising agency when I was eighteen as a copywriter – no use at that. They were very friendly people, I got the job through friends, and then they tried me out at layout and then they put me back to copywriting again. I did it for about eighteen months and I cost them a lot of money. When I was doing the layouts there was something four inches by four inches on the front page of the *Daily Mail*, and I unfortunately marked it to the blockmakers four feet by four feet, which was rather larger than the *Daily Mail* was even then, and I waited and kept telephoning about this block and finally a taxi arrived and two chaps came in lugging this great thing. That was that. It was a lot, a lot of copper. And the *Daily Mail* appeared the next day with a very nice little empty space which said 'reserved for Mullards Powells'.

When I went into advertising I knew I wanted to be an actor, but I didn't know how to become one. I didn't know anyone in the theatre but one of the girls in the office of the advertising agency said: 'Why don't you try for a scholarship?' It had to be a scholarship at RADA, I had no money, and I finally thought well that's all right, I'll try for that. I did get a scholarship, not through RADA because when I turned up there, having got the day off from the office, I was met by someone saying I'm very sorry we're not giving any scholarships this year. You know I'd had the appointment and paid the entrance fee and all that and I was in a terrible state because I thought when I get back to the office they'll think it had all been a great big hoax, but I ran into a girl who I'd known when I was a child on the beach at Eastbourne and I wept on her shoulder a bit and she said: there's the Fay Compton Studio of Dramatic Art and I know that they're holding auditions tonight, and I went along there with no appointment, rushed in and got the scholarship and that was that.

I lived on about twenty-seven shillings a week, in a little attic in Bayswater. Friends were very good to me; a couple of chaps from my advertising days used to take me out to Lyons in the Strand every week and give me a brunch which was a really good meal with tomatoes, sausages, chips and bacon, the whole thing and a cup of coffee all cost about a shilling. That really kind of kept me going for the week. The rest of it was jam sandwiches from fellow students and baked beans out of tins of course.

I very seldom nowadays consciously observe what someone does but my son had polio when he was about twelve and was paralysed from the waist down. He's fine now, I mean he plays rugger and rushes around does whatever he wants, but when he was recovering and walking again, it was obviously a very stiff strange walk. I had a little cine-camera and I remember taking shots of this when he was first walking and then when we saw it on the screen my wife and I persuaded ourselves that he was fine, he was walking fine, but obviously deep down inside one thought, 'Oh Lord, he's going to limp for life.' Years later when it came to doing the scene in *Bridge on the River Kwai* I found myself doing the identical walk that I had seen on that little cine-camera from five or six years previously. I'd entirely forgotten, I didn't know I was doing it, it was only when I saw myself on the screen I thought where on earth did that curious, slightly lurchy, bent walk come from. It was the same as I had on the cine-camera. I mean it's how you use your own children and it's monstrous isn't it, but not deliberately done.

When I first went to Hollywood, this is an unlikely story but true, there was a party on at the Beverly Hills Hotel where I was staying, an enormous party. I hadn't been asked and it was being given by John Wayne and he suddenly heard I was in the hotel and very kindly, about midnight, turned up and said: 'Come down, put on a black tie and come on down', and so I was thrilled and went down to this great gathering. It was the first time I'd ever met Betty Bacall and I was talking to her, she was ravishing and marvellous, when a well-known Hollywood agent came up and dragged her away, and said 'Oh you mustn't be seen talking to that limey, come on', and I was so furious. I'd never clocked anyone in my life and I clocked him. And I flew out in a rage back up to my room and ripped off my black tie, back into bed, crossly done, ashamed of myself, but also very angry with this chap. Then the phone went and it was John Wayne again saying: 'Come on down, now you've got to make it up.' So down I went with the black tie again and I behaved very well and by then of course it had become something of a scandal and a lot of people had gathered round and he said: 'I want you to shake hands with this man' (he's dead now, though not through my blow), and so we solemnly shook hands again, rather coldly but solemnly, and with a lot of applause because I clocked him again. Well, it was something he said again, I don't know what it was but it drove me mad. But John Wayne was marvellous about it, he was very kind and comforting and I received a huge box of cigars the next day, I don't know who from.

On my very first night in Hollywood, I met James Dean. It was a very odd occurrence. I had arrived off the plane – the planes took a long time in those days, about sixteen hours flight, and I'd been met by Grace Kelly and various people, but I found that I was alone for the evening and a woman I knew telephoned me and said: let me take you out to dinner, and we went to various places, but she was wearing trousers and they wouldn't let her into any of the smart Hollywood restaurants. However, we finally went to a little Italian dive and that was full and so we were turned away, and then I heard feet running down the street, and it was James Dean. He said: 'I was in that restaurant when you couldn't get a table and my name is James Dean', and he asked us to join him and then going back into the restaurant he said: 'Oh before we go in I must show you something – I've got a new car', and there it was in the courtyard of this little restaurant, some little silver car, very smart all done up in cellophane and a bunch of roses tied to its bonnet, and I said: 'How fast can you drive this?' and he said, 'Oh I can only do 150 mph in it', and I asked if he had driven it, and he replied that he had never been in it at all. Some strange thing came over me, some almost different voice and I said: 'Look, I won't join your table unless you want me to, but I must say something, please do not get into that car because if you do (and I looked at my watch), it's now Thursday (whatever the date was) 10 o'clock at night, and by 10 o'clock at night next Thursday you'll be dead if you get into that car.' I don't know what it was – nonsense, so we had dinner, we had a charming dinner, and he was dead the following Thursday afternoon in that car.

I would hate to sound a sort of pessimistic or gloomy person because I'm not. Everything is a disappointment, in one way. Of course you know you rejoice if something's a success but I think T.S. Eliot wrote something about every achievement being a new kind of failure, and for me it's always: why didn't I do that, why didn't I have that mannerism, why did I . . .? Once I've done a film it's finished. I never look at it again, unless I have to.

1977

JOHN MORTIMER

The idea for *Rumpole of the Bailey* came in a way from my father who was a divorce barrister. He was like Rumpole in the way that he always quoted poetry to me and he was rude to solicitors. I grew up in an atmosphere of divorce as that is what he specialised in. He used to come home at night and sit on the end of the bed, but instead of *Goldilocks and the Three Bears* I used to get '*The Duchess and the Three Co-respondents*'. He would say, 'Today we managed to prove adultery with evidence of inclination and opportunity. A great part of the evidence was footprints upside down on the dashboard of an Austin Seven parked in Hampstead.' Then he told me that divorce was never dull because it was always connected with sex and so I went into it.

Other barristers are very fond of the character Rumpole and they all pretend to be him – they all sit in El Vino's drinking claret and it's really got rather tiresome. I think judges quite like him too. I am rather a ham barrister, you know, I rather orate, which Rumpole does. I catch myself saying the most 'hammy' things in court; I remember once in the Uxbridge Magistrates Court I was defending a lady pop star for passing rather curious cigarettes through London airport and she was there in the dock in a black dress, tearful and dramatic and I actually heard myself say to the magistrates: 'Give her justice, which is what she has waited and prayed for all these weeks, but let it be justice tempered with that mercy that is the hallmark of the Uxbridge and Hillingdon District Magistrates.' She was triumphantly acquitted!

Barristers are very much performers and I often go from court to a rehearsal room where actors are doing a play and I think I've got into the real world at last. My father was a very dramatic old barrister. He was blind and then he became deaf and then he couldn't stand up any more and by that time he was absolutely irresistible – no judge could possibly refuse him anything.

My first job was as an assistant director in a government propaganda film unit during the war. The man who ran it had seen my Punch & Judy show when I was about eight and he was so impressed by it that when we fought Hitler he thought I was just the man to work on propaganda films about the war. I learnt how to write film scripts when I was very young which has stood me in good stead, and I have written about thirty or forty films which luckily have never been made. If ever you are hard up for a penny, you can always write a film which you hope won't get made because they pay people to write scripts so that they can then decide if they should make a film or not.

I wrote a novel while I was in the Army but my father always told me that if I was a writer I would stay at home all day and my wife would leave me, because it is dreadful to have a writer stumped for words hanging about the house. He offered me the Law just like girls who want to go on the stage are offered secretarial courses – something to fall back on. I've been falling back on it ever since. In my early days as a lawyer I did divorce cases and I divorced people like shelling peas because they all got divorced after the war. Then divorce suddenly became easier and old people who had been living happily together for about fifty years suddenly got divorced and remarried, and as I married a lady who had four children and I had to support all those, I just divorced people night and day.

You learnt all sorts of things about writing in this environment, for example, that there were two languages in courts: often my clients, after the judge had passed judgement didn't know what had happened to them, whether they had been condemned to death or awarded enormous damages.

Once I had become a QC, I took to crime because the 'heart' had really gone out of divorce. Although, in a way, your own beliefs don't enter into what you do in court, I am profoundly opposed to censorship in any form – I don't think anybody has the right to decide what I read or what I think or what I write – so therefore one of the risks that you take if you believe in that is that there will be pornography. Personally, I find it an acceptable risk and I don't think it is particularly harmful, but that doesn't necessarily mean that I welcome pornography – I just think it's part of what you've got to have if you believe in free speech. I don't think it should be inflicted on people who don't want it and I suppose to some extent that children should be protected from it, but I think that people have a very strange view of what children are like and what they can accept. I do think you defend pornography much more satisfactorily if you don't read it.

I always defend – never prosecute – I would find it distasteful to use my skill at cross-examining people and appealing to juries in order to put someone in prison. Personally, that is something that I wouldn't want to do. I think that the present institutions with three or four people crowded in one cell with their chamber-pots for very long periods of time are inhuman, totally useless and do nothing at all but solidify the criminal classes into their own patterns. I think that there is a very small proportion of people who have to be immunised from society – like the Kray brothers and gangsters of that sort who live by murder – but a great many of the people, probably about seventy-five per cent or even more, that are in prison need not be there. They are there because of their inadequacies, their environments and so on. There are all sorts of different criminals, and the criminals that I want to defend are those who blunder into crime – most murderers fall into this category – as most murders are usually either an extension of a Saturday night punch-up or a domestic disagreement, and those people are not really criminals in that sense. There are professional criminals for whom prison is part of their whole way of life. It is totally ineffective to stop them being that – it does them no good, it does society no good, but nobody takes any time to think of an alternative.

I don't believe in original sin. I have usually found my clients are people who are stupid, live in environments that they can't cope with or else are brought up in environments where crime is the normal behaviour. Just as I, whose father was a barrister, want to succeed in the Law, so I think there is a whole part of society in which crime is the acceptable way of getting on.

I have never refused to defend anybody. One of our prides, and I do think it is a pride for people who are against lawyers, is that there should be nobody so unpleasant but that their case shouldn't be put by someone who can do it as well as possible. Therefore you do feel that if you dislike someone, you should defend them even more, and for that reason I have defended people in the National Front, Fascists and so on.

1979

BEN TRAVERS

About forty-five years ago, I was a great friend of Tom Webster, the famous *Daily Mail* sports cartoonist, and he was a great friend of all the leading lights in the sporting world. He used to put up with me as an opponent in golf and I remember on one occasion he suggested that we played golf at a course somewhere near London, I forget which one, so down we went. In the middle of lunch, an individual came to join us and I in my ignorance did not know who he was and Tom Webster told me that he was going to play a round with us. It was only on the way to the first tee that I discovered that he was one of the leading golf professionals in the country, in fact I think he was a champion at the time. I declined to play with him because I was not a good golfer, but said I would be delighted to walk round with him and watch. However, he insisted that he wanted to see my style and was obviously very serious-minded about the whole thing. He said 'Come on, let's see how you stand', so I got up and my ball was teed and I got ready to swing but he told me I wasn't standing right at all. 'Stand to make water,' he said, 'and in your imagination, let your urine fall six inches behind the ball, and you will be in the correct stance.' So I repositioned myself but it was obvious he thought he knew where I should stand better than I did! Well, I hit the ball about thirty yards along and of course it was all wrong. 'Ah, I told you' he said, and for once in my life the apt retort came to my lips: 'In the first place,' I said 'I would like to know one thing. Do you teach many ladies this game?'

I am still writing plays; I finished one just a few months ago and tore it up last week! That is the natural process of writing plays – I always tear them up and I think most playrights ought to. You get your first version, read it through, keep the little bits that are useful and tear the rest up. I've done that with every play I have ever written, sometimes five or six times. At rehearsals too you add or alter things and I think on three or four occasions I have gone away and rewritten a whole act after rehearsals.

Of course, farce is very complex because there is action going on the whole time but I have taken to writing comedy now and that is not so difficult. You sometimes get ideas from some conversation, for example, the domestic troubles a friend is having. I did come across a rather curious, and I think quite useful, subject for comedy, in a strange place. It was in Singapore about five or six years ago and there was this advice column in one of the local papers – you know it gave advice on social and domestic problems and especially to teenagers. This particular column was run by a man and one particular letter to him read as follows: 'I hear you will sort out teenage problems. I wonder if you can help me, although I am now twenty one. First I loved a girl madly, then I met her sister and loved her and now I have met her cousin and love her as well. My three girlfriends are not understanding and do not wish to share me – they want all my love each. My first girl says she will kill herself; the second says she will kill the third and the third says she will kill me. This is terrible. What can I do?' There is a subject for comedy. I'm not going to use it myself but if any of my fellow playrights would like to they are welcome.

I am now ninety years old and I don't know what to expect from the future. My mother died in 1910 never having seen an aeroplane. I don't think she had ever been to see a motion picture either, and here am I, one generation later, with mother never having had those privileges, if that is what they are, and I sit and watch television and what I see on television is men walking about on the moon. That's happened in roughly sixty-five years. I'm about to die pretty soon now but I don't fear death itself; I am afraid of the process of dying but not of what comes next. You have spiritualists who tell you what happens in the afterlife and a lot of it is very instructive and interesting, but there is only one thing that anybody knows about what happens when you die, and that is that you *don't* know! But there is a greater thing than knowledge – there is faith, and faith is stronger than knowledge. If you have faith, you can face death with great comfort and indeed happiness and optimism. Many righteous and good people don't believe that we shall ever see our dear ones who are dead again, and we think of them as they were in this life, but they won't be anything like that if we do meet them again. It will all be taken care of and you have to be very optimistic about the future life.

1976

ALISTAIR COOKE When I went to New York fifty years ago, I had preconceptions; I had no real notion of what the country was like – it was based on Douglas Fairbanks and I wanted to meet Al Capone – I was that illiterate. But New York was splendid, with majestic architecture – the Empire State Building and Chrysler Building were just finished, and Le Corbusier had not yet imposed on the western world with these ghastly monoliths with the eyeless windows which have taken over London as well – buildings that look as if they were put up by a man who had heard about a building but never seen one. We didn't have that then, we had these majestic buildings with spires and decorations and where New York wasn't majestic, it was garish – just as London where it wasn't graceful was seedy, and I find that fifty years later, New York is more garish and London is more seedy.

The first big shock was arriving at the very pit of the Depression which it seemed to me had not affected the middle class in England quite as much as elsewhere. In America, one third of the nation's workforce was out of work – today we have nearly nine million unemployed. Very well dressed business-men stopped you on the street and asked you for a dime and a quarter. One big difference between America as it is now and as it was fifty years ago is that you could then go anywhere in the country – there was no violence, even in the most poverty-stricken places. More superficially, I was horrified by paper towels and paper napkins and these awful things sticking up on the 'sidewalks' called parking meters, and they made tea in the most barbaric way with little tea bags.

I think the most profound influence that America has had on me is the journalism. To sum it up, at that time, when you were writing anything potentially libellous in England, you didn't write it; if you were writing it in America, you wrote it because the libel laws practically didn't exist. Now, of course, it has done a complete reverse – American libel laws are much tighter today. There was such raciness in the writing, it was so idiomatic, so direct. The great journalist of the day was H.L. Mencken who was as famous in those early days in America as George Bernard Shaw was in England. He to me was, and probably still is, the journalist of the century. He was against all establishments – labour unions, Republicans, Democrats, conservatives and golf. He defined democracy as: 'The theory that the common people know what they want and deserve to get it good and hard.' In any other country he would have been thrown in jail for being against the Establish-ment. His definition of an idealist was: 'A man who on noticing that a rose smells better than a cabbage, assumes it will also make better soup.'

That time too was the golden age of American humourists. S.J. Perelman was, I suppose, the drollest writer. He could take the language literally and take an idiom and divest it of the idiomatic quality and ask what the rest of it meant. He really invented Groucho Marx who learnt this art from him and he wrote the Marx brothers early movies. He died last year and some friends of mine were dining with him the night he died – he was in great form – and they dropped him off at his hotel at midnight and as he was getting out of the cab, the cab driver said to him: 'Have a nice day Mr Perelman' and Perelman said: 'Listen, don't poke your nose into my affairs – I'll have any kind of day I want to.'

I call the American humour 'the humour of the soured immigrant.' When you get into the 1840s, when the people began to break through the Appalachians and go out on the prairie, that's where the new politicians came from. These people had to be very down to earth and the whole language changed then. So many of them who arrived in New York were conned by the railroad agent: 'Come to Kansas and we'll give you 160 acres free', which was true if you could make a crop grow in five years. That's the rural soured immigrant. In the cities the soured immigrants were the millions of people, especially the Jews, who came into New York. They enriched the culture of New York by way of their music, both classical and popular, the theatre and so on. There are five times as many Jews in New York City alone as there are in Tel Aviv and there you get the humour of the man who was told that the streets were paved with gold and found himself working in a sweatshop, and it has become now a kind of benign cynicism, which goes through from Mark Twain to Woody Allen. The Jewish influence was felt in Hollywood – you always think of Hollywood smart guys, but these people had to have that quality for survival. The legend of Goldwyn spread around the world was that he was a sort of divine stumbler, but he knew what he was saying when he said about a verbal contract: 'It isn't worth the paper it's written on.' There is one Jewish legend which I think summarises their appreciation of idealism, of generosity of sorts, of always having one eye cocked for the man's real motive – that's the thing I love – they are not fooled and it comes from experience. This story is about a Rabbi who is dying and he was so loved by all his congregation that the people came from streets around and as he had insisted that he die in the Synagogue he is brought there and the assistant Rabbi leans over and says: 'Rabbi, before you die, the people would like to have a message, a final word of wisdom from you.' So the Rabbi says: 'Life is a barrel of water' and this is passed right down the congregation out to the people in the street, and at the end of the line there is a little man who says 'Yes, but what does it mean?' So this is passed all the way back down the aisle back to the assistant Rabbi. By now the Rabbi is almost gone and the assistant Rabbi says 'Rabbi, the people are deeply moved by your message, but what does it mean?' And the Rabbi says 'So it *isn't* a barrel of water.'

Obviously I read reams of criticism of the Americans by the British and the British by the Americans and a great deal of it is extremely clever, but is it true? I don't believe in national character. I believe that people in Siam and Croydon and Lancashire and Chicago are much the same and those are the people I try to talk to. Dr Johnson said 'Patriotism is the last refuge of the scoundrel' and my humble emendation is that a strong belief in national character is the first refuge of the anxious. It is so easy to solve problems by saying: 'How typically British, how typically American, how typically French.'

1982

LILLIAN GISH

I have come over here to watch 'myself' on stage – there is a show called *The Biograph Girl* in which I am being played by another actress. I have just come from seeing it and I am very excited. The one playing me looks like me I think and the one playing Mary Pickford looks like her. I think it is a wonderful idea and I never thought I would see me up on stage – I thought you have to be dead for that and here I am living to see it.

I've been around the world three times in the past five years and all the cities look alike, all the people look alike and I think it is because of film. I think it is the most important invention of the twentieth century; I think it has more power over the minds and hearts of humanity than anything else.

At the age of eighty-four, I still exercise for an hour or so every morning on an upside-down board. When the blood flows to the head, you begin to think clearly for the day.

When I first went to Hollywood, I got together with D.W. Griffith, the father of film. I met him through Gladys Smith, who became Mary Pickford and that time they were making $275 a week and they had an automobile and I was most impressed! He took my sister and I upstairs to see if we could act and we thought we were in a madhouse – he recited a plot with the rest of the company and at the end he took out a gun and started shooting at the ceiling, chasing us around the room! He saw film as the universal language as quoted in the Bible, and thought that when all men could understand each other, they would know their problems and we would cease having wars. He made the first serious movie *The Birth of a Nation* but the movie theatres wouldn't take it as they didn't think people could sit through two hours of film. All men loved him, all women loved him but he died a very sad man and completely broke.

I never married; I would always listen to actors talking about their troubles when I was young and it always had to do with something called a wife or a husband. Then my mother for me was the most perfect human being I ever knew and she hadn't made a success of marriage so I thought I had no chance. Anyway, a wife is a twenty-four hour a day job and I was working so why impose that on some poor man? I never fell in love with an actor. I wanted to be around writers and people who knew a great deal and I was a good listener. I decided that actors didn't know any more than I did but I loved them all and I was friends with them all and I have never had difficulty with anyone in my acting profession. I love my people and my world. I think that it's maybe because that we are in a world of make-believe that we are all still children in a way.

D.W. Griffith gave film its form and grammar and nobody has added anything to film except Disney since him. He took the responsibility of everything he put on the screen very seriously. He thought that The Keystone Cops taught children a disrespect for the Law and look at us sixty years later – was he right? I firmly believe that the screens are responsible for the way the world is today.

Everybody was very young when I started in the film business because the lighting and photography were so bad, everyone looked as though they had been dead for two or three weeks. You couldn't possibly have an old hag of eighteen playing the heroine – you had to be about twelve or thirteen! I never picked money, I picked people – the best story, the best director, the best actors, the best camera men. I just wanted a living wage and a little bit of the profits – but nobody would give me that.

I can't remember a time when I wasn't working, so I don't know what I would do if I stopped now, I just don't know how to do anything else.

1980

SIR JOHN BETJEMAN

I was delighted when Jim Parker wanted to put my poems to music. He is a very quiet, modest man and his music really seemed to capture the verse. I can't sing a note in tune. I know about rhythm – I think, and the sound of words – but I'm not really musical. My forbears were musical – Gilbert Betjeman introduced Wagner to Glasgow and when the music started the audience began to laugh so he tapped his baton and said, 'Are you going to listen to this music or are you not, because if you don't I shall go home and enjoy a whisky-toddy.'

I think the best of the lyric writers is Cole Porter. I can't write lyrics because I can't keep a tune in my head to write words to it. As I get older it gets harder and slower to write poetry – it doesn't get easier and I only think of something when I wake up and I write it down and then I look at it at breakfast and it's awful. I add to it during the day – I find walking about best for writing poetry. I longed to write poetry all the time and I felt that every time I didn't write it was wasted time. Part of the pleasure is writing it on the page and seeing how it looks and reciting it time and time again, and then trying it out on a friend you can trust. You can tell if they like it. If they cough, then it's a bore. I am now motivated to write by places, faces and eyes. I think people speak through their eyes and you can catch someone's eye and talk – I think they are our antennae. I don't look at eyes too pointedly or one gets into trouble!

I didn't like being a copywriter very much. I started as a journalist which taught me to write things simply, like government department forms. I think sitting in the underground was an inspiration for advertising slogans, like:

> Whatever her party, the sweet young thing,
> It's certain she'll vote for a Bravington ring.

> She was bashful, she was shy
> Give her a Bravington ring
> And the cloud will pass by.

They didn't pay me for that, I've just remembered.

My first poem was appallingly bad. It was a crib about the Faerie Mountain. The last line was a complete failure, and it is the last line which counts in any poem – it's the one to be remembered.

My childhood was comfortable. I had kind parents who on the whole left me on my own or sometimes with nanny. But I always preferred my own company to that of others. I didn't know anything about sex – I didn't know what it was. I used to be told vague things about plants and then I thought it was very wicked – a sin against the Holy Ghost. I had terrible crushes and I've never felt so sick with love as in my teens. I wrote poems about it.

1981

ARTHUR MARSHALL

I am very fond of all things British and of all the British institutions I have observed, my favourite is one which I am afraid the next thirty or forty years may remove – the British Club. I belong to a marvellous Club called the Reform Club. I have never been quite clear what it wanted to reform, but no matter. It is an absolute haven in the middle of London's noise and griminess; it has a marvellous library, beautiful rooms and a lot more. I was given a very good lesson once at the Reform Club; it was at Coronation time and the Queen came down Pall Mall where the Club is and a lot of the members had been toasting her rather liberally! One member, who I must call Mr X toasted her extremely liberally and was highly intoxicated and there came a moment when he thought he would like to rest a while. He lay down to rest in the entrance hall and after he had been there for about two hours, I thought perhaps I should do something about this so I went to the secretary, apologised if I was interfering, but that Mr X had been lying down in the entrance hall for two hours. The secretary just looked up and said, 'Is he breathing?' 'Well, not only is he breathing, but he is actually snoring rather loudly.' 'Is he being a nuisance to anybody?' and so I replied that apart from having to step over him to get in and out he wasn't being a nuisance. The secretary said, 'In that case, I shall do nothing. If a member wishes to lie down and sleep in any part of the Club, he is at liberty to do so. Good afternoon.'

I love travelling by train, but I don't really like trains that go tremendously fast because it is so lovely in a train – you've got your sandwiches, your thermos, nobody can get at you, the telephone can't ring and its beautifully restful with the countryside passing. I wrote somewhere that as a schoolboy I hadn't wanted to be an engine driver because in those days the drivers were on exposed platforms but now that they are all covered in and you sit right up in front, I thought how lovely it would be. This article was seen by British Rail and they very kindly arranged for me to write an article and they put me in the front of a high-speed train from London to Bristol. I wasn't allowed to drive it of course, but I was right up next to the driver. Everything went well until we drew slowly into Swindon and there were a whole lot of passengers lining the platform waiting to get on the train. When they saw me at the controls, blood drained from their faces and they hurried into the waiting room to wait for the next train!

I do get asked to 'open' things quite a lot these days. At school I always longed for some royal person to come down and close something because so many of the buildings at school were ghastly. I do open a fête or two here and there and I do do a certain amount of talking to things like Women's Institutes which I love. The atmosphere is so wonderful; these ladies are entirely devoted to good things. I wish I'd known that marvellous woman Lady Baden Powell. She was a dear creature and head of the Girl Guides. She told a wonderful story how once when she was in the Girl Guides Headquarters on the first floor, she tripped and fell all the way downstairs to the ground floor and landed with a frightful clatter at the bottom. The secretary came rushing up saw Lady Baden Powell lying there, looked very relieved and said, 'Oh, it's only you, we thought it was the new Hoover!'

I am now working on a compilation of prep school reminiscences because I think in twenty or thirty years' time, prep schools will be very few and far between. I was at a very, very rum prep school. It was in Hampshire on the Solent. It was just after the First World War and I suppose I was eight or nine. A master came to teach us Latin and he was very peculiar; halfway through the term he started to confiscate anything of value that we had – our penknives and fountainpens were all confiscated. Then one Saturday afternoon he went into Gosport, pawned the lot and eloped with a chorus girl from the show on the Pier! The headmaster was a dear fellow and tried to do the best for us. At the age of twelve, we were wondering about sex and were rather muddled and one day all the boys in the top form were sent for to go to the headmaster's study. He looked fairly genial when we went in and asked us to sit down and then said, 'I expect you've all been wondering how you got here.' We hadn't been wondering at all – we had come straight along the passage! Of course, he meant how we had got into the world. He told us that it was all quite simple, and explained it like this: 'When a lady and gentleman love each other there is this little thing provided by the gentleman and this little thing provided by the lady and they meet in the lady's cave and they form up and make a baby. Any questions?' So out we came feeling totally bemused and the first thing we did was to look about us for a little thing. We found that without too much difficulty!

Sport was absolutely compulsory and you had to play 'footer' whether you liked it or not. Much worse from my point of view was that you had to play cricket. When I went to my public school, we had to be soldiers twice a week and we dressed up in uniform and marched about. In due course I became a schoolmaster and went back to Arundel and was an officer in the OTC and we had swords and had to do sword drill. We were inspected by a General every so often who thought the boys were all marvellous but that the masters' sword drill was a total disgrace.

I was in the Army during the Second World War, at Dunkerque. It was very noisy and I don't recommend it. The French at Dunkerque were really extremely disagreeable. Of course they had good reason to be because they thought we were deserting them and as we were waiting to get off, the French would come up and say 'Pas encore parti?' with an odious intonation. I don't like them any the more now. Look what they've been doing – refusing our lamb, sending over all those apples and then they come over and pinch all our fish. They're a terrible lot. I think the idea of a channel tunnel is perfectly ghastly – they will come pouring down in droves.

I do enjoy watching soap-operas on the television, but lately everything has been a disaster. Take *Coronation Street*, the Ogdens longing for that new house, Fred and Eunice with nowhere to go. *Dallas* has the price of oil going up and down and Pam going right off her nut. But of course the whole thing pales into insignificance compared with *Crossroads*. It is like a ship without a rudder now that Meg has gone. I long to be in 'Crossroads', do you think they might have me? I would like to be an extra in the reception area, to walk across looking tremendously wooden and say 'Where is my key?'

1979 and 1982

PENELOPE KEITH

There's no theatrical background in my family. I was always taken to the theatre as a child as a school holiday treat. Apparently I came home, aged five, from school and sat in the bath and told my mother I was going to be either a nun or an actress when I was older. She was a bit taken aback and said, 'Well, darling, nuns can't wear pretty clothes,' so I decided to be an actress.

I suppose I was quite an outward going child – I was probably a bit of an extrovert. I was a great talker and if anyone was speaking in class and the teacher asked whoever was talking to stand up, I immediately stood up because it was bound to be me – even if it wasn't! I was very tall, very plain and very long. I suppose this was where the comedy came from because I knew I wasn't going to get very far on my looks and so I thought I'd better be the 'gag' girl. When I first started on television I did a play and I had a very small part as a secretary. During rehearsals, the director did a lot of lining up and eventually after a long time said, 'I'm not going to get you in love', and I remember saying: 'Well, I'll bend my knees', and I did. I spent the whole three lines walking from one set to the other, you know, crawling! As a child I was always seeing aunts and uncles I hadn't seen for ages and they would say, 'Hello, haven't you grown!' It's dreadful the way one says things like that to children. They weren't setting out to be cruel, it's their first remark, not, 'Hello, don't you look well.' So my mother and I developed this defence mechanism whereby I'd walk into a room and say, 'Hello, haven't I grown!'

When I started in the theatre I was always given the character parts because if you were tall you weren't young. It's changed a lot now – this was sixteen years ago. In retrospect, it was very good for me because one had a bash at all the character parts of playing nineteen to ninety which broadens one's range. I remember one time I played a nineteen year old – I think I was younger than that at the time – and a little boy came up to me in the local theatre club and told me he thought I was wonderful. He thought it was wonderful for a woman of my age to play a part so young! I was established as old and eccentric. Even fairly recently, a sweet, lovely guy who I was going to play a love scene with came up to me and said, 'You are tall, aren't you?' I have never in my life gone up to a man and told him how small he was. I think I'm going to try it now.

It was wonderful when I joined the Royal Shakespeare Company because I'd been a medium sized fish in lots of little ponds and suddenly there I was, the minutest fish in this very big pond working with the great stars like Peggy Ashcroft and Donald Sinden. It was fascinating to see how they worked. I had one small part as Mrs Simpcox in *Henry VI*, a real beggar woman. I was bound up with tatty old rags – the only actress in the entire company who never wore pretty clothes. I felt a bit unattractive so every night I went on reeking of the most expensive scent I could find, dressed as this old beggar woman!

A lot of people say of me that I am a comedienne, but it is not true. A comedienne for me means someone who is funny, and I am not funny. I am funny if I am given a good part to play in a comic situation but I couldn't stand up now and be funny. I am an actress who happens to play comedy. When you are rehearsing comedy, you go through phases of thinking that it is never going to be funny and wonder why you ever thought it was funny in the first place. You have to go through these great processes of finding the truth of the situation before the situation becomes funny.

I am now going back to the stage, after a gap of two years and I am nervous about it, but then I get nervous about every single new job. I think my roots are in the theatre and I am looking forward to going back.

1977 and 1980

GLENDA JACKSON

What I dreamed about (selling pills and medicines) at Boots, was to get onto the cosmetics counter, but I never made it. As a child I wanted to be a doctor, and then I thought I might like to be a missionary, then I wanted to be a dancer – that was my first theatrical dream – I wanted to be a ballet dancer, and I came to acting really quite late. I've never regarded it as being glamorous because when I left RADA the principal said to me: don't expect to work much before your mid or late forties, because you're basically a character woman and you know there isn't much work for you at the moment, and that was true then. So I never thought the theatre was glamorous really.

I always judder when people say 'You're a great actress'. I don't like it because I don't know how you ever define it. The thing that I have is a great deal of luck: I was given opportunities at a time when I could exploit them, when I was ready for them. I know people that I worked with in rep who are as good and in some instances better than me, who will never be given those opportunities, and will never be able to show what they can do. And they just die out in weekly rep, because there comes a point where you can't actually recreate anymore. The failure just gnaws at your soul and there's nothing left. And I've been very fortunate, I've worked with very good people and very good things, and I've had chances to extend myself, but I don't think there's a recipe.

Success and fame could corrode me, if I wanted it to. It would be very easy to believe what you read about yourself, and always expect to be given preferential treatment, and that of course is terribly corrosive, because it would separate you from people, and acting is about people actually. But if you can exercise a certain amount of restraint, and coming as I do from a largish family who send me up rotten if ever I try to put it on, that's never really been a problem.

Acting is about the observation of people and what obsesses them. Really I mean the recurring themes in human nature, life, if you like to put it that way, and if you separate yourself totally, you put yourself in a tiny ivory tower, or adopt only an élitist attitude, you cut yourself off from the roots that feed you. It's not the major tragedies that fashion us, it's the everyday irritants. It's waiting in a bus queue – and rain comes down or the bus is late or you go into the shops and they haven't got what you want. That's what tempers you. I think we can all cope with major tragedy, the extremes and the dramatic parts of life, it is the day to day tedium of it that actually fashions you.

I don't think you have to use deliberate devices working for a camera. In a way it's easier, because all you actually have to do if it's that close to you, is think. The amazing thing about the human face is that you can be thinking absolute rubbish but it need not necessarily be visible on your face. I'm thinking of the great example at the end of *Queen Christiana*, where Greta Garbo is at the prow of that ship and the wind is blowing and the sail is billowing and it is on record and verified that the director told her: 'Think of nothing', and that is what she did. You see this, and your imagination, having seen the whole film, fills her being with every single emotion that you actually imagine, so in that sense you're doing the work for her, but they've programmed you to do that.

I think one must make clear that acting is not behaving. There is behaviour which is one thing, but that is not what acting is. I would like to be able to define clearly and lucidly for you the difference but I can't. But I know that it is different. You have to be able to repeat time after time after time in acting, and behaviour changes second by second and minute by minute, but acting you have to repeat and repeat.

1976

DIANA RIGG

The television series I did in America was a terrible flop and I see no point of absolving myself of the responsibility of taking on a series which is named after you. Having said that, one then has to qualify why it was my fault. I didn't throw my weight around as much as American stars in their own series do. They control absolutely everything from the scriptwriters to who is in the show, who directs it, the line that the show takes – they know the way they want the show to go and they control it totally. I thought I would lay myself at their mercy, which I did and that they would know better, and I discovered that, in fact, they didn't and that I was being churned out as this second-rate Mary Tyler Moore creature in an American environment with three of the most extraordinary scriptwriters you have ever set eyes on in your life. They were all very, very small and they were also misogynists which didn't help at all, being a very large woman. Anyway, there I was, surrounded by everything that everybody imagines as the trappings of success – a house in Hollywood, a swimming pool, a series named after you, and it was a disaster. It was failure on an enormous level and I think that in order to exorcise failure you have to embrace it and say 'it was my fault'.

It taught me to be very careful before I commit myself to something again. I don't want to start being arrogant and start throwing my weight around, but I should have said that I wanted to see six scripts before I do the show. The curious part is that I am still being offered series in America, but I don't care about reputation – I care about what happened inside myself and it was very painful, but out of any kind of failure, providing that you embrace it, I think you can turn it to account, you can learn from it and not be destroyed by it. My confidence could have been totally destroyed by it.

The talk-shows in America are a kind of death arena. Most of the fellows who have their own shows are latent, failed comedians. Johnny Carson, if he could, would be a straight stand-up comedian, but he can't quite do it by himself, so the interviewee goes on as a stooge, which is fine up to a point. I don't mind being a stooge but he does put you at a terrible disadvantage. You can't top what happened to Dick Cavett. He was interviewing a man about health foods and this man was seventy, and he had lived solely on vegetables, no meat, exercising every single day and he was expounding the virtues of this life when he suddenly keeled over and died on the spot! Johnny Carson cannot top that.

I am a very independent person and I have found independence can be a plus or a minus. In terms of relationships, it can detract because whenever anything is remotely rocky, you withdraw into yourself very fast indeed and that may not be the answer. I figured out that it probably started at the age of seven when I was sent away to school. If you can imagine that all the things that you have taken to be permanent as a child: your mother, your father, the house, the regimen, what you eat, the teasing, the intimacy, the loving and the knowing – all that is suddenly cut off completely. You are put into a strange building with a lot of children who are totally strange and a discipline which is very strange to you because it is a discipline that exists for the good of the community as opposed to just yourself as a child. This makes you survive as a sole entity – you have to learn to rely upon yourself. I did rebel against the institution, but rebellion is self-destructive in lots of ways and I rebelled constantly in school and it wasn't until I left school and didn't have to rebel anymore that I began to develop.

I knew at that stage that I wanted to be an actress but it was a very unpopular decision – the headmistress and teachers considered it useless and I was out on a limb, but following something which was instinctive without much encouragement. My parents encouraged me because they loved me but they didn't understand what it involved. Technically, you have to learn to be an actress. You must learn technique to be on the stage, but it cannot intrude – it has to be very much secondary to your instincts. I love to watch people, I learn from that and I like listening to people. Sensing what people mean, what they are, what are their fears, is our responsibility as people, but if you are an actor or actress, you take it to a very fine degree – it is part of your trade to watch, listen and try and understand because the permutations of human behaviour are infinite and fascinating. I love it.

I have absolutely no sense of snobbism about what I do. I think whatever I do, providing that I learn from it, is valuable – my criteria is that I should learn from it. I'm not too chic to do this or that or the other, I'm really not and its not a question of economics either. It's just relish. I love working, great actress or not. I defy anybody anyway to be described as a great actress in her lifetime. I don't know, it's awfully dangerous, the whole number. I just keep plodding and enjoying it. I have fallen flat on my face before and you can always pick yourself up and laugh.

I've taken to motherhood rather well actually. I didn't think I would. My pregnancy was just wonderful for an aged lady – because over the age of twenty five they call you elderly – and I was thirty eight. I had a wonderful time and I drank champagne from morning to night – I just couldn't have been healthier. Came the baby and it was the most joyous thing in the world. The first time I pushed her out in the street, a man walking along the street recognised me and he burst out laughing – me and a pram seemed utterly wrong to him. I take my daughter to a nursery and I do get rather daunted by those professional mothers that are there – those *Guardian* 'Women's Page' mothers – I read my Women's page and I admire what they do but there they are in the middle of January with no stockings on their feet and open-toed sandals, out pops breast and they feed the baby and I feel that I am not quite in there with it. I discovered that motherhood was competitive in the sense that you show how good a mother you are, and I am not in that race either. Children's behaviour is compared as well and Rachel has let me down totally. She discovered nose-picking and you get so tired of saying 'Rachel, don't pick your nose.' I was pushing her through a London store, a pretty kind of high-class one, and she was terribly quiet in her pram and I knew exactly that one finger was lost up one nostril, so I decided not to say it for the fiftieth time that day. There was a long pause and suddenly this little triumphant voice called out – 'bogey!'

I can't resist biting my baby's bottom – I mean it's there! I say: 'Rachel, come here, I have to bite your bottom' and she is now two and three-quarters! But that skin, that flesh, you just have to sink your teeth into it! I have had letters from women saying how dare you bring filthy sex into your child's life. I don't care. It's not only my child – I'll bite anybody else's as well!

I had to bare my bottom when I did Tom Stoppard's play *Jumpers*. I *had* to reveal my bottom – it wasn't just one of these cases where the director thought it would be good for the play – it was actually in the text. The only way I could do it was to make my bottom up. Every night I used to put three layers of make-up on my bum, otherwise it just looked like a piece of old cod. Bottoms do.

I love a live audience and I can never understand it when actors tell me they don't like looking at the audience – I love watching them all, I love that communication that you get with an audience – even the ones who are fast asleep – they are telling you something! I think possibly that communicates itself, I think that must be the clue. I feel an audience before I go on stage, as a physical thing and I love it, I love the challenge of going on each night and there is a different audience and you can't just go through the motions. The miracle of it is that in this day and age when they can sit at home and watch television or alternatively a big screen in a cinema and it's all presented for them, they still come to the theatre where they have to use their imagination, and pay a fortune so to do. The power of live theatre is so fantastic.

I believe in having fun on stage. Naughtiness. I found that Lady Macbeth was a great bore to do and at one point the director had Dennis Quilley sliding his hand down the front of my bodice and massaging a breast, and I was whispering to him (it must have been a matinée): 'down a bit, left a bit, right a bit – golden shot!' Dennis collapsed, as he giggles a great deal too – thank God.

I think that every actor who is truly honest remembers their worst notice, because it actually carves itself on your soul, you live with it for weeks before you finally exorcise the pain of it. Mine was from a gentleman in New York who was writing about the nude scene in *Abelarde and Heloise* and he said: 'Diana Rigg is built like a brick mausoleum with insufficient flying buttresses.'

Now that I am approaching forty two, I look forward to playing the more mature roles, if they are good parts. I certainly don't want to play juvenile parts because it would be macabre wouldn't it? But you see, that's the wonderful thing about the theatre, that if I had been a movie star I think I would probably be working about three times a year now, whereas the theatre gives you a longer life and you can go on for ever.

I am going to do *Hedda Gabler* which is statutory playing for a mature lady and one other Noël Coward play and after that, I really don't know. I'm not on that treadmill anymore – I used to be, but now I quite like being at home, biting my daughter's bottom!

1976 and 1980

JACQUELINE BISSET

When I first came across the script of *Rich and Famous* I was looking for something I could get my teeth into and this script just jumped right out of the pile. I had decided I was going to search meticulously for something and not do anything else and not go to work for anybody other than, to a degree, myself. I did help to get the film made – I formed a partnership with a man called Bill Allen and the funny thing was that he had had a great deal of trouble in getting the thing mounted and had had the project for five years. As co-producer of the film, as well as acting in it, I felt very emotionally tied to it and it made me a little more stubborn and a little more difficult. I decided that I was not going to go through the usual process of being 'Dear Jackie' and winning the popularity contests as it hadn't really taken me to a satisfying place in my work. I don't believe that getting tough is the way to do anything, but I did not regret getting rather difficult because I felt that the work was coming out on screen the way I wanted it to. It was not the most 'fun' experience in that sense, because I don't particularly enjoy tension and I do tend to put myself in a state of tension when I'm doing something as it helps me work.

When I went to Hollywood I worked with a lot of very major stars and a lot of good directors and I thought then that if I was really smart, I would keep my eye open to see what was going on, to learn how to behave on a set, the structure of the business, and I hoped that one day I would be able to apply it. I am proud of what I have put together, I am proud of having gone there and made a success, I feel good about it. At the same time I felt rather ambivalent about it because I had a European career and an American glamour-girl career and I never felt that I was either one or the other – I felt there was an internal person in me who wanted to get out, and I found it, to a degree, in Liz in *Rich and Famous*.

There was a tremendous culture shock when I first went to America, but I don't really have any reservations now about the American lifestyle. I think the world is what you make of it and there were a lot of things in America that got me moving. I think that if I'd stayed in London I would have continued being a little spoilt, running around having a great time, but when

I went into the rather bleak area that I felt Hollywood to be at the time, I had to really look round and decide to start shaping my life up for myself. The energy of America on a traditional English background is terrific.

1982

MERYL STREEP

All Americans think they can do British accents, just like all the British who come over think they can do American accents, and we all hold our noses. The inflection is easy to catch, but the specific sounds are very, very difficult. I think it's easier to learn and reproduce a different language than to do one that's slightly like your own. It's very daunting being the only American working with a British cast, because in America we still feel intimidated by British actors and feel secretly second-rate, compared to them. I wasn't prepared for the warmth and welcome that I had on the set of *The French Lieutenant's Woman*, and the first day I felt as if I had lived in the midst of these people all my life, and that's the hyperbole that theatre people talk about, but I realised that theatre people are the same in America or here or anywhere – it's just a community of like souls. To prepare myself for playing the part of Sarah, I wore a corset for five months which has a lot to do with the way you bear yourself and how you feel at the end of the day, and it forces a kind of look on the face – it's pain, just pain all day long.

I played Shakespeare in New York and I didn't regard it as being the special area of any one people – it crosses all sorts of cultural boundaries but I suppose Americans can't really do it as well. It has to do with the difference of the culture here – a more literate culture, people are more involved with words. There is no emphasis on words and articulation at home.

I don't react very well to being acclaimed a huge star so suddenly. I do miss my privacy and I didn't make a pact with the devil when I started to be an actress and I never imagined that I would have this kind of success. I've had a lot of good luck and I am very happy with the parts I have been able to do, and I am very grateful for that. At the same time I hate being worried about the security in my house, I hate fearing things and not being able to watch people because that's my stock in trade. I think that people are more polite here in London – in America they are far more aggressive.

My next venture is *Sophie's Choice* which is a wonderful novel written by William Styron which was a bestseller in America and almost from the time it was published, people wondered who would play the part when they made the movie. I really broke my neck to get that one.

1981

100

GOLDIE HAWN

The idea for my last film, *Private Benjamin*, was given to me by three writer friends and I thought that I would like to produce it as well as star in it. We put our heads together and got on with it. It has been a huge success in the States and I would like to think that the audience gets two things from it; one is that it is hilariously funny, and the other is that it has something to say about women and their situation today and it makes a little statement about a particular cross-section of society. It's nice to be able to make people laugh and enjoy themselves and at the same time learn something.

I think a lot of women identified with the young woman in the film and it's basically a story about choice. A lot of us girls grow up thinking that we've made it if we marry a man who will take care of us and the truth is that it doesn't usually work out. Life doesn't deal you such a simple set of circumstances.

My mother worked and I never thought for a minute that I wasn't going to work, although I used to dream of staying at home and looking after the family. I think you have to choose between being a housewife or going to work – you can't do both.

I studied dancing from the age of three so I always had a purpose to my life, a reason to exist other than just school. It was very difficult to get jobs in New York so I sold-out and got a job as a go-go dancer. I worked in some terrible places; I danced on tables and in cages with men pressing their noses up to the cage, and it was quite grotesque. I'm not sure how I survived it, but it didn't scar me permanently – I still like men a lot!

It was *The Laugh-In* that brought me to attention both here and in the States. The dumb blonde image was at first accidental, and then contrived. When I first started I was so nervous that I made lots of mistakes; I would look at the cue cards and get all mixed up, and luckily I have a sense of humour about myself. The producer loved it and didn't change anything – except my life! I haven't found it a problem to shrug off the dumb blonde image and I'm quite happy with the way things have gone.

I've now had two broken marriages and although I'm the first to admit that I'm not the easiest person to live with, the outside extenuating circumstances were bigger than the three of us. It's very difficult to find out where the balance of power is when a women is more successful than her man. It's unfortunate when you realise that a relationship is based on power, money and position, rather than on deeper things.

1981

'I was very tall,
very plain
and very long . . .
I wasn't
going to get very
far on my
looks so I
thought I'd better
be the "gag" girl'
Penelope Keith

BOB HOPE

My parents were not poor, we were an average sort of family. My father was a stonemason and had a lot of work. We didn't have underwear all the time – my mother used to paint black buttons on our stomachs. I think the first time I made somebody laugh was when I was born – my mother was hysterical! I had a variety of jobs before I became a comedian and one thing I used to do was box. I used to love climbing into the ring – I don't remember ever leaving it though.

As a young man struggling to get into show business, my heroes were Jack Benny, Frank Faye, Phil Baker, Crosby . . . Even though I have never taken anybody's style, I think when you are watching other comedians you soak it up unconsciously. I didn't actually start as a comedian, but as a dancer. Then I had to announce an act and it was a Scotsman I knew so I got out there and said: 'This guy had to get married in his back yard so the chickens could get the rice', and it continued from there. I kept adding jokes and it was then that I decided to become a comedian. The competition was very fierce and I starved for about a year when I started. Then I finally got one date for $25 and it made me – from that time I got very lucky and things got steadily better.

I first got into movies through a show called *Ziegfeld Follies* singing a song 'Can't Get Started With You' and a director saw me and wanted me to do a juvenile lead in the film *The Big Broadcast of 1938* which is where I sang 'Thanks For The Memory' which has become my signature tune. However, it was really radio that provided the big breakthrough for me as it was the ideal medium for my style of comedy. I fooled around with it while I was on Broadway doing shows but it never really got started until I got the Pepsident show which came over here during the war. I think it was speed that singled me out on the radio; Jack Benny was a tremendous hit, but working slow, which was his style, and I had a lot of writers and we picked out jokes and I told them very fast. We would do maybe 140 jokes in half an hour and that's what caught on. I think it is true that I was using more writers than most comedians when I started, but nowadays all comedians seem to have about seven or eight which is what I have had for the last twenty five years. I think the secret of my success is experience and editing. I know from experience what the audience will laugh at and that really is the crux of the matter.

Gene Wilder makes me laugh today, I like him and that other modern comedian, Tommy Trinder. Is he really playing football? I knew Lennie Bruce very well and of course, he was the original 'sick' comic, but very funny. He had a great sense of timing – he was born backstage. He was a very bright fellow and came in with original material and it was a great shame he got mixed up with drugs.

I use very little blue material on the stage. However, at the golf club it is very different! We tell sensational jokes. I seem to go down quite well with the younger generation in the States – I wouldn't be on television as long as I have been on if I didn't go down well with them. You know, the kids of nine, ten and eleven are in charge of the knob on television sets there. They are the ones that turn it on and select the programmes, and their elders go along with them.

How did I first meet Bing? Well, I was a boy scout and I saw this old lady waiting to cross the road. So I went over to help her across and it turned out to be Bing. Seriously though, I met Bing around 1932 and we played at the Capital Theatre in New York. When I went out to Hollywood, before the 'Road' pictures, we did an act together there and the boys from Paramount saw us, thought we worked well together, and put us in this picture *Road to Singapore* and that is how the whole thing started. We have never had a row – you just can't have an argument with Bing because he just walks away. I was the loudmouth if anything happened – Bing would tell me to go and find out about it and he would go off to the golf course and wait. He does take life very easily, but he loves to be on, he is as hammy as anybody and I admire him for it because you have to be in our business. I do work much harder than him but it's because I really enjoy it, it is not slave labour. I get so much out of entertaining so it's therapy for me. I feel better after a show than before it.

My traditional Christmas work of going out and entertaining the American troups was the most exciting part of my life and the most emotional part. There was more gratification connected with that than anything. It was the feeling of getting out with these guys who were making the sacrifice and doing a great job for their country. I did it from 1941 until 1972.

I've known quite a few American Presidents and I must say I am very fond of Richard Nixon for a lot of reasons – especially bringing the kids home from Vietnam. Watergate has in no way changed my opinion of him. The whole thing is a very long story but he was very loyal to his staff and it got him into a lot of trouble. Although he is discredited now, I think he will go down in history as a damn good President for some of the great things he did.

I would never go into American politics – they tried to entice me about ten years ago but I'm not fit for that and anyway I like what I'm doing. Politics is a lot like show business – one day you are drinking wine and the next day you are picking the grapes.

I have no ambitions left apart from directing comedy pictures – that I would like to do one day. I don't find being famous difficult to live with at all – it leads you into good things, and when you are famous you can help people. I don't have any trouble; I travel on commercial airlines and people are nice – you get on the plane and everybody stays away until they have had a couple of drinks then they come over and lay it on you! I certainly have no thoughts of retiring yet – I have to save up a little money first!

1975

JIMMY TARBUCK

The last three months for me have been like being discovered all over again and it has been terrific. One critic recently said that like wine, I was improving with age. I don't think you are a comedian until a certain age – you're a cheeky personality and that is what I was when I went on at the Palladium in 1963. I think I have only just become a comedian now that I am forty – you need the experience to talk about different subjects with any sort of authority and make people laugh at you. Timing is the all important thing.

The programmes that really make me laugh on television are *Dad's Army*, *Rising Damp*, *The Two Ronnies*, *Eric and Ernie*, and Les Dawson. I also like programmes like *Survival* – it's all about Chelsea! Did you know that ground rhino's horn is an aphrodisiac? The trouble is it does have a side effect – you keep charging range rovers!

I do tell blue gags, but I wouldn't tell a joke here that I thought would offend any lady or youngster in the audience. For instance, there is this guy who goes on his holiday in France and he ends up in a house of ill repute. Anyway, he says that he has been recommended to a lady named Rose and the patron says what a wonderful choice that was. He calls Rose in and this beautiful red-head comes down the stairs. However, before the guy can do anything, the patron tells him it is £200, but he pays and has a wonderful time with Rose. The next morning he says he would like to book her again for the following night and has to pay another £200. This happens again the night before he is due to leave and as he is leaving, she asks him where he is from. He tells her he is from Liverpool and she replies that she was brought up in Liverpool as a child and they discover that not only did they live in the same town, but also in the same street. She asks him if he knew a Mrs Cohen at No. 76 and he replies 'Know her? I saw her last week and she asked me to give you £600!'

When I was eighteen, I was on rock and roll shows with Marty Wilde, Billy Fury and everybody like that and they did a one-nighter in Paris which turned out to be the most embarrassing thing of my life. All the musicians in the band told me that they would educate me in the ways of life and I was taken out with them and we ended up in 'one of those places'. There was this lovely little Chinese girl who was delightful, but she was the equivalent of £6 and I had £4 so I ended up with this little French girl and it really was a very nice education for me. Years go by, I had been on television a few times, and I was invited to play in a golf tournament in Paris. I went over there with my family and we were eating in this restaurant and all of a sudden there was this girl standing in front of me. She said 'Do you remember me? I'm Angelique.' There I was with the wife and kids and she told me she had someone she wanted me to meet; she brought in this eight year old little boy who was the spitting image of my own little lad and she said: 'This is Jamie.' Jamie told me he was very pleased to meet me and that he had heard a lot about me and then he asked why it was that Mama spoke French and I spoke English. I said, 'If I'd have had another £2, you would have spoken Chinese.'

1981

TOMMY COOPER

The fez came when I was in Egypt. I was in the army there and we did a show at the YMCA. I used to wear a pith helmet. One day I forgot to bring it with me so there were waitresses with fezes on so I took one off her head and I've worn it ever since.

I was in the Horse Guards and I remember being stationed in Pirbright and we were under canvas and we used to go out and gallop up the mountains and down, over the waters, through the fences and gallop along the fields and back again and I took a horse with me.

When you get on a horse, as a recruit, when you put the girth around (I didn't know this) the horse blows itself out because it doesn't want it to be tight. You're supposed to wait for a while and then you get it on quick. I didn't know this and I put on the girth and we were all on parade and he said, 'In front of your horses, prepare to mount', and so you put your foot in the stirrup and he said 'mount' and I put my foot in and the saddle went right underneath. Everybody else was on top and I was underneath.

We had a sergeant and he used to have us out for roll-call at 4 am – pitch black. The corporal-major used to come out with a hurricane lamp and he used to say 'Good morning, men' and we used to say 'Good morning, lamp' because we couldn't see him. This corporal-major, a big man he was; he hated anybody with a face. The sergeant used to come round to wake us up and he'd say 'Good morning, good morning, good morning' and he had a bayonet in his hand.

I've got this mongoose – a man-eating mongoose. It's very unpredictable – sometimes it's happy and sometimes it's not. When I got this I was out in the middle of the Conga jungle and a friend, who was stationed with me, was writing home to his mother. I remember he said: 'Dear Mum, I'm out here in the heart of the Conga jungle, eating bananas and coconuts all day. I'm getting as brown as a berry; incidentally, the tribe are head-shrinkers and they can shrink your head to the size of a small orange.' And he puts: 'P.S. If you can get me a bowler size 1½ send it over.'

I think inventions are marvellous – you know wherever they put petrol pumps, they find petrol. Take Van Gogh, a marvellous painter. He cut his ear off to send to his girl-friend and they said 'Van Gogh, you're a genius' and he said 'Eh?'

1979

KEN DODD

I do find it rather difficult as a comedian having these perfect features! I did think of having my teeth straightened once, but let's face it, there wouldn't have been anything left to laugh at if I had! I think a comic has to learn very early on to let people laugh at him as well as with him and he has to take it all in his stride. I really don't mind.

I have just done a season in Blackpool and they always start all these conferences up there when I'm there. Blackpool is a very up-market resort –

they get a much better class of seaside hooligan there; in Eastbourne and Bournemouth they get Mods and Rockers, in Blackpool they get the TUC! Anyway, Mrs Thatcher came and was gracious enough to come and see the show and she actually did laugh all the way through it. It's all right telling jokes about people, as long as you don't attack the dogma and one joke I tell is about Sir Geoffrey Howe – how he wants to get us out of this mess as soon as possible because he's got another one waiting for us. I've been telling that gag now for twenty years at Blackpool, so it shows you how long we've been in a mess!

I've got this thing called a 'Giggle Map'; when I first started in show business I decided that I would keep notebooks on which jokes went down well and over the years it has developed into this Giggle Map that tells me what sort of gags people like in different parts of the country. Take Yorkshire for instance, they're a very odd lot! They have one trait, which is their strength and their weakness – they are stubborn and very gritty. One joke I tell is about this old lady who went to a stonemason and asked him to engrave her husband's name on a memorial stone as he had just died. He asked her if he should put R.I.P. on it so she said OK but put T.I.C after it. He asked her why and she said that her husband had spent all the club money, all the money that they had saved in the teapot – he had drunk it all down in the Dog and Duck: 'So put R.I.P. – Rest In Peace and then T.I.C. – Till I come!'

When you go further north, the Scots people love jokes about themselves: there was this Scotsman went into a drapers and said he wanted to buy twelve thimbles. When the assistant remarked on what a lot a sewing he was going to be doing, he replied, 'No, we're just having a wee party.' When I visit Liverpool I tell jokes about unemployment. They were taking men on at a building site there the other week and the foreman was asking for each man's name. One of them said 'F.W. Woolworth' so the foreman told him to clear off as he didn't want cowboy names. The next man gave his name as Mark Spencer, so he was told to clear off too. The next man came up and said his name was Ken. 'Oh, that's better' the foreman said, 'what's your other name?' 'Tucky Fried Chicken', the fella replied. Liverpool people have a great enthusiasm and a complete blind spot as regards authority.

I've been involved with mentally handicapped children over the past year. About a year ago I saw a performance of a circus by some mentally handicapped children and I was really struck by the way they knew how to act daft and to be funny. The headmistress told me that these children are great mimmicks and they love people like Laurel and Hardy. I have just seen a performance of *Coppélia* by these children and to see them work together was very moving. Somebody said as they were leaving the school where these children performed that they felt they had been to another world, and I think that this Year of the Disabled, as well as raising money, has focused the attention of people, who perhaps averted their eyes before, on the disabled both mentally and physically. Now hopefully we won't look away so much.

I have now been in show business for twenty-six years; it's a lovely game, it's a business where we get paid for trying to bring happiness, you know, getting their chuckle-muscles working.

1981

SPIKE MILLIGAN

I was one of the great unemployed in about 1934/35. I was at the Catford Labour Exchange – which is like being born dead with cancer – and the fellow two in front of me in the dole queue suddenly fell down and the chap in front of me said: 'He's dead' and the bloke behind me said, 'Someone must have offered him a bleeding job then.' I was a communist in those days and a very active one. I didn't actually do anything but I was very active. Then I got a job playing in a band and you automatically leave the communist party when you get rich, they won't have capitalists! I think it may be my communist connection that has kept me off the honours list. I mean, we've got Sir Harry Secombe haven't we? Mind you, I think they went in for bulk buying there. And I'm a mate of Prince Charles too, although we do clash about blood sports.

My father had a profound influence on me – he was a lunatic! He went bald when he was very young, about seventeen, and so he used to wear a wig which in those days looked like shredded GPO directories. He was a romantic Irishman and he always thought the worst thing that could happen to a man was to go bald and have piles at the same time, and of course, he got piles. Napoleon had piles too you know. He had all these piles during the battle, and they were all hanging down and the only way to get them back was to take his trousers down, bend over a bucket full of cold water and a bucket full of hot water and keep splashing himself, one after the other. That's how they lost the battle of Waterloo! My grandmother had rheumatism in her ankles, and I never understood as a boy why she left a trail of yellow powder everywhere she walked. Then I discovered she used to put mustard powder in her socks. When she went dancing with my grandfather, people used to wonder why they all look jaundiced when they came off the dance floor.

There are several people who have influenced me and I suppose it started off with me taking a liking to Jesus. I thought that he sounded like a good guy, I liked the sound of him, I liked what he did and I think his Sermon on the Mount was one of the most beautiful pieces of delivery I have ever known – Caesarian mind you, but beautiful. Then I took a liking to a Captain Ball who was an air ace in World War I. When he got dropped over the lines, the English would go up and say 'Please can we have our Ball back?' Then I got into Marxism and Trotskyism and was very influenced by Lenin who seemed to have the right doctrine, but you can't run it on that line unless you become like a glutinous jelly, so I left them behind and got into Louis Armstrong, Bing Crosby, Albert Schweitzer, Socrates and men like that – I could go on, but I'll save it for the repeat.

I think true stories are funnier than when you make them up. I don't like dirty stories, but this is a true story. A friend of mine, who shall remain nameless, got dysentery and things were getting a bit bad – people in the office were keeping out of his way and they suggested he went home early. He had to walk to Waterloo, and it was about half an hour before the rush hour started, and on the way to the station, he had a terrible accident. He thought he couldn't go home like that so he saw this supermarket, rushed in and asked for a pair of underpants and a pair of medium-sized trousers, while keeping on the move around the shop. He grabbed the plastic bag, rushed up to the train and by then it was rush hour. By this time he was really reeking so he went to the loo on the train, locked the door, waited for the train to start, took his trousers and pants off and threw them out of the window. Then he opened the plastic bag and there was a lady's pink cardigan in it! Anyway, he wanted to get off the train, so in desperation, he pulled this cardigan up around his backside, and suddenly realised that where the neck was, all his wedding tackle was hanging out! So, he did what any Englishman would have done – took his trilby hat off and used that! That story is absolutely true, I swear it.

1980 and 1981

EAMMON ANDREWS

I think the reason why I have been successful in television, and managed to stay there for thirty years, is my shyness. I am very shy and it's hard to say that in our business, but I forced myself to face up to the lines. I was certainly thumped around a lot at school due to my shyness – and bullied. I started to learn how to box when I was about fourteen: I got a real thumping one morning by a fellow who shouldn't have thumped me – he was much smaller and I should have been able to deal with him. There was another guy in the same school even smaller and he was an Irish schoolboy boxing champion – he was very light but brilliant, and I thought I must do something about this and I joined the boxing club. I won a number of titles as a juvenile but I never thought of taking it up professionally. I gave it up because I don't think anyone should box for too long, and when I got a job as a junior clerk in an insurance company I used to turn up with the odd lip and the eye and the chief clerk said that either I appeared with a whole face or not at all, so I stopped boxing. It was a very boring job – as junior clerk I did the filing and it was dreadful. Eventually I started to hide the files and for a while I was able to keep investigation at bay, but then I was caught and sent for by the general manager who couldn't decide if I was lazy or dishonest, but eventually decided I was lazy and told me I would have to work overtime to put all the files back.

I'm not quite sure where my ambition to 'go on the boards' came from. My dad was an amateur actor, but I think it was just a way of escape from anonimity. I really didn't want to be in show business – I wanted to be a writer, a journalist. My first big break in television was *What's My Line*, in which I was to share the chair with Gilbert Harding, and fortunately for me, and I think for the programme as it so happened, I did the first week and Gilbert did the second week. Gilbert, who as you know and remember was very irascible and short-tempered, had this 'challenger' who was a male nurse, but unfortunately, Gilbert had the cards out of order and he had 'motor mechanic' written down and when asked if he (the challenger) used instruments, tools in his job, the poor fellow said 'Yes' and Gilbert said: '*No, no you don't!*' and it gradually blew up into such chaos that Gilbert said he would never do it again, and he went onto the panel where he was much better. I think ninety-nine per cent of his temper and arrogance was real – sometimes he would put on the act, but he did get very irritated and would 'bend the elbow' a bit before he went on anyway. In those days it was very hot in a television studio and I could see him sitting there and I would see it rising in his face – whatever he had had, and I had to hope that we would get off the air before it really went, you know . . . I loved him. He loved the fame, even though he protested about it; he loved being a character. What he didn't like – because he was an intellectual – was that some of his friends used to tell him that he shouldn't be doing such a stupid programme, and he sometimes felt it was beneath him. But he was an unhappy man; his drinking was monumental and I always remember he was up somewhere in the Midlands at some civic function and he arrived paralytic, unable to appear, returned to his hotel, went straight into the bar and ordered 'a double treble'.

My own worst moment in the thirty years I've been in television, not only for me but for the viewers, was when I sang. I remember coming home to my wife and telling her that I was going to sing and she said 'Don't!' but I went ahead and having missed a key change in rehearsal (not really knowing what that was anyway) I got it right when it came to doing it live. However, the lad in the wings who had been training me was so pleased that he went off happily singing the tune and I heard him, thought he was trying to put me right, and wobbled all over the place. I had a big number at the end – 'How Deep is the Ocean' with the Vernon Girls Choir, but by this time the phones had started to ring and the public were saying 'Get him off – he *can't* sing again.' Of course, I had to go through with it and every retired journalist came out to write a piece about me – it was in every paper all over the country.

I enjoy what I'm doing – I wouldn't know what to do otherwise – it's great fun.

1981

VAL DOONICAN

I can remember all the things that happened to me as a child so well. I was the youngest of eight children and we lived in a small two-bedroomed house, and when I think back on it now it is incredible compared with the luxury that we live in today. I just do not know how my mother managed. It was a very happy childhood even though times were very hard. My father worked very hard and my mother spent her whole time washing, ironing and looking after us, but in those days, it was a common thing; standards today are so much higher. I look at my children and wonder if they could live that way, although I suppose they would cope if everybody else was in the same situation.

My father died when I was about thirteen which absolutely broke my heart as I adored him. He left an enormous impression one me; he was a hard man, he drank a lot and I think he did a lot of things in his life that he always wished I wouldn't do. He never got the rewards out of life that he wanted me to get and as I was the youngest, he spent an awful lot of time with me. He was a magical man; during the later part of his life, maybe because of the restrictions of the house as we were all growing up, he moved out of the house and lived in a little hut at the end of the garden. I used to go up and down to him all the time. He had a handlebar moustache, a completely bald head and he used to wear a bowler hat on Sunday and a cap for the rest of the week. He used to tell me the most marvellous things – he was so full of wisdom and he would never let you get upset about anything. I was heart-broken one day because he wouldn't take me to a football match and so he suggested that we went for a walk. I was sulking and I didn't want to be friendly with him. We were walking along the street and he hit me on the head and said, 'You're really upset about this match aren't you?' He pointed to a farm labourer leaning on a gate and asked me if I knew him. I didn't and he pointed out that that man didn't know me either, but that *he* thought the whole world revolved around *him*. The message hit home and I realised that that man's life was of no importance to me at all and mine was of no importance to him. You can get so obsessed with your own life that you really do forget that everybody else's life is just as important as your own.

On Saturday afternoons, he would finish work at 12.30 and he would go to the boozer to get something to drink and on the way home he would go to a secondhand bookshop and buy six books. He would read until 5 am and you could see his oil lamp on in the little hut. Then he would have a couple of hours sleep and go to work again. On Sundays he used to take me for a walk, seven or eight miles into the country and back again, and he would go into the pubs along the way. I would sit outside and he would bring me out a glass of lemonade. He would always walk right down the middle of the road, reading a book and I used to tell him that he would get run over. He replied that it was only when you walked on the side of the road that you got run over!

He died of cancer of the throat. He knew that he was dying, but he didn't want my mother to know, or any of us. The loneliness of the whole thing really gets me – there he was down in his little hut in the garden trying to cope with it on his own. Finally, he had to go into hospital and I used to go and see him every day when I came home from school. My mother used to send him up his tobacco, matches and daily paper and I would take them to him. As time went on, his whole face disappeared into bandages, but the last thing he said to me has to be the most profound thing I have ever heard in my life: I sat by the bed talking to him and he told me that as he was going to die pretty soon he didn't want me to come and see him anymore. I got up to say goodbye to him and he told me that he had something he thought he should say to me – 'You think I'm terrific don't you?' I replied that I did. 'Well, I think it's only fair that before I die you should know that I'm not. When I'm gone, I'm sure a lot of people will tell you that I'm no good and there is nothing that would please me more than for you to say: yes I know, he told me that himself!'

I think my family background has stood me in good stead for my career in show business. I meet people now that knew me when I had just started and they say that I haven't changed a bit. I have been so lucky and I am eternally grateful and when I think back to those childhood days and think of the hard life my poor old mum and dad had, it makes me realise just how lucky I am.

1979

JAMES GALWAY

There was a lot of music around me as a child – everybody in the street played something; we had a lady who played the banjo and some played accordians and a load of people who played flutes. There were so many flute bands and we played Mozart and Beethoven with thirty three flutes, eight sidedrums, base drum, cymbal and triangle! We didn't even know if it was classical or popular music, we just played it.

I like all sorts of music. The only kind I don't like is the 'gin and tonic' sort that they play in lifts. I listen to all sorts of music and recently I went through a stage of Ella Fitzgerald. I would put her on when I got up in the morning and keep it going all day. I do like pop music as well, mostly rock music like the Pink Floyd and Supertramp perform, I really like the sound they have.

I do have an awful lot of music sent to me as people seem to think that if I play one of their tunes they will get famous, but they are so wrong you wouldn't believe it. But they keep trying and I have about three hundred tunes up in the office but I don't intend looking at any of them and I'm not going to play any of this modern music that people send in because I know the composers I want to write for me and I ask them to do it. I know the music I want to play and I have my programmes well organised three years ahead – not only where we are going to play but exactly what.

I never thought as a child that I would become a famous musician. Everybody played something and we all went through a tin whistle phase and there was constant rivalry between the children in the street as to who could play the fastest. Even when at the age of ten I won the 'All Ages' competition for playing the flute, I still did not realise I had a special gift – I just went along and did my bit and somebody had to win it anyway. I think I was at an advantage because at that age I wasn't allowed to drink and I was probably the only sober one there.

When I think back to my rough and tumble childhood days, there is one guy who really stands out in my mind and he was called Alec Robertson. We used to call him 'Buck' Alec and he was a really tough Belfast man. We used to go round to his area every Saturday night because he was always fighting and people would quite easily come flying through the window of a pub or doorway. Then the police would come round and it always took about six or ten cops to hold him down. The best thing about him was that he lived in a little two-up, two-down house like everybody else, but in the back yard he had two lions. He used to take these lions for a walk in the street. He is still alive, but he has given up the lions and he has two St Bernard dogs now.

My parents were absolutely distraught with us, they just didn't know what to do with us next. Most of the mischief was directed at the neighbours and I still meet the people I used to terrorise as a child at weddings and wakes because it is the only time the community ever gets together. Wakes are great once you get over the initial impact of howling your head off, and then everybody sits down and drinks a fantastic amount of alcohol, swapping stories about the deceased. They stay up for three days and then they all go to the funeral; I'm surprised that they actually don't drop the coffin in the street!

I think the present position I'm in now is due to myself playing the flute and my manager, and the two of us doing a thing together that nobody has actually tried to do before. That is really building up the career of a musician. Some people are a little bit surprised that I actually talk to an audience. I wished the audience a happy Christmas the other day in the Festival Hall, and that was considered to be 'far out' by many classical musicians. I like audiences, they are nice people.

There has been a phenomenal revival of flute playing and as far as I can see I am going to go on spreading the flute gospel indefinitely.

1980

BERNARD LEVIN

My passion for music started late and it was nearly poisoned early on because when I was a child I was taught the violin very badly. I was never told that there were symphonies and concertos that would be fun to listen to, I never learned the name of a single composer. All it was was these appalling black dots on the page and here was I making this appalling noise in the effort to reproduce them. After a couple of years I gave it up completely and only much later did I come to like music, and then, of course, the unassuaged regret of my life was not being able to play any musical instrument.

I have two real conductor's batons and late at night I will play music on the gramophone and draw out my baton and the feeling in my heart, not to mention the noise, is absolutely, unbelievably marvellous. There are two things I actually want to do in an orchestra – one is to play the side drum in a performance of Ravel's Bolero and the other is to play the tambourine in Haydn's Toy Symphony.

To me, the greatest single fallacy in the whole of art is the belief that opera is boring. There can be boring performances of course, but opera seems to me to be the greatest form of art. It marries the two greatest arts of all, music and drama, and at its best I know of no artistic experience to touch the performance of a great opera by fine performers. I think I can say that I have been more deeply moved, more deeply affected, more uplifted in an opera house at the performance of a great opera by great performers than literally almost anything else in life. It is an experience that anybody, anybody at all can have – you don't have to know anything about it, you don't have to study music, you don't have to know how to read the score – this overwhelming experience is open to everybody for the price of a seat. I'm blowed if I know why it's not more popular – I think it's because generations have painted it as a highbrow art which 'ordinary' people think 'is not for us', whereas they are missing one of the greatest pleasures of life – really they are. Take Mozart, who is my god, and my hero. You are absolutely transported, you are taken utterly out of yourself and you experience something that is as close as we can get, I reckon, unless you have a profound religious conviction, to touching the divine principle. And then you think 'Well, who was this Mozart?' And you realise that he was a perfectly ordinary human being and if you met him in the street you would not have the faintest idea that he was one of the greatest souls that had ever been born. If, when you contemplate the fact, you do not stop and think: what is art? where does it come from? what is it for? who are these people who are singled out by providence to be a kind of channel through which it flows? – then you might as well go bang your head on a wall and finish your life. It is to me the most fascinating and profound question in the world. Mozart was a conduit, a pipe through which this music flowed, but who was putting it in at the other end? That is what I want to know. My idea of paradise is listening to a new Mozart opera every week in the company of the woman I love.

1981

GEORGE SHEARING

I was born blind, and for as long as I can remember I have always been very independent. I have always liked to do things for myself, walk around the neighbourhood on my own and I used to ride a bicycle when I was about twelve or thirteen. I remember one day I was just walking round the corner when I fell down a beer cellar and although I am sure this would be a joy for some people, to me it was rather tragic because I didn't know when the end was going to come! I've even driven a car once or twice.

I had a guide dog for about twelve years, but I don't have one now. During the time I did, we were on an aeroplane on our way from Los Angeles to New York and we had a couple of intermediate stops. We got as far as Chicago and the pilot came through from the cabin and asked if I would like him to take the dog for a walk. So, I thanked him and gave him the dog and about twenty minutes later my fellow passengers noticed that there were some twenty people milling around outside the aeroplane, reluctant to get back on because they noticed that the pilot had a guide dog!

It was pretty tough for me when I first went to America – a great ego deflater! I had auditions with some of the top agents in the country and was not at all successful for a while. My break came when we discovered our new sound, which all happened by accident really and it became my trademark. I wrote a little tune called 'Lullaby of Birdland' in ten minutes over a steak in my dining-room in New Jersey. You know, I've been back to that butcher to try and find the same steak but . . . What I do now is to take all song titles that have the word 'love' in the title and I substitute the word 'lunch': 'I'm in the mood for lunch', 'One night of lunch', and 'Lunch is lovelier second time around'.

I draw inspiration from classical music for my jazz quite a bit, and I do play purely classical music as well. I learn a classical score either by braille or by tape; the beautiful thing about learning it by braille is that after all the lights have gone out at night, I can still be memorising it. There should be more braille menus in restaurants, more braille numbers on elevators, a complete directory in hotel rooms with all the services in braille. The things I envy sighted people for most are playing tennis, driving a car and sight-reading music, rather than taking several weeks to memorise it.

I was born in Battersea but I have lived in America for a long time now, and I am an American citizen. But it's a funny thing, every time I come back to England I feel that there seems to be a greater welcome home atmosphere than the last time and my final wish in life would be to spend six months in England and six months in the States – that would be an ideal year for me. I really miss the English sausage and I am tired of the ritual involved to get my tea right in the States! I also miss cricket of course.

1980

SHEILA HOCKEN

'Sheila Hocken is most simply described as a very remarkable woman. She was born blind and for twenty-nine years she lived in a world in which phrases like 'green as grass' meant nothing, where she didn't know what the man she had married looked like, where she read and told the time by braille. Then two years ago, the miracle happened – she had an operation and for the first time in her life she could see.'

I was lucky in a way, I went to a sighted school and I had to get along with the other children, but I couldn't see to read the blackboard and a lot of the books and children don't understand that sort of thing. Sometimes if I went out to look at the blackboard they would shout: 'Get out of the way', but I think that was a good thing because I got the knocks then instead of when I grew up.

The public do try and treat blind people well, but they go about it the wrong way. You might be standing somewhere in town waiting for something and before you know where you are, you are at the other side of the road when you didn't really want to cross. They don't realise that you want to be asked first instead of grabbed and if you see a blind person, you should go and ask them and don't push them first – that is awful.

I have called the book I have just written *Emma and I*, Emma being my guide dog. She made such a profound difference to my life. Before I had her, I had to go out to earn my living as a telephonist so I had to go to work and back, but I would never go out anywhere else. Maybe I wanted to go out in the evening and I would ask someone to take me, but they didn't want to go where I wanted to go, so once I got Emma, it was really like being let out of prison – I could go where I wanted and when I wanted and it was so fantastic. The relationship a blind person has with his guide dog is much closer than a normal pet relationship; you have to believe in your dog and they know this and if you don't believe in them they just won't work for you. Emma and I became one person with six legs and a chocolate bit down one side – you become so close. At first you have to learn together because it is like driving a car, you can't just get in and go and the dog will only respond to basic commands like 'right', 'left', 'forward'. They know what a shop is but then when I had had Emma a while, if I said 'fish and chip shop', Emma would take me to the fish and chip shop, or chemist, or No. 49 bus stop or wherever – she just knew everything. One thing that guide dogs aren't trained in is good manners. I used to go to work with her on the bus and she would never go the end of a queue at a bus stop, she would always put me straight in front. When we got on the bus, she always had a favourite seat which was right next to the heaters and if somebody had got there first, she would just stand there and stare at them until they just had to move.

Once we started going to work, I told her the way which was straight across our market square, turn right and find the bus stop which she obeyed and did for about a week. One morning we got into the square and she wouldn't go, and not being able to see, you don't know what has happened. She got up and turned right instead so I had to follow her and she crossed a couple of roads, turned left and sat down. I hadn't a clue where I was and thought I was going to be late for work. I heard somebody passing and asked them where the bus stop was and this little fellow told me that Emma was sitting right there. I thought it was odd, but forgot about it and the next day we got to the square, and Emma wouldn't go straight across, but turned left and crossed a few roads, turned right and there we were at the bus stop. It took me about a week to realise that she hated going to work the same way every day so she just picked a different route out each morning.

Guide dogs are taught to disobey a lot of commands which is hard to teach them. The first time it happened to me, was when I was still at the training centre and our trainer took us to a railway station. I hated railway stations because they are noisy and there are lots of steps and when we arrived, Emma took me in, down a couple of flights of steps and along the platform while he was parking the van. When he came up he told me that Emma had taken me right to the edge of the platform and that there was about a six foot drop in front of me to the railway lines. He told me to tell Emma to go forward and off he went. I was absolutely terrified and I think I whispered 'forward' hoping that she wouldn't hear and she got up and pushed herself in front of me and pushed me back. I have always trusted her since then. She has never really made a mistake but she has a human sense of humour. We have a shopping centre in Nottingham and they made a braille map of it and we were testing this out. All down the middle of the shopping centre there are big pillars and what they did was to stick braille labels on them with numbers so that you could relate to your map. What I forgot is that Emma would not take me to a pillar because she had been taught to avoid them. So I had to walk down the centre with her and listen, because you get an echo back from obstacles. Every time I thought we had reached a pillar I would stop and go and have a feel and it all went very well until she twigged to what

I was doing. We stopped and I thought that there was a big pillar there, let go of her lead and went to have a feel and it was this little fellow's trouser leg!

When you can't see, you have to pretend that you never will in a way because if you don't, you won't get on with living as a blind person. But always in the back of your mind there is a little voice saying that you've got to see, that you can't go on without seeing, but you have to suppress that. I had my operation on a Friday, and I knew they wouldn't take the bandages off until the Monday and that weekend was like a million years. When I sat down on the Monday morning for them to take the bandages off, I remember gripping the arms of the chair and thinking that I wanted to stop them because if it hadn't worked I just couldn't have faced it. Suddenly they were all shouting at me to open my eyes and I got hit by an electric shock of brilliance – it was so fantastically brilliant out there, I just had no idea. In front of me was white – it was a nurse's apron and it was so dazzling white I just couldn't bear to look at it. I looked away and saw greens and blues and all sorts of different shades and they were the nurses' uniforms. It was *so* beautiful. I had never seen people before and however you touch things, they don't give you the same impression as visual things do.

I didn't really see people in the hospital as they only took the bandages off for a couple of minutes every day, so the first person I really saw was my husband. I had never wondered what he looked like until the moment came for him to pick me up and I realised that I wouldn't know who he was. I recognised his footsteps coming down the ward, looked up and there was a total stranger – I just didn't know him at all. I thought he was handsome and was ever so pleased. When I got home I just had to go and look in the mirror and again, I was a total stranger – I didn't know it was me but it had to be. Then I saw this huge great thing sticking out from the middle of my face and I touched it and it was my nose. I was absolutely horrified and thought that all my friends had kept it quiet all these years and I was really upset until I started looking at everybody else and realising that they all had them.

Nothing was at all as I had imagined it to be. I would see something as simple as a cup and not have a clue what it was until I touched it and then it visually turned into a cup. What really struck me was that things are so beautiful – the grass – I just couldn't believe it, it was so fantastic. People never go out and say 'Oh, doesn't the grass look beautiful', but it is not just green, it's yellow and brown and deep and pale and absolutely gorgeous. I had never heard anybody rave about sunsets either but they are so beautiful. The very first night I could see I saw the most fantastic sunset and all I had ever had was second-hand sunsets and you just cannot believe that the sky could go from blue to golden red – it is so fantastic.

The relationship between Emma and myself has completely changed since I got my sight back. She realised I could see one night when I spotted that she was pinching the cat's food and shouted at her. She leapt up in total horror and came up to me and leapt all over me and made such a fuss and the next day when we went out, she didn't try to guide, she was just like a hooligan – she barked at all the dogs and dragged me from lamp-post to lamp-post. She is super-human.

1978

ITZHACK PERLMAN

Having contracted polio as a child, I didn't go to a special school. The only thing weird about me then as far as my friends were concerned was that I had to practise three hours every day. My parents moved to a neighbourhood where there were a lot of other children so that I could have friends and there was a school about a block away so I walked to school everyday. I did play football a lot – I was usually very much sought after as a goalie because I could stop any ball with my crutches!

I was about three years old when I first became aware of the violin. I listened to it on the radio and it really attracted me – the sound. At the age of three and a half, my parents bought me a violin and I am now beginning to understand what I felt then because my six year old daughter is now in the process of trying to play the violin and I try to play it and I can't – part of the thing that is so discouraging about a little kid playing the violin is that those little fiddles just don't sound very good. My case was no exception and so I got really mad and threw it under the bed. I got polio when I was about four and at five I just continued to play. I hated to practise very much, nobody really likes to practise; the love of music is really very important, very necessary, but obviously the discipline in a five or six year old child is really not there. I really can't say that I was more driven to the violin because of my handicap, I can say that it hasn't stopped me. People's attitude towards handicapped people is that they don't really want to see it and it really happens everywhere – on television as well!

At the beginning, I really didn't want the handicap to have anything to do with my playing – in other words, I wanted to prove myself as a player rather than as a handicapped player. I didn't want people to say: 'Oh well, for a handicapped person he plays very well.' As a matter of fact, one of my first reviews when I was already seventeen years old said that they didn't know if my standing ovation was received because I played well or because I was handicapped. I have newspaper clippings from that period where every single review said: 'Mr Perlman stepped on the stage and hobbled along with his silvery, shining, aluminium crutches. Very heavily he plonked himself on the chair and picked up the violin . . .' and then they forgot everything. This doesn't happen anymore, but now I've come a full cycle I want to let other people know that it is very possible to achieve things with a disability and that a disability in a person is only what you make it – in other words you have to eliminate what you can't do – obviously I am not going to ski – the splits I do all the time!

In the days when I wore tails for everything, I went to a recital and was waiting for the elevator and all of a sudden I heard a crack and thought is it the left foot or the right foot? So I looked and there was a brace broken. So I hobbled back to my hotel room and I have a little kit, screwdrivers, oil and every conceivable engineering device and there I was unscrewing a shoe, finding another shoe and fixing the screws and bolts and my hands were greasy and there I was in my tails, white shirt and tie. I was about twenty minutes late for the performance. I almost fell off my chair once when I was in Israel – it was during the last movement of the Brahms Violin Concerto and I was really making the musical statement, I was leaning this way and that, and all of a sudden I felt I was leaning a little bit too much, so I tried to correct it but found I was leaning to the left all through the performance. I finished playing, picked up my crutches, got up and the chair fell – the leg of the chair was bent and had I leaned just a little more, it would have broken.

I am willing to try anything in the musical field, not just classical music. I have just recently done a jazz recording with André Previn and Jim Hall on guitar, Red Mitchell on base, Shelley Mann on drums and we had a fabulous time together. In jazz there is an element of improvisation that is not always in classical music – in fact in classical music if you change three or four notes everybody notices, but in jazz it is really a way of life. For me it was a great experience. I think that Stephan Grappelli is wonderful. It takes a special technique to loosen up or just be able to improvise at a moment's notice and still stay in the same harmonic progressions and then get out of it on time. I always admire people that can do that.

My wife is my best critic – she is the person I go to for advice. I must tell you how I met her. I went to a music camp in New York and I played in one of the student concerts and a girl came backstage, shook my hands and asked if I would marry her. That was it. I was seventeen years old then. We became friends and got married. Fiddle players don't formally have coaches, and I think it is very important and so whenever you have somebody that you respect, and besides my wife I have a couple of other people, you should use them; you have to have a rapport with your critics, you have to be able to accept criticism from them and this is very, very important.

I don't think you ever get to a peak – you shouldn't think of it as a peak – you should think of it as part of the road. You can say well I'm now thirty-five years old and I've played this particular piece the best that I can play it at this moment and hopefully in about two weeks or two months, or a year I will be able to play it the best that I could play it at that moment, and hopefully, it will be better. In other words, for me the growing process of an artist never stops, because the minute it stops, you stop growing and if you stop growing you don't stay in the same place, you just go down and down.

1980

LUCIANO PAVAROTTI

I am very nervous before a performance and sometimes during it. Five minutes before is when I do not wish my worst enemy – if I have one – to feel so bad, but the moment I put my feet on the stage another person comes inside me and everything disappears if the voice is there. If the voice is not there, which sometimes happens, then I concentrate on the technique I've learned in twenty years of stage experience.

I saw Beniamino Gigli live when I was twelve. I remember it well because at that time I had already decided to become a tenor. I asked him how long he had studied and he replied, 'I have just finished now' – he had been practising for the evening performance and it was a very good answer. I took his suggestions to be an eternal student and never satisfied with oneself.

The normal human voice is baritone and the tenor is an artificial voice which you must construct. People in my country go to hear the tenor voice because they think it is the most exciting. Very few prefer baritone.

I am still looking for the perfect sound, but what I achieve pleases me and more importantly, it pleases the critics. Sopranos are superstars, but tenors are a good match. I respect my colleagues who reach the top rather than being envious. There is no professional jealousy between me and sopranos but between sopranos and me – probably!

1979

PLACIDO DOMINGO

I am going to make the film *The Merry Widow* this summer (1982) and at the moment it looks as if Julie Andrews will be co-starring with me. I don't think there is any resistance to this by the purist opera fans – in the old days it's what all the opera singers used to do, it is nothing new. Anyway, I think there are only two kinds of music, the good and the bad and so if I think something is melodic I will sing it. I don't believe that music should be compartmentalised. For me, the music of Henry Mancini, or John Denver or Andrew Lloyd Webber has the quality, the melody of any leider by Schubert. The only thing that is different, perhaps, is the treatment, the harmony and the rhythms.

I never actually had a singing lesson in my life, but I think I learned by imitation – my parents were both professional singers of Zarzuela – music of the Spanish people and I listened to records. I think the recordings of Caruso were my main inspiration, because he is untouchable.

Out of the eighty or so roles that I have played, I suppose I could do about thirty of them at a moment's notice, if I am in good shape. Another twenty I would have to think about for a couple of days and for the rest I would need a week. When you are involved in an opera, you have to know everybody else's part as well and it is fascinating to know the whole thing. I don't even try to study – I learn because I love to.

Otello is my favourite role because it combines two geniuses – Shakespeare and Verdi – it is the most demanding role for acting and singing together. The acting is so demanding that sometimes I have forgotten about the singing and when I am really concentrating on a performance, I don't think about the singing, and that's the marvellous thing about this role. It is such a difficult singing part because the second act of *Otello* is an opera in itself and you really have to measure your strength from the beginning of the act to the end and it puts a tremendous strain on your voice. After you finish the second act, you can say 'it's done' so you can enjoy the third and fourth acts. I have decided that I will not do any more than ten to twelve performances of *Otello* in a year because it takes so much strength – more emotionally than vocally actually because the role has helped me to feel vocally better for lighter roles.

I remember the first time I played *Otello* was in Hamburg in 1975. At the end of the first evening, we had forty-five minutes applause and I don't know how many curtain calls. I just did not know what to do – I was about to ask the conductor to start the opera all over again! If at all possible, after a performance of *Otello*, I would prefer not to see anybody, but just to be in my dressing room and to fall asleep. But that is impossible – I always have to see people and just have to keep going and then I cannot sleep until five or six o'clock in the morning. You have to be physically fit to take on this sort of role. Hours before the show, you start thinking the character and walking like the character and you feel the tension of the character. By the time you finish the performance, you have been working almost eight hours under tremendous strain.

I think the art of singing is adapting your voice to the part you are playing. You have to express pain, love, anger etc. and in three bars you can be colouring completely different emotions. One thing that helps me interpret the opera is the singing of songs. Let's face it, how much does the audience understand of the text when you are singing opera? Especially when it is in a foreign language. Everybody is waiting for the beautiful melody but a very small part of the audience really knows the text. When you are singing songs, everybody wants to understand the words.

I like to think I bring peace with my voice – that is really the meaning in my career. For the two and a half to three hours of a performance the audience are sitting close to each other with no differences of colour, religion, races, ideas – they are only in a communion with you – they are just thinking of what you are singing. I would like to reach more people through opera because classic music goes deep into your soul, but I also sing popular music and I do a lot of television performances of opera because maybe somebody will hear me in this way and if they like it, they may decide to go to the opera to see how I sing there. My main feeling is peace and I do not think we can do enough to achieve this.

I don't want to go on singing until people get tired of me. I would rather they say 'Why isn't he singing anymore?' There is a certain age beyond which you cannot perform anymore – you cannot play Romeo or Alfredo when you are approaching fifty. You should be selective about your repertoire when you get older. When I stop singing, I will still dedicate my life to music and my dream is to go to a beautiful place with a nice climate and to establish something that hasn't been done before. Rather than being the director of a big opera house with many problems to face every day, I would like to establish a school – a theatre-cult school – and I will choose about twenty to twenty-five young singers from around the world and I will say: these singers are going to be absolutely first-class singers for every opera house in the world in two years. It's the other side of the coin, you know, because you hear so many people singing who don't have any talent, and there are many who have a lot of talent but haven't got the right opportunity and I would like to ease the way for them.

1980 and 1982

BUDDY RICH

I've been touring all over the place. When we left here last year we went to Japan and did our usual tour. We were the first jazz band to go to Afghanistan. We were sent over by the State Department and we did a tour of about five months, playing in most of the depressed areas in the world – we got to India; we played three nights in Afghanistan. The audiences were different! We played at a thing called the 'Chesham Fair'. This was the first musical event that ever happened and the people of Pakistan and the Afghani people came down from the hills. We had thirty thousand people on the opening night and since they weren't familiar with Western customs, instead of applauding at the end of a piece of music, they hum – if you can imagine thirty thousand people making a sound like that. I thought that perhaps they were coming up after me.

I enjoy playing music and I hate bad music – I hate bad anything, I hate bad people. Music transcends all that, I think music appeals to everyone of all ages and I think it is something that is beneficial to the world.

I have very strange feelings about Donny Osmond's kind of music and about ten years ago we played Nashville which is the home of that kind of music and the opening night I was asked by the Press what I felt about country music. I gave some terrible answer and the following day the owner of the club – a place called the Exit Inn – got a call that they had threatened to bomb the place if I showed up there that night. Most of the country people were offended by that, not realising how many people they offend by the music they play! I don't like it because what is it? How can you like it? If you can't hear it, you can't see it, feel it. I don't understand it, it isn't real to me. It's popular bad music.

When we are touring at home most of our work is in colleges and high schools; we appeal more to younger people nowadays. The people who come there are very early twenties and strangely when I first started with the band in the 1960s everybody was concerned with the success of the big bands because rock music had taken over completely. I decided that I thought it was time for a change and as big bands weren't happening, it was time for a big band. I took the band onto the road and we had very little success the first time out – in fact I think we played a hotel in Las Vegas and we were the only band to be cancelled on the opening night! It's true – on the opening night the pit bosses came back and complained to the main man that we were making too much noise for the gamblers! Then we went on to New York. Great success – in fact the very first time when we played there Harold Davison was in the audience and he asked why I had never been to England and I said, 'Because no one has ever asked me', and he said, 'Well, *I'm* asking you.'

We came to England about six months later – our first tour and we opened our very first night at Fairfield Hall, Croydon and I was anticipating a huge success. We had about three hundred people in the audience in a hall which seats three thousand, and I was a little disappointed and decided to give the best possible performance that I could give, and by the time we had finished the tour (which was four weeks later) we were sold out. It's been that way ever since which is absolutely marvellous.

1982

'It would be
extremely difficult
for me to choose between
singing Elvis Presley songs
and scoring a century for
England, but I think
I would choose a
century for England'
Tim Rice

MARVIN HAMLISCH

I started playing the piano when I was about seven years old. My father was a musician and my sister was having piano lessons and I started by mimicking her, playing by ear. I knew at a very early age that I was going to go into music. I was actually trained in classical music and was supposed to become a concert pianist, but I was much too nervous for that. It was when I started writing material for our school productions that I realised I wanted to write.

Normally when I'm going to write a song, I sit down and decide what kind of mood I'm in and then I like to work to a title. It's very rare for me to write a complete melody and then send it to a lyricist – I have to have a title or about six lines of lyric before I can write the music. I get a kick from hearing my music wherever I go, but I don't want to make a big deal out of it. After all, I'm just a shy, retiring Jewish boy!

I adapt a lot of music for films, but you know you're only dealing with background music. When you're writing a musical it is very different and it's very exciting to write a show that travels around the world.

1981

SAMMY CAHN

The ideas for my lyrics come from phone calls. The phone rings and someone says 'Will you write a song?' – that's actually how it starts. The title that they thought was most difficult was 'Tender Trap'. When I hear the word 'trap' I think of the word 'snap', so that's the song written – 'trap' and 'snap'. What more do you need?

The main business is selling the song. After we write a song we spend an enormous amount of time preparing it for demonstration, because that's the moment of truth. When I walk in to sing a song for the first time I'm in the bullring.

I do more parodying of my songs than actual songs. Dirty is what they are!

> The girl that I marry
> will have to be . . .
> A nympho who owns a distillery

> You made me love you –
> You woke me up to do it

> Kiss me once
> And kiss me twice
> And kiss me once again –
> It takes a long, long time.

I looked under Jordan
And what did I see? –
Mrs Jordan

This is my first affair
And what goes where?

It's impossible to make love
In a Toyota – *it's* impossible.

I have a marvellous, marvellous mother who gave me some very good advice: 'never lie still or they will throw dirt at you' – I keep moving.

The business has changed a lot. When I was hustling songs in Tin Pan Alley I was writing fifteen songs a day, which is no exaggeration. Every day I would take one of these songs to the office of a music publisher and he would turn it down. After eights months of this the fellow I was writing with said, 'Why do we keep going back there?' I said, 'Because he lets us in, that's why we keep going back.'

Writers today are infinitely better than we were. They have better word imagery. I'm not talking about the noise, but the songs which have meaning and lyrics. The Beatles have left a great treasure of words and songs. My favourite lyric writer of all time was W.S. Gilbert. He is the total lyric writer. Next is Johnny Mercer, Cole Porter and then many others.

1980

TIM RICE

I never had the ambition to be 'in' pop music when I was younger; it didn't cross my mind when I was a kid that you could be in it – it was the kind of job that people like me didn't do. I had a really good, middle-class upbringing, incredibly happy, but you were kind of programmed into doing fairly respectable things. Obviously, if you wanted to be a doctor, lawyer or accountant twenty years ago the oldboy network was an advantage, it would help you get to university. Now, thank goodness, it isn't quite so important, although it still helps. It's perhaps true to say that in the world of popular music a slightly posh voice might not be an instant advantage. I know that Andrew and I are probably regarded as boring old twits by the rock industry, perhaps partly because of the way we speak. It didn't cross my mind at all that somebody like me who went to a public school could actually get a job in the pop business, even though I had a pop group at school and was always singing rock and roll. I was gripped by the charts and until I was about twenty three, the only things I could talk about were popular music or cricket.

It was Elvis Presley that got me in the first place, and also the facts and figures, because I've always been absolutely besotted with facts and numbers. My first interest when I was about six was astronomy and the solar system. In 1951 I went to the Festival of Britain and there was this fantastic thing called 'The Dome of Discovery' which had a marvellous model of the solar system and I read in the paper that it was being dismantled when the

Festival was over. I wrote to the organisers of the Festival asking if I could have the model. I didn't get a reply but I did get *The Evening News* coming round wanting to take photographs of this precocious young man who was interested in the stars. It was when I was ten that I got off the rather intellectual pursuit of astronomy and got into the pop music charts. In a way, my interest in cricket began by following all the averages – it's a statistician's paradise.

Andrew and I have been very lucky of course. We were lucky in that we were doing theatre writing when everyone else was influenced by the Beatles. We were influenced by them as well, but we didn't set out to write for pop groups or make records, we set out to write for theatre, and that was Andrew's ambition. I think we have been commercially successful partly because there aren't so many people fighting us, we are almost number one in a field of one. That's not strictly true but in England there are not that many other people who are even trying to write musicals. My brother came up with an interesting fact; the money that everybody has made out of *Jesus Christ Superstar* in the first two years, including producers, promoters etc., could have bought a Ford Cortina for every member of Everton's home gate for four consecutive Saturdays!

I have written with one or two other people apart from Andrew. One-off songs mainly – with Marvin Hamlisch – who I think is the only theatrical composer who is in Andrew's league in the world. I've written with Mike Batt, of whom I'm also a great fan, and with Elton John. I am always keen to do other things if I can, as Andrew has done with Don Black and other people. I think when it comes to theatre it would take a lot to get me not to work with Andrew. We are always fighting and all that but . . . we do have ups and downs inevitably – we are very different personalities and it is hard to think of something to follow something that's gone quite well. Andrew had this brilliant idea of *Cats*, and the lyricist was there already in the sense that T.S. Eliot had written these poems. I would rather do nothing at all than do something just for the sake of it.

I do get a bit narked at times, being a fully paid-up member of the Lyricists Union, when a song is referred to as a Burt Bacharach song. Burt Bacharach is a wonderful composer but not many people know that Hal David wrote the brilliant lyrics. There are exceptions like the great Sammy Cahn. He is one of the few lyricists who actually comes out and emphasises that the guy who writes the words does also make a contribution. There are some shows where the words are better than the music. On the other hand, there was a very nice tune recorded by little Jimmy Dickens in 1964 which would have been a wonderful song if it hadn't been called 'May the Bird of Paradise Fly Up Your Nose'. I am amazed it was even a small hit because it is a very unattractive title. There are quite a few songs which I think can be clobbered by their lyric. A bad lyric can sink a song, a mediocre lyric might not matter, certainly not in the pop world, but in the theatre the words are usually pretty important.

I must say that, having had tremendous success, I now find that the incentive to write is less. *Cats* was good for me, because Andrew had a big hit and that really more than anything got me going again. Obviously, there is no financial incentive whatever. It is difficult. In fact, one of the lyrics in *Evita* was all about that, the song called 'High Flying Adored', and although it did fit into the plot moderately well, it was really about how *do* you follow up a big success because if you have another big success, so what, you've done it before, and if you flop, you'll be absolutely distraught. In a way you can't win.

I've got about 25,000 records at home – I'm one of the few people over thirty who still buys singles – I automatically buy every record that hits the charts every week, just because I love pop singles. I was greatly influenced by Elvis Presley, Buddy Holly, The Everly Brothers and Cliff and the Shadows. This is all pre-Beatles of course – there *was* good pop music before the Beatles, even in Britain, although obviously the Beatles changed everything. Elvis recorded one of my songs once, just before he died – it was the last track on his last LP! We sent it off to Elvis about four years before he died and the publisher who was our contact kept telling us that he was going to do it, but we were absolutely convinced after two or three years that he wasn't going to record it. But he did, and we were thrilled. I met him once, three or four years before he died, and I must say that he looked great.

It would be extremely difficult for me to choose between singing Elvis Presley songs and scoring a century for England, but I think I would choose a century for England!

1981

BILL WYMAN

When we go on tour it's really like an army on the move. We have about eight or ten semi-trucks (those thirty ton trucks with trailers), about sixty crew who build and break down the stage, and there are about sixty people that go with you on a private plane – secretaries, publicist, photographer, doctor etc., and you've got to hotel them and move them about the country. It's an enormous logistical problem. We have total involvement with this organisation because we don't have a manager as such because they're too expensive and they organise things for you without asking you. It's the only business where the manager doesn't work for you – you work for the manager. When we need something done we just employ the best person for that particular job. We spend an awful lot of money doing the tours so although we got twenty million on the last tour it probably cost us about ten million setting the tour up.

The TV guys were interviewing people at one of our concerts in San Francisco on this tour and asked: 'Are you Stones fans?' – these kids were about sixteen or seventeen, and they said, 'Yeah, we've been fans for years,' and the TV guy said, 'What was the first record that ever turned you on?' and one kid said 'Some Girls' which was the album we released in 1976! That was our thirty-first album and yet he said he's been a Stones fan for years. It really makes you think.

I always thought that if I got involved with drugs I would probably enjoy it and there would be problems; it's like starting smoking – if you never start you don't seem to need it. And I thought of all the problems if you do start – like trying to get them, especially in certain countries. It's a permanent hassle trying to obtain all the things you need. I don't drink very much, I have the occasional cigarette – I'm very boring really!

I came from a very working-class background. South of London. In fact the first time we had a bathroom in the house and a toilet was after I had been in the Stones about a year, and we moved into a modern flat; before that it was always a toilet in the garden and no hot water and no central heating – nothing. I still love baked beans. I live in the South of France and you get all these wonderful things and people think you're drinking champagne and eating caviar every day and all you're doing is phoning your mum at home and asking her to send you Branston pickle and Bird's custard. The French have got no soul. They are all pretentious and pseudo-intellectual. I can't deal with it.

I don't think we've changed at all really from the beginning. I think the world about has changed. They say now: the Stones are in middle age, they've toned down, becoming very reserved and quiet and all that. But it's really that the things we rebelled against were very small things which were built up at the time – like long hair, no ties in restaurants and things like that, and not smiling in photos. All those little, little things created a kind of image for us but everyone accepts them as normal nowadays. I think it's people around us that have changed, not the Stones.

The band is still the most important thing to me but the rest of the time I do my own thing because I'm a workaholic.

1982

BOB GELDOF

I was hopeless at school. I was OK up to the age of eleven, but after that I went downhill very fast. I won a prize for the debating society and I won a prize for Gaelic when I was eleven – 'The Man in the Iron Mask' in Irish, which was a lot of use to everybody! After I left school at seventeen I had a variety of jobs, including teaching English in Spain. I was sent to a town in the desert, in south-east Spain and a desert was a pretty good place to spend a year I felt – I was in bad spirits at the time. I enjoyed my six to ten year olds, and we used to have tea parties every day with their mums making the cakes. They would tuck into the lemonade and I would tuck into the wine. I had a class of teenagers who were hopeless. At this stage I had pretty long hair, flared jeans, and no shoes and their class was after the siesta – and I spent the siesta guzzling back the old vino. I would arrive in class half pissed and would allow them to smoke and we would look at photographs together, but then they started taking advantage of the freedom. I put one of the guys up against the wall one day and threatened him with immediate face battering – it was a fairly liberal education, but I think they learnt a lot from it. I also had a class of septagenarians including a NATO admiral, the governor of the bank, the head of the history department at the university and a couple of other nobs. They were the funniest because there was this specimen walking into class complete with bottle of wine and they would all jump to attention and recite the Lord's Prayer in English.

I worked in a pea factory in Peterborough when I was sixteen and I haven't been able to eat a pea since. After I came back from Spain, I worked in a meat factory in Dublin which was quite an experience. I would start at about 5 am and put on my overalls and the wellingtons and there was blood up to both my ankles. There was a guy there called Paul who used to come into work with an axe down his trousers and his sole aim in life was to get these guys – the 'Five Lamp gang', and he would come in after the weekend and show me his knee or something where there would be an axe gash or some splinters in his head where somebody had got him. I tried to do my middle class, educated thing and find out *why* he did it, but he just said he was doing it because he wanted to do it. He ended up in 'Rat Trap' – the song isn't necessarily about him, but he started off the line of thought. He was a hideous person, he was a very stupid person and there was no particular reason for the violence. It was meaningless.

It is usually something I see, something somebody says, an emotion that starts me writing a song. The object of the song is to make people spark off a similar emotion when they hear it. I talk a lot when I do a concert – probably only because I like to hear my own voice – but a concert is largely an exercise in mass communication and if you can't communicate, I don't think you should be doing concerts. I think I'm a bloody awful singer and if a Boom Town Rats track comes on the radio, I'll turn it off. I think my voice has character, because I have adenoids or something and some people think it's a good voice. But then again, I should worry – John Lennon must have thought he had the worst voice in the world, Dylan *has* the worst voice in the world but he sounds great, Bowie learned to sing about four years ago, but was brilliant up to that time as well.

I think, in the general scheme of things, in what's important and what's not in the world, rock and roll is probably very unimportant. I think that Lennon probably realised that and thought that peace was far more important and worth fighting for and he used rock and roll to achieve it. You can achieve things through it. It's not so much an instrument of social change, although I think most people would like it to be, but rather it mirrors and articulates social change. If we talk about things that are very important in this world, I think rock and roll would come pretty low on the list.

1980

ADAM FAITH

When I was a kid I didn't want to be a train driver, I didn't want to be a pilot, I wanted a big house at the end of a long drive with big wrought iron gates – that was all I wanted. I didn't start out to be a pop singer but a film director. I went to see James Dean in *East of Eden* and when I came out my life had changed basically. I was so stunned by it. I wanted to be a director then. I didn't think someone from Acton, working class, whose old man was a driver on a bus could become an actor – it didn't occur to me so I thought I would be on the technical side.

It was an accident really that I got into music. When I was about fifteen I had a mate called 'Ergie' and we used to sit on the wall at the park up by his house and the girls would be swinging on the swing and I used to sing Lonnie Donegan songs for all these birds, and when I was eighteen we started a skiffle group and there was no one to sing so Ergie said, 'You can sing – you must sing – you sang on the wall in Acton – sing now.' So that's how I started to do it.

I didn't rate myself as a singer and was very grateful for songs like 'What do you want?' because they didn't demand a great deal as I couldn't have competed against great rock singers of the day. Tommy Steele was the first pop star and then Cliff Richard and I came along. For a while it was just Cliff and I. It was great on the road in the early days because it was always fresh – and fun. No one had had rock'n'roll and no one had had one night stands like that before – and kids were screaming and blocking the roads – it was fun. There was nothing to do on the road and Colin Berlin, who was my agent, was a stamp collector and he got me into it, and I liked antiques. That's basically what we used to do – mooch around. It was a very pleasant existence. I remember the first thing I bought when I had money was a house and then I bought a car.

All the time I was singing I wanted to act so it was a conscious decision to leave the pop world. I remember one day I woke up and I said to the missus: I can't do it anymore, today is the day I am going to stop. So I wrote to all the rep companies to see if they could fit me in. When I was an actor on about £300–£400 a year I didn't live like I did before or since, because I figured that it might take me twenty years to become an actor and earn enough money to live well so I'd better be careful. So I bought an old mini for £100 and rented a house and sold mine – I battened down the hatches for four years.

I'm happy with my life the way it is – it's a nice kind of life. To be really big in the films there's got to be a period in your life when you live in America. I couldn't live out of England even though I have worked in America. I gave up cigarettes nine years ago and that was harder than learning to fly the helicopter. I also haven't really ever drunk although I did when I was fifteen or sixteen but when I was eighteen I packed up drinking. I drink wine now. There weren't many drugs around in 1959 either.

I don't have any sympathy with anybody that is in show business that talks about 'pressures' because any job in show business, *any* job, whether it's sweeping the floor or something is better than working in a factory, ten times better. It's a fantastic job – like sport. I used to look to the future but since the car crash I had I don't do that anymore. I only look to my kid's future and my wife's future because you make provisions. If you have gone through a smash like that you reassess your future – it's true – which is why it's become a cliché. I wake up good or bad and anything that happens is a bonus – whether good or bad, it's better than being dead which I nearly was.

1980

CLIFF RICHARD

My inspiration, my starting point in a musical career was Elvis. There were some wonderful singers around like Bing Crosby who was singing as well as ever when he died, but although I recognised them as fantastic singers they didn't make me want to be like them. Crosby and Sinatra for example didn't inspire me – and I think there was a whole generation of us who weren't inspired by those men and then suddenly Elvis came along. We suddenly realised that that was the sound that made your hair stand on end and made your skin creak, and so I chased that. I never dreamed that I would actually do it. We couldn't afford to dress like him in those days, and even though there is supposed to be a recession at the moment I still think that there is more money to fling around on things like clothes. It was just a matter of doing local pubs, singing in them, and if you got a picture in the local paper and you happened to be caught imitating Elvis then it made the whole thing fantastic. Extra custard at school, all the girls behind the counter. . .

I changed out of the Elvis image due to the fact that I worked with a really terrific TV director called Jack Good, and when we did the *Oh Boy!* show together he told me that he didn't want me to sing the 'A' side of my record but the 'B' side and if I wanted to be on his TV show I had to sing the 'B' side. I am very grateful for that because it was the song that was called 'Move It' which was the first hit record I ever had. Jack Good said to me: 'Whether you like it or not there is a resemblance', and I think that's what it was. I really didn't look like Elvis but we modelled ourselves on guys like that so you did tend to stand a bit like him, and perform his intonations when singing and your hairstyle – my hair was all swept back. I'm not receding or anything, I just prefer it all down forward now. The main thing was to get rid of the guitar and the sideburns – because they were the big Elvis thing. However, I should say that if it wasn't for Elvis I wouldn't have even started, but I had to get away from that pretty early on and with Jack's help and guidance I moved away from that image quite quickly although the press didn't let me get away with it. For example I was doing TV shows then and a newspaper quoted me as 'this crude exhibitionism by Cliff Richard on *Oh Boy!* last Saturday' etc. and 'don't let your daughter go out with people like this' and things going round. It was just ludicrous because the Shadows and I, along with Marty Wilde and Billy Fury were the only ones doing that kind of American thing.

People either 'loved Cliff' or 'hated Cliff' and the other one that you loved was Elvis. There was a great battle going on for years, and a lot of Elvis fans don't like me even now – no one is going to replace him. I get some very bitter letters from Elvis fans, they call me 'scum of the earth'. But the Elvis fans to a certain extent always bought Elvis records, even though they may not have been artistically good and I don't want my fans to buy everything I do just because I've done it. Although it would be rather nice, artistically it wouldn't be very good, as then I might go on in that direction although it might not be right for me artistically. For example, 'Hey Mr Dream Maker' was one no one actually bought and I find that rather healthy. I have actually gone into print as saying that I felt that Elvis gave so much pleasure to millions of people and yet when you think of the latter days of his life he obviously wasn't having a great deal of happiness and joy himself. Elvis's fans love him to a point of deifying him – which I don't think is necessarily right, but the fans don't get to you. They send their love in letters, but it seems to me what Elvis needed was someone who was really close and who was willing to tell him what he sang at times was rubbish or fabulous – someone truly concerned for the person and it seemed to me that Elvis missed that somewhere along the line. The guy shouldn't be dead.

I didn't compare my career directly with that of Elvis, but I did find that after about two years of singing, although it was great in so many ways, I suddenly didn't feel elated any more. It was not the way it should have been – I was expecting a lot more from it. I found that conversation centred around sex, politics and religion and believe it or not, religion was really on top of the list. Everywhere we went people were talking about it and so I just chased it really. Coming from a Christian background, I went straight to the Jesus syndrome and found a reality that I didn't think was there, and a rationality. A friend of mine always says that you don't have to commit intellectual suicide to become a Christian but I always think that you have to to an extent – you have to take this black step of faith. But it's not that black and it isn't such a shaky step because there is so much reading and understanding that it gets you to a point where you are so convinced that it is true that then you can step out into the unknown.

I now donate some of my earnings to an organisation which sends out nurses and doctors and general relief to stricken and poor areas. Having become a Christian, I started to feel very guilty about earning so much, but now I don't feel guilty any more, I now feel grateful and feel that quite a large part of this has to go back. I now do Rock Gospel tours, presenting Jesus in a rock'n'roll way because a lot of people still feel that rock'n'roll and Jesus just don't go together.

1982

DR BILLY GRAHAM

I did come from a religious family – my father and mother were Presbyterian and we went to church very regularly. I found it very boring and as a boy I never enjoyed church. One of the reasons I wanted to leave home was to get away from the church because I just couldn't stand going to church. I tried to get out of going to Sunday school and church, using all the excuses I could, and my parents were very concerned about me.

Then one day, something happened to change all that. An evangelist came to our town and he stayed about three months. I went to hear him out of curiosity and I found a man with a Bible, explaining very profound truths in a simple, ordinary way and I got a great deal out of his talking. I went to hear him night after night, and one night he asked all those who would like to receive Jesus Christ as their Lord and Saviour to get up out of their seat, come forward and make a public commitment, and I did that. I had no emotion about it, I didn't shed a tear and when I stood up I felt like a fool and wondered why on earth I was doing it. But when I went home that evening, I remember looking out across the fields in the moonlight and asking God to change my life for me if He was real, because I did want purpose and meaning in my life. From that moment on, my life did change and I could detect something working inside me and now I know what it was – the Holy Spirit.

I never liked the word 'Evangelist' – I associated it with emotion, anti-intellectualism, anti-church and big money and I had determined that I would never hear an evangelist. When I started in evangelism, which I never meant to do, I made a list with some of my colleagues of all these criticisms and I determined that we were going to do something about it. We have tried to correct each one of these points through the years and I think we have succeeded, at least to a point. My salary and income is published in the United States and personally I have not made a lot of money. Our organisation is named after me but it is run by a board of directors, twenty-five in all, black, white, men and women. They meet every month and they are my bosses – they could fire me any time they want to. We spend everything we take in purchasing television time, radio time around the world, publishing a magazine and producing religious motion pictures. I think Christ would have used television and I often wonder what television would have done with Jesus Christ. For example, when he raised Lazarus from the dead, think of all the cameramen fighting to get a position!

During the depression I had a job selling brushes door to door and of course, if you sold $2 worth, that was a tremendous amount. What you tried to do is knock on the door and when it was opened, get your foot in so it couldn't be closed. Then you would say that you had a brush that you wanted to *give* her and it was always right at the bottom of the case and in getting to it, you would lay all of your brushes out and hopefully her curiosity would induce her to buy a brush. I realise now how dishonest that was. It was very good training though, because I was quite shy and I would still consider myself slightly shy. I also had a slight stammer which I had to work hard to overcome.

It was when I was in Florida that I felt I was called to be a preacher, or that I was called to Christian work anyway, so I started preparing messages; I prepared four talks and then I went out into the swamps and practised those sermons out loud with nothing but the alligators, birds and snakes to hear me. And for about ten years, I didn't preach a sermon that I hadn't practised about twenty-five times first. I don't practise at all today, but I should as I would be better at it. The first time I ever preached in a church, I had these four outlines that I thought would last thirty or forty minutes each and I preached all four in eight minutes!

I was here in England during 1946/47 and it was the coldest winter I can ever remember in my life. I preached all over Britain and there is hardly a town in Britain that I didn't preach in during that period of time. I must say that I learned the basis of my present day evangelism here.

I spend ninety per cent of my time with just ordinary, common people and I don't find it more difficult now that I have become a 'star'. I can't even get on an aeroplane without people gathering around me wanting to know more and sometimes I have conducted a Bible class from Los Angeles to New York.

It is said that in the thirty years of my life as an evangelist I have had 1.7 million 'inquiries' (I don't like to call them converts because it is God that does the converting, not me.) I don't know who keeps those figures because the only figures that really count are the ones kept in heaven and God isn't making any mistakes. Anybody that is keeping figures down here will be totally wrong. For all those that do stand up at the end of a meeting and give themselves to God, there are some for whom it is an emotional moment and not necessarily a lasting thing. Jesus gave us the parable of the sower and he said that he himself was the preacher and sower of the seed. He gave us four reactions: one was that the Devil would come and pull it away immediately, (in other words they don't last hardly the night out); then there is another group that when some troubles and temptations come along, they fall away; then another group for which the deceitfulness of riches chokes it out; but then the other group really stands. Now if you take those as percentages, that would be twenty-five per cent, but I don't think you can take it as percentages.

I have known seven American Presidents and I don't think that one of them has ever exploited me in that it was good for his image to be seen with me, although I think it is possible that their staff might have tried to. I knew Eisenhower very well as I knew him before he became President as well, and I was also very close to Richard Nixon. He was a very successful President until Watergate. I have read the books, I have spoken to him and I don't know how he fell into Watergate and I don't think he knows all that went on. I am told that the language on the tapes was from a Nixon I never knew and that it was like two different Nixons; it comes to a certain point on the tape and it just goes downhill and they sound like thugs sitting around planning something that Al Capone would be doing. He wouldn't allow me near him at this period and it is said that he told his staff not to let me near him because he didn't want me tarred with Watergate. I did try to get to him – I tried even the night before he resigned, just to have a prayer with him, but I couldn't even get through to him on the telephone. I see him now and I talk to him quite often on the phone.

There is hardly a social issue that I don't take a stand on, but because my message is centered in Christ and getting people to Christ and so individualistic, these other things get forgotten. For example, abortion: I am against abortion except in cases of rape or incest or where the life of the mother is at stake.

I have had doubts about what I was doing, and they came after I received Christ. I had doubts about the Bible, about Christ himself and my big intellectual hang-up became this – was Jesus Christ who he claimed to be? Was he a maniac, was he a liar or was he truly the Son of the Living God? and I had to decide that. I decided it on the basis of faith because I couldn't prove either one. I believe that the Bible is God's revelation to man and that when we read the Bible we are reading what God wants man to know.

When you look at the world today, I wonder if I have made any contribution to it at all! The contribution that I see is that I have been able to announce the Kingdom of God, to preach the Gospel, to sow the seed and as in Wesley's day he did not see the results of his ministry – it came along fifty years later. I am not comparing myself to Wesley but I would say that the full impact of any little ministry I have had may not be seen for years to come, and may never be seen in this life, but it will all come out at the Judgement.

1980

COMMISSIONER BRAMWELL-BOOTH

I am now ninety-five years old, and my memory goes back to when I was three years old. I remember that I had gone to dinner with my grandmother, and after dinner, she knelt down in front of me and said, 'Oh, Cath darling, such a lovely thing has happened, God has sent you a new baby sister and Mama wants me to take you to see her.' It didn't strike me as strange that my mother was in bed, and beside her was this beautiful cradle with pink muslin and I was lifted up to look into it and I burst into a howl of misery – I had never seen anything so dreadful – like a red beetroot covered with hair! I had an idyllic childhood and I think people would find it difficult to believe how very happy we were; I never remember quarrelling – we had plenty of disagreements, plenty of arguments. We argued in the nursery and we have been arguing ever since – my sister and I have been arguing about this and that in connection with this show, but I have never quarrelled with people I love. I live with my two sisters now, one is eighty-four and the other is eighty-six, and Dora, the youngest, chops the logs.

I didn't go to school – I don't really know why not, but I don't think obligatory schooling was in when I was young. My mother and father educated me and I wouldn't change what they did for me. They brought me into touch with life, they opened so many avenues; the love of reading, the love of beauty, the love of music – the door was opened to us. Today we have gone quite to the other extreme – think what a proportion of their lives children spend shut up in school now. My mother used to say that there was no need to put children into school until they were ten; they could learn to read at home. I think now we are putting such a burden on little children – youngsters, six, seven, eight years old, and we are pushing them not only to learn but also to put upon them things that belong to another age in life – all this absurd talk about sex. I can't imagine myself growing up burdened with that sort of thing. Childhood is the most beautiful time of life, when everything is new in the world and you can be enthusiastic and it is not carefree enough now.

To please my father was the highest joy you could aim at when we were children, and my father was devoted to his father, and so we had to keep in touch with our grandfather as much as possible when he was at home. I remember on one such occasion, he asked me what I had done that morning at our little church and I told him that I had sung a solo that Sunday. 'How did you get on?' he asked. 'Well, I did my best', I said and he suddenly seemed angry with me, and he could really shout – 'Your best! What's the good of that, Catherine? You won't be any good to me in the Army if that's all you can do.' I felt dreadful, I should have liked to burst out crying, but I felt I would be letting the others down if I did. Then he suddenly stopped and changed and said 'You see, dear child, when we believe in God, and God helps us, we can do better than our best.'

We were taught to shout as loud as possible in the Salvation Army, and also to walk backwards! In those days, the Salvation Army procession wasn't always a very large one, but in any case, large or small, we were liable to be attacked by ruffians. So the Captain had to walk backwards to see what was happening to the march behind. And of course, we also had to go into pubs with the *War Cry* and don't forget, this was in the Victorian days, a good age! In those days, only a certain class of lady would go into a pub, but I was trained to do it, and as an Army Captain that was my duty and I wouldn't have missed it for anything. I was thrown out once, but it was my own fault; I had gone into a pub one afternoon and started talking to this man and all of a sudden he asked me to pray with him there and then. So I went to go down on my knees and that was my mistake – the barman leapt over the counter, took me by the shoulders and threw me out. It took me all my time to stagger across the pavement, but I didn't fall down. It taught me a lesson – there was no need to go on my knees and make a display of it, I could see it from his side – he couldn't have me starting a meeting!

In Bath, we used to carol-sing all night from Christmas Eve to Christmas Day. My father and mother were never home on Christmas Day. They were always visiting hospitals and shelters where the poor and lonely were gathered in, and they had a great feast on Christmas Day. When we were a little older my mother used to take us as well, and I remember going to the big women's hostel. The three of us – we were just three sisters in the family – used to sing together and I used to strum a guitar. People think that they have brought in guitars lately – not at all. The Salvation Army had guitars going strong in so many places. It was a strange sight, all these bedraggled looking people, all ages, young and old, and the light, and us standing there singing. One of the excitements when we got home was to count how many fleas Mary had brought back – Mary was my sister. It was an extraordinary thing, she used to attract them. Of the three of us, Mary always had the most.

In the Second World War she was imprisoned by the Germans and very badly treated. She spoke German and so she asked one of the guards to help get rid of the bugs because it was really awful. He said he couldn't do anything and besides they were not German bugs, they were brought by the Poles – they were Polish bugs!

It's a wonderful thing to be brought up and to know that all the people I loved best like my parents, my grandfather and our friends all took it for granted: they believed the Christmas story, the story of Christ's birth, the Angel coming with the message, was real. It never dawned on me until I was well on in my teens that people could imagine that it was a fable, or imagination, or that it never happened. It was the most important thing that has ever happened. It's a wonderful foundation for life and it's so beautiful.

Since we have retired, our family motto is: 'We plan for life, not death.' You are thrown on the dustheap, they don't want you any more when you're retired and it's an awful feeling. I should have liked to have continued working for longer, but the powers that be decided that I should retire and I had to make the best of it. I should like to finish my old age as Moses did. It says in the Bible 'His eyes were not dim' – well, that doesn't apply to me because I already have to wear spectacles! 'And his natural strength was not abated.' That is what really attracted me. Just think how wonderful it would be to be as strong and vigorous at ninety as you were when you were nineteen. I should love to reach the age of one hundred.

If you had known me when I was younger, you wouldn't have thought me a remarkable person at all. I was shy and my life has been in contradiction to my nature, this publicity of life. My darling father gave me some very good advice once when I had been training for about twelve months: 'Cath darling, it doesn't matter how much your knees tremble as long as the people don't notice it.'

1978 and 1979

DAVE ALLEN I have stopped smoking – the cost has a lot to do with it, and not being able to breathe. I haven't given the amber fluid up – I will die for that. I came from a family of smokers, and the first time I gave up smoking was when I was eight when I'd been smoking for about four years because I copied my brothers. They would hold a cigarette very tightly and give me a quick drag. I used to follow my mother around too and she used to forget that she smoked so she would leave a cigarette lying around while she did something and I would have it. When she came back she would say, 'I thought I had a cigarette' and light up another one and so on. My father believed in practical lessons and he caught us smoking (not knowing that we were already hardened smokers) so he said he was going to teach us a lesson. He was a cigar smoker and he used to roll them in cognac and then let them dry. He made us sit down with him and smoke one of these cigars each, so we sat there smoking while he waited for us to go green and yellow and vomit and nothing happened.

I was brought up in a religious manner. I remember when I started school, it was really like the Gestapo in drag – the nuns. The first day my mother left me at school with two nuns who were supposed to be looking after me and I didn't want to stay there. They kept on giving me sheets of paper and a pencil to draw something on, and I kept on refusing and so it went on all day. The next day, I went to school but I turned round and went straight back home and told my mother there was no school that day. Then there was a knock on the door – it was like the KGB – and there were two of them standing there saying, 'We have come to take your son' and my mother gave me away! When I think back to the things I did – I don't think I was absolutely wild but I did things. I found it extraordinary to be told at the age of seven to go into this little dark box and confess, and I used to make them up. There were also damaging things. I was told as a child that Protestants had no chance, that they would burn, but my mother was a Protestant and it used to worry me because I thought my mummy would burn. Then she would clout me for something and I would think 'good, good'.

I honestly believe that your own mind is very important and I believe that everybody has a responsibility – every parent has a responsibility, every teacher, every part of society has a responsibility to the individual's head, because what you put into the head is very important. I firmly believe that if religion didn't exist in Ireland, there wouldn't be the problem we have. What has happened is that two supposedly intelligent sections of society have got into the head and created differences when there basically aren't any. My responsibility on stage is to make people look at it, to think it out. Blasphemy is generally associated with traditional religions, and traditional religions will protect themselves against ridicule, in a sense, by bringing on a word like 'blasphemy' – blasphemy is a sin. If you were somebody in the world who worshipped stone turds, would it be blasphemous for me to make fun of them – because they actually worship them and believe in the great God 'Turd' who is up there?

I do not ridicule religion, I ridicule some concepts of what men believe religion is. I firmly believe that if anybody wants to do anything in their life, they have the right to do it. It is not the right of any man to step on another man's head and tell him how to do what he should do if he doesn't believe it. Religion gives a great deal of joy and pleasure to people and if it does that, then all well and good. But it doesn't at the same time control my thinking and my way of life. I'm an atheist – thank God! You have to hedge your bets a bit. Look at the alternative – its either Nick or Him. They say to me if I'm good in life I will go to heaven and if I'm wicked in life I'll go to hell. That's the extraordinary thing about religion – why don't they just say, 'Be good for the sake of being good, be pleasant for the sake of being pleasant'? There is always this great threat – 'If you don't do that, you'll burn.' It's reward and punishment which I think is the wrong basis. Then I think I wander through life and I have met a lot of what I would call good people and they are goody goodies, creepy goodies 'God I love you' and thinking 'me' all the time. That means heaven is going to be full of that lot. Can you imagine being stuck with that lot for eternity? It means hell is going to be full of the most interesting people, so I'll be happy to go to hell, but then I suppose that God would know that hell would be heaven to me so he'll send me to heaven, and that's going to be boring!

1981

EDNA O'BRIEN

When I am actually writing, which of course is about one day in seven, I cope by little dodges – it's quite nice being a woman in that sense – you have to cook the dinner and peel the vegetables. All these writers who say they work for four hours every morning – they'd have written *War and Peace*, lengthwise anyway, several times over. When I'm writing, I'm – excuse this word – but I'm transported for a while and then I'm praying and waiting in between, really for a kind of inspiration. I'm always accused of being bawdy and realistic, so it's not mystical. It's really like waiting to be charged. You know when you look at a painting, a great painting, say one by Turner, there's something more in it than just a canvas of a sky with lightning – it's energy, it's electricity, it's God – I don't know what it is, but one is always waiting for that charge. It isn't enough to write just a good story (although that's hard enough) it needs that other thing, it needs that throb and that doesn't come any old day.

I think the Irish, for better or worse, have a greater sense of imagination, a greater longing for imagination and for that old fashioned thing: wonder. They also are very much more addicted to the supernatural. Fairies etc. originated in Ireland and it feels in that sense an older country. It's not an affectation or anything. If you were to ask me the quality in this world I love most in another human being, I would say magic . . . I would add humour and kindness and sexuality and about sixty other things afterwards.

My book about Arabia began on a dull day in my own house, November, the rain, no money – need I go on with these depressions? And somebody rings up and says how would you like to go to the Persian Gulf for six weeks in the Spring? Now Persian Gulf, I think, exotic, Sir Richard Burton, Arabian Nights, Turkish Delight, women all reclining – me also – and the desert would inspire me. I really am a very, very stupid person because I rarely relate what is to what – my imagination makes this leap . . . So that was November and I set out on St Valentine's Day and I went to Abu Dhabi, which is where *Arabian Days* is set, and it was an extraordinary and drastic contrast. It's a very new place. It was nothing five or ten years ago and it's concrete, concrete as far as the eye can see. It's very rich and instant riches bring a lot of traumas to a place as well. And the women I really could not see. For one thing they are masked behind their cardboard – the richer women's cardboard has sort of gold spray on it, but it's cardboard too. They were very, very frightened of me and they had the advantage of being able to peer out through these slits, and I can't imagine what they thought of me. They were very reluctant and very suspicious of me, but I can understand why, it's like people who live in very lonely parts of the country in Ireland – they are very, very frightened that you are coming in to trespass on them or to take their secret away. And what we all dread is to have our secret taken from us.

I think travelling as a woman alone is no joke, and travelling to very distant places is less of a joke. It is a very male orientated society, nobody raped me or anything like that I'd like to add, but I didn't feel that I could enter into it all. I couldn't really feel sad on behalf of the women – I felt they were guarded and hidden, but I don't know their story. I imagine, and I'm not defending their position, that they were very unawakened. We who (speaking of myself) earn our living and have been divorced and all that, and have a great number of little battles to contend with all the time, we do it because it's what we want to do or what fate has commanded us to do. But looking at their palaces – they call them all palaces, they are very like the foyers of cinemas, there is a lot of carpet, a lot of artificial flowers – drinking orange juice and cups of tea might be quite nice for a week.

I think the very root of our behaviour and our degree to be happy or to be unhappy or to be stressed or to be anything, is right from the womb and I do think with all due respect that mothers are the most important and the most wonderful species of all because the child is nearest to the mother at first.

I had a very violent upbringing in a very backward part of Ireland and violence was almost as natural as anything else, as nature, if you like, and I have a dread of violence. Thrashing was taken for granted and in schools it was the order of the day that children would be flogged. I always say that people are potential murderers or suicides – sorry for that depressing remark – but the violence makes you one or the other. My violence is against myself – I don't actually slap myself but it all goes inwards whereas many people who have had a violent childhood then tend to take it out on their wife or on the next generation. And I think that in the streets now, in London, the sort of power of near violence is very, very strong and life has deteriorated very much in one particular area, not just money, but in the area of random human behaviour. People are crosser and more aggressive and more frightened – which is the saddest thing. I think one other reason for the discontent in the world is that in the sixties, due to television, due to magazines, there was a great sort of illusion that everybody was going to be what Andy Warhol said – a 'superstar'.

Because women's condition has improved to some extent and because they have a little more authority and they earn their living, men are more edgy and are more threatened. They are going through a kind of transition which they don't let on to be going through, but they are.

Writing *The Country Girls* was very instrumental in the ending of my marriage. Now if you were to ask me would I undo that, the answer is no, because I believe and indeed my children have proved it to me, you can be a woman and a writer or an actress or a social worker, whatever job and it need not change the family life, but there is that thing of jealousy which we can't ignore. People are sometimes jealous of people's careers. I parted from my husband – I did go out of the door one day and I haven't had any other husband or any potential husband in fifteen or sixteen years, not because I'm old and grey and full of sleep, although I nearly am, but I think because my actual work is a bit of a threat to men. I think men are frightened of certain professions, particularly of writers. And I would say that I have had to pay, to pay that price in my life and it wasn't that I wakened up one morning and said I choose my career rather than a happy, loving, lovely domestic life. I actually want both, but it doesn't seem possible.

1978

ANTHONY BURGESS

For a Lancashire man to live in Monaco is the height of poshness. I had lunch with Princess Grace and Prince Rainier the other day. It was all right – she was a very good actress. I didn't choose to go to Monaco – in fact the last few years I have been chased out of countries; forced to leave countries. I was chased out of Malta for criticising the Government. My house was confiscated. I went to Italy and my young son was next on the list to be kidnapped in the district we were living in so my wife (who is Italian), my son and I dashed off to Monaco which is a neutral zone with not many tourists or kidnapping yet.

I started writing novels quite late in life. Up in Lancashire and especially in the Catholic regions in Manchester there is no real literary tradition I think because there is no real educational tradition. It was only in the first third of the nineteenth century that you allowed us English Catholics to get a higher education – it was only the Catholic Emancipation Act that allowed us to go to university or to public schools and for us there were no lawyers or doctors or school masters in Catholic families. If we had talent or temperament we used to go into the entertainment business – which partly explains why most of our great comedians or music hall comedians are of Lancashire/Catholic origin e.g. George Formby, Tommy Handley, the Beatles etc.

I always thought of myself as a musician, a composer of music but one day I was looking through somebody's window and I saw someone tapping on a typewriter with two fingers and it struck me: that's a damned easier way to earn a living in the field of arts than getting a piece of scoring paper with thirty lines, paying £300 to get the parts copied and then selling it to someone who doesn't play it. To write a novel there is at least a chance that a publisher will turn it down politely. So I began to be a novelist and have been a novelist ever since. The publisher to whom I first sent my first novel kindly called me into his London office and gave me a glass of Empire sherry and said: 'You know, we like your novel; it's funny.' I was surprised because I had always seen myself as a creature of gloom and sobriety. But he said, 'Nevertheless, we can't publish this as a first novel, it has too much of the flavour of a second novel; will you go back home and write a first novel?' So I went back home and wrote a first novel and at that time I was undergoing something that happens to us Catholics in the North – something called 'Guilt' and I wrote a very guilty novel which was promptly rejected and I said to hell with the lot of them and I went off to Malaya and there I was so impressed with the mixture of cultures, religions and languages that I began to write because I had to.

I was told that I was out of touch when I came back here and I couldn't get a job and that I had better go abroad again. So I went to what is probably the last of our dependencies which is the little oil state of Brunei in Borneo and I taught there. One day I was so bored, so thoroughly frustrated when I was teaching some kids the elements of American history and there was a cobra coming into the classroom with her young and the fan had stopped spinning so I did the only thing possible in the circumstances I fell on the floor and said in effect, 'Let someone else take over!' Well, they brought a stretcher in and put me on a plane and sent me to the Neurological Institute in Bloomsbury and there they said, 'We've been having a look at your brain and there is something in it!' And I said 'Yes, that is talent.' But they said, 'No, we rather suspect there is a cerebral tumour, we cannot quite see it but nevertheless all the evidence shows that it is there so the best thing we can do is to give you a year to live.'

I found a flat somewhere and this is the interesting difference between a romantic film and real life. In the film the person with this death sentence hanging over him is usually well-heeled and falls in love, goes on a last holiday and fades out in a kind of romantic mist. I had a wife and had a year to live and I had to get a job. So I went to various educational authorities and said: 'Please give me a job', and they said, 'How long are you prepared to stay with us?' When I told them they said there was no future in it. So I began to write professionally and in that terminal year I wrote six novels and after that I was all right.

It bothers me a good deal that I am always associated with *The Clockwork Orange* because it is not a typical book. It is a book which deals with juvenile violence and I became associated with violence chiefly because of the film made by Stanley Kubrick. In consequence they have turned me into some kind of expert on violence which I really know nothing about. The point of the book was not the depiction of violence but rather a kind of projection of a possibility that we'd become so worried about – juvenile violence. I feared that possibility that the State was all too ready to take over our brains and turning us into good little citizens without the power of choice which is why I wrote the novel; that the State might decide to do something radical with these young thugs, because I had some talks about not putting them into jail but rather putting them through some course of conditioning turning them into effect clockwork oranges, no longer organisms full of sweetness and colour and light like oranges, but machines.

We all have the right to make moral choices. But these moral choices must be, as it were, educated. We must know what 'good' is and we must know what 'evil' is – it's as simple as that. Right and wrong don't matter so much because these change all the time. What is right one day may be wrong the next, according to the Government. We all ought to know what is good and what is evil all the time and we must choose. It seems that we have to subsist as some kind of double creature. I am scared that if we burn out of our minds this element of violence we may not be able to be what we are – and we are highly inventive and creative creatures – I don't know but this is a possibility. We have to recognise the capacity in us for committing violence – it is in all of us. There is a lot of evil around today and I use the term very deliberately. The crimes that are being committed today are no longer merely acquisitive crimes such as robbery, but gratuitous violence which are acts merely performed for kicks, which is a pure manifestation of evil in all of us.

My latest novel, *Earthly Powers*, was most acclaimed in France. I seem to be one of these Englishmen who belong to Europe more than my own country, which I don't like. It may have something to do with being brought up in the north west of England where we are mostly Irish, and when I was a boy Rome was closer to us than London because it was where the Pope was and Paris was on the way to Rome. In my old age, I feel the wheel has come full circle and in my end is my beginning, and that I've become a European even though I no longer subscribe to the beliefs of my family.

I don't think England likes its writers. If this country is remembered in the history of the far distant future, it is as the country that produced a great language – I think English is the greatest language in the world – and for producing a great literature. Not just Shakespeare, but a continual procession of writers who have been perhaps more appreciated abroad than in their own country. We are scared of writers here because they tell the truth and in general the British are not prepared to get down to reality in the same way as the French. This is a virtue, but the British have never been very good at thinking – they take things from day to day and solve problems as they come along and don't work out philosophies of problems. So consequently, they are a bit scared of books because they set out philosophies, whole visions of life.

One of the reasons I live abroad is because as a writer, I can see England better when removed from it. As a man who has travelled widely I can say that England is the most civilised country in the world. It's a gentle country, despite the violence of racial problems.

I have a great love of language – I have invented two new languages, one for *Clockwork Orange*, a sort of futuristic slang, and one for a film called *Quest for Fire*, which was about stone age man and the discovery of fire. It was felt that it would be stupid to present this film in English, French or any other language, pretending that these were primitive people. I tried to make them speak a language that they might well have spoken in the Stone Age. We don't know how people spoke so long ago, but we can guess because we have at last been able to reconstruct the language that was spoken in Europe and India thirty thousand years ago, so add a step back from 'Indo–European' and imagine a language which eventually became the mother of the language we are speaking now.

The women's liberation movement has the idea at the moment that men invented language to keep down women. They are going to such absurd lengths at the moment in their effort to 'desexualise' language that we are not allowed to use certain words – we can't talk about 'chessmen' but have to say 'chesspersons'. The most horrible example of this attempt to castrate our language is what happened with the word 'testimony'. In ancient Rome, when you provided a testimony, you put your hands on your testicles to show you were telling the truth, 'May I be detesticled if I'm not telling the truth!' It's really the other way round – the testicles are a testimony that you are a man. There is the story of the man who applied to her ladyship for a job as footman and she told him to take his trousers off so she could see his calves and then she asked to see his testimonials. For lack of education, the poor man lost the job! Now a woman doesn't have a testimony, she has an ovarimony – she swears upon her ovaries. Things are going too far. Language is not as simple as that, it's a very arbitrary thing and sex doesn't come into it.

1980 and 1982

145

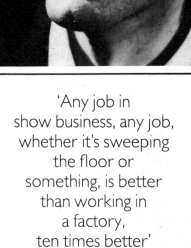

'Any job in
show business, any job,
whether it's sweeping
the floor or
something, is better
than working in
a factory,
ten times better'
Adam Faith

'A woman in the
House of Commons is a
contradiction
in terms . . . I don't
think any woman is ever
fully at home there'
Enoch Powell

ROALD DAHL

I had no thought of writing at all until I was over twenty, when I was wounded a bit in the War and sent to Washington. I was sitting in my rather grand office in the British Embassy wondering what to do and there was a knock at the door and a tiny little man came in with thick glasses and said: 'Excuse me, are you busy?' and I said: 'No, not in the least, do come in.' I thought he was going to ask for a job but he said: 'My name is Forrester; C.S. Forrester' – one of my heroes, great man, one of the great writers of the time – and he said, 'Now you've been in the war, America's only just coming in, you've been in action, I'll take you out to dinner or lunch – tell me your most exciting exploit and I'll write it up in the *Saturday Evening Post* and we'll get the British a bit of publicity.' I said: 'Well, I don't have any wildly exciting stories, I haven't done half the things that a lot of the fighter pilots have done.' He said, 'It's all right, come on,' so we went out to lunch – I remember we had roast duck. He was trying to take notes and eat this bloody duck at the same time and he couldn't do it. I said, 'Why don't I scribble it down for you this evening in a rough way and you can put it right when I send it to you?' So we finished our duck and I kept looking at him, he wasn't very exciting (writers aren't you know!) and no sparks were flying out of his head or anything. We finished the meal and I went home that evening and wrote the thing out and sent it to him and I got a letter back about a week later saying: 'I asked for notes, not a finished story. I didn't touch it, the *Saturday Evening Post* have bought it at once for a thousand dollars; the agent takes ten per cent; here's my cheque for nine hundred bucks.' I thought 'My God, it can't be as easy as all that' – but it was!

I like the short story format because you finish it quicker than you finish a novel – I'm a lazy sort of chap and I'm absolutely terrified every sentence and paragraph I write that the reader is going to shut the book and say 'I can't get on with that book', and throw it away. Now a novelist can't do that because a novelist has got to spread himself and take a lot of time to describe scenery and the sunlight coming through the pine trees – I couldn't do that because I would be frightened of losing the reader. You run out of ideas for short stories in the end you know. You keep your eyes open. Someone once said to Stravinsky, 'Maestro, where do you get your great ideas; while shaving? In the bath? Or while strolling in the woods in the evening sunlight with the long shadows . . .?' And he said, 'At the piano' – there's a lot of truth in that. It's three-quarters true for a writer, but the other quarter is obviously the spark of the plot which is going to have to come into your head and you rattle it around and buzz it about; has got to come from something you see – somewhere or something you hear. It's got to, you can't just *think* of it, something sparks you. I don't know what it is and then you sit down and try to make a plot of it.

My son got hit when he was a baby – his nurse pushed his pram into a taxi, in New York, and he got severe head injuries which developed into hydrocephalus – it's too much cerebral spinal fluid in the ventricles and you get pressure in your brain and one suffers damage unless one is very swift and quick to relieve the pressure. This was sixteen years ago and they did have a tube with a valve in it with which they could drain the fluid out of the ventricles and put it in a place in the heart where you hoped it would be all right – in the right auricle of the heart or the peritoneum; but they weren't very competent in those days, although much better than nothing, but he had to keep going back for operations; he had five altogether, but the shunts kept blocking.

I thought of a lovely man who I knew as an inventor, who I had been flying model aeroplanes with. What I admired so much about him was that instead of these tiny model aeroplane engines, he'd made them all himself and turned them in his workshop so I went along to him; his name is Stanley Wickham, and said 'how about doing this?' (i.e. making new valves). He said all right and I was only the catalyst and the medical liaison who went to watch operations at Great Ormond Street. We had the enormous advantage in the Head of the Neurosurgery at the hospital, Kenneth Till, who was a tremendous co-operator in this. He told me exactly what was wanted and I told Stanley and he really did it; not me; produced this splendid little valve. It's very complex and this is still used on children in Great Ormond Street and especially in underdeveloped countries such as India and Kenya where they can't afford to pay a hundred quid for the American valve which is a profit thing. Theo (my son) is splendid now, quite all right.

I'm not very keen on the movie industry. I only had one lovely experience – that was doing the Bond film. All your experiences when you are in a movie or are a writer for a movie have to do with the director, and Lewis Gilbert was director there and that was splendid. But most directors of big films are monstrous; beastly; egomaniacs with no taste and no knowledge of how to make a movie – everything is screwed up – *Chitty Chitty Bang Bang* was screwed up. I've given it up now. I did it for the money and now thank goodness I can afford to give it up which is one of the great luxuries of life.

1978

DR JACOB BRONOWSKI

I have to confess to an extraordinary mental capacity of which truly I'm not very much aware. I had the great good fortune of being born of rather clever and rather modest parents, so what mental gifts I have, I inherited from my parents. But I also inherited from them something which was given me by their culture, not by what I was born with – namely a simple feeling in the family that all human beings were pretty smart. You know, we were obviously much cleverer than monkeys and cats, and some people were *very* much cleverer than monkeys and cats. I was never aware, at home, that what I could do was extraordinary. And to this day I never approach a piece of work, whether it's writing, thinking, science, or this evening, in any other spirit than, 'That sounds interesting – let's do it.' And if I don't do it very well, I'll say afterwards, 'You know, you just didn't work hard enough.'

I was in Germany as a child. The war broke out in 1914 when I was six; it came to an end in 1918 when I was ten. I was very patriotic as a German, but in fact I was a Russian by nationality, so I was an enemy alien. We were not very well treated by the Germans. But I think it just made me at home in the world. I've always lived in countries that I haven't been born in. You know, I was born in Lodz, and the last time I was in Lodz was in 1913 – that's sixty years ago.

I had difficulty in learning to speak English as well as I do, because I'm not a very good mimic. But I had no difficulty in learning English as a literary language, and you see it's a very beautiful language. When I had been in England for about a month, a boy at school took me to the Whitechapel Library and there the elderly librarian said to me, 'Well, if you're going to learn English you should start by reading a simple book,' and he lent me *Midshipman Easy*. And I remember that I was struck, in *Midshipman Easy*, by the use of the phrase, 'hoist with his own petard' which I later discovered had not been invented by Marryat at all but by Shakespeare, but of course I didn't know any better at the time. But I thought that was lovely, and English has always struck me as a language which is full of these marvellous historic metaphors. Very concise, very precise. It's a language that I fell in love with.

I never thought of myself particularly as a scientist or literary figure, but I loved them both because of this sense that one was unpicking the world, finding the strands that run through it. Language was the key to that, and each way of looking at the world had a language of its own. I will tell you, if I can remember it, a very characteristic poem that I wrote – it must have been about 1965 or '66, when I had just settled in California. I had discovered that California was a country that everybody went to as if it was an El Dorado. They went full of ambition, and they all thought that the Promised Land was there. And naturally they all wanted the Promised Land without working for it – you know, that's what stops most people from doing anything, they think they're going to win it in the Pools, and you can win everything in the Pools except the desire to live. Well California struck me that way very much. I was very upset about people wanting to have success so easily, and I wrote a poem which goes like this:

> This is the coast the lemmings reached,
> They did not drown, but simply beached.
> Hereafter agonies and less,
> They found the go-go star – success.
> The goddess in the wilderness
> Who shook her breast
> And blessed the West.
> She beckoned from the burning blast,
> Medusa with the face of glass,
> And with her sunset fingertip
> Wrote as in magnesium strip
> A raincheck on the Hall of Fame,
> 'Make a cross and put your name'.

I have had many Bohemian friends. For instance, for a short time, towards the end of his life, I knew Dylan Thomas quite well. I liked him very much as a person, and he was always very charming. People are not in awe of me in the street, but friends who come from poetry or the arts and so on, have just that touch of awe which makes them behave somewhat better with me than they do with others, and Dylan I think behaved exceptionally well. And I thought that I just couldn't stand his life. I just thought that the notion that you would wake up very late in the morning and say to yourself, 'Have the kids gone to school? Who's driving my wife to the supermarket? Who has the car?' and so on, was too deeply ingrained in my outlook for my ever being able to dismiss them. Now I was very sorry about this, because I also realised that you can't write poetry like Dylan Thomas's without a wonderful air of irresponsibility, where you say, 'To hell with the second car and the supermarket. This is life, this is how I think.' All this rather tidy poetry that I write comes from a different temperament. Do I regret it? Well of course I regret never having written poems as beautiful as Dylan Thomas's.

I have been fortunate in having an immense enjoyment of life and happily I enjoy what are called intellectual pursuits marginally more than mere physical pursuits. Would I do the *Brains Trust* again because I enjoyed it? No. I *would* do it again, though, because I came to it from a deep sense that science was reaching a stage where those scientists who had a special talent for speaking simply and explicitly also had a great duty laid on them to do so. I would have done, no doubt, more academic scientific work if I had given more time to it and less time to gossiping with you! But whether I would have done anything half as important in the spread of a liberal attitude towards the scientists, towards the sciences, and above all towards intellectual ideas – no, I don't think I would have done. I don't think I could have done better with my talents than I have.

When a foreigner like me comes to this country, he is encouraged to speak the language like a native at the earliest possible moment, he is even encouraged to change his name as soon as possible – which I didn't do, because like musicians, scientists on the whole do better to have outlandish names. In America, none of this is true. I mean, as you will know from the example of Dr Kissinger, it's a positive advantage to speak English with a foreign accent in America, and I don't mean an American accent. It's always astonishing to me. The first time I went to a very secret American atomic energy establishment, I heard so many Russian accents that I said to the head of the establishment at the end, 'You know, I wonder if I go to Omsk I'll find that everybody speaks Russian with an American accent.'

America is not very homogeneous, therefore everybody brings their own traditions to it: they will behave like the Quaker stock from which they came or, in the case of most of my colleagues, like the Polish stock from which they came. You know, people stop me in the street in America who actually know me. They speak to me in Polish, a language which I don't speak any longer. And that makes all questions of moral values very difficult in America because people don't share common traditions.

Now that leads to the second point, which is that it's a tremendously do-it-yourself society. I'll tell you a little story. I arrived in America in 1953, and it was a very difficult time. The McCarthy Committee was just sitting; the McLaren Act had just been passed; it was very difficult to get a visa. I as a university teacher had to go to the American Embassy and take a test to show that I was free from venereal disease. My wife, as the wife of a university teacher, did not have to take such a test. Now I arrived on a very cold day at about five in the morning, on the quayside in New York, from a French boat called the *Liberté*, and my luggage was unloaded, and I had brought with me copies of my book on Blake which had newly been published. And a very small man, in a great coat and cap and covered with badges and so on, began to go through my luggage and held in his hand the piece of paper on which I declared what was in there. Well, I come from that kind of simple European stock where I had actually written down what I had, and it said, twelve copies of a book on William Blake. He said to me, 'You know, by rights, bud, I oughta read every one of those.' I said, 'Be my guest' and sat down on one of my suitcases. He blanched at this and he opened one and he looked here and there. There's a bit towards the end about Karl Marx which I suddenly remembered, and I thought to myself, 'God, I shouldn't have said that,' but there it was. And he looked at it and he looked at me and he said, 'You write this, bud?' So I said, rather proudly, 'Yes.' He said, 'This ain't never going to be no bestseller.' That's just true. And I bet you that man thought he said the most natural thing in the world. You know, literary criticism is obviously a natural gift of customs officials. Well that tells you all. There is this curious feeling that everybody is the judge of everything, and that makes life very different from this country.

I wasn't very keen to go to Auschwitz because many of my relatives from Poland had died there – horrible. But the point of the series *The Ascent of Man* was that it wasn't an entertainment, it was about life the way it is, the way it has been. And we just made up our minds to do it. We arrived at the station, and I went through these terrible wooden and iron gates that say 'Arbeit Macht Frei' at the top – work makes free – to these unhappy people who went there to their deaths and to the gas ovens. I was particularly keen to see Bunkers 12 and 11, where people were beaten and shot for breach of regulations, because I felt that you must see it all. But it turned out that the things that were far more moving were the ones that I couldn't have imagined at all. The Germans are terribly methodical, so there would be whole areas which contained nothing but old spectacles, all very carefully collected. They weren't the slightest use, but the Germans weren't going to throw them away. There was a terrible area which was entirely full of wooden legs and crutches and artificial limbs, and the most pathetic area of all was one which was just full of little tin chamber pots that children who had come to the camp had brought with them and the Germans had collected.

The most awful thing was that there were pictures in the corridors of prisoners, which were just the ordinary pictures, you know, front face, number one on the bottom. But many of them were pictures of quite young people, children, and to see these pictures of people taken as if they were criminals, with the tears streaming down their face, was just unbearable.

Then we drove over to the pond and we had arranged that I was just going to say a piece at the pond to close that programme, which would arise out of what I'd seen in the morning. So I walked up and down for five minutes, making up my mind what I was going to say, and then we did it – one take and we'd go home. We'd made up our minds that it was a piece which you couldn't possibly do twice. You just had to say what came into your mind, and the thing that came into my mind, absolutely out of the blue, was the phrase from Oliver Cromwell that I'd heard, 'I beseech you, in the bowels of Christ, think it possible you may be mistaken.'

But Auschwitz was – it was just hopeless. You know, if a civilised country could allow that sort of bestiality to become part of its relation to other human beings, I just felt that the future had fallen in, that how were we ever going to make people understand that human beings are individual. I'd like to explain one thing to you. You see the most awful thing about Auschwitz was that you realised that the people who'd been killed in the gas ovens, they were just dead, they were the fortunate ones. But the people who shoved another lot of people into the gas ovens the next day – they were characters out of Dante's *Inferno*, living in endless hell, because they'd lost all sense of human feelings and were going to repeat tomorrow the unutterable bestiality that they had practised today.

In my opinion, there is no difference between unutterable crimes, between the man who killed a single child in Auschwitz and the man who killed 80,000 people at Hiroshima. I think those crimes are absolutely on a par. We must learn that crime is something to do with our relations with human beings. When you sit and press that button, there should be a person at the end of it and the person should look like your sweetheart and you should say to yourself, 'It's her. It's somebody for whom I have feelings.'

Now you ask the question: what about the scientists? I thought, what about the chaps who actually invented the gas that they were using at Auschwitz? One is faced, at many moments in one's life, with a conflict between loyalties which are not compatible. And during the war many, many scientists were faced with a very simple important question, which was 'Do I feel strongly enough about the civilisation in which I work to do anything to resist the Nazi threat to make a bomb first,' and we all felt yes about that. All of us, and I have no doubt that all of us would do that again. We felt quite certain that to allow what was then going on in Central Europe, what we'd seen films of in Poland and Russia, to become normal all over the world was something which we must resist by all the technical means which we possessed. We felt we would be traitors to the intelligence we had been provided with, to turn round and say to Mr Winston Churchill, 'I know you want the bomb, but you're a warmonger, I'm a peaceful man, I would rather go to jail.' I think an individual *can* say that, but I don't think you can blame an individual who says, 'No, I can't do that.' The questions arise about what happens at the moment when other people make up their minds to drop the bomb, because I don't have to tell you that no scientist was asked about dropping the bomb, and those who knew it was going to be dropped were very much against it.

In the fifty odd years since I came to this country we have widened the intellectual interests and aspirations of people, oh, a thousand-fold. We have invented intelligent programmes like this; we've invented the paperback – well, I know that some of the pictures on the covers obviously are not very revealing about the contents . . . But you know, if you can sell Plato with a naked girl on the cover, good luck so far as I'm concerned. Plato and I would be of one mind. We have invented an ability for people in all countries, but in Western countries in particular, to share not just wealth but the intellectual wealth. You know, fifty years ago what organisation in the world would have put up that money to put out my programmes on *The Ascent of Man*? But we still have far too few people to bring these gifts to. We still don't know how to satisfy the leisure aspirations of most people.

Above all, we don't know how to provide enough jobs which are fundamentally interesting in themselves.

You see I don't believe in problems which are always other people's problems. I have four children – and I just would think it impertinent to say to any person in the world, black, white, yellow . . . 'It's OK for me to have four kids, but you mustn't.' I don't think there are too many of us. I think that what we haven't solved is the point to which I come back, of giving people very satisfying jobs. The things that the hippies tried hard to do, but failed, and the things which a few privileged of us do, like you and I, are so good. I think I've had the most wonderful life in the world because like any scientist, I share with prostitutes the only really satisfying job. I'm actually paid to do what I like doing.

My life has been happy, because although I have suffered many conflicts of loyalty which I spoke about earlier, I've never had any uncertainty about the meaning of the word 'good', the meaning of the word 'true', the meaning of the word 'beautiful', and the meaning of words like 'original', 'new'. I've always had a tremendous pride in being a human being, and being born in to the twentieth century. I'm terribly sad that, you know, thirty years from now I shall be dead because – not because anybody will miss me, but because so many more marvellous things will be known. Now, should you listen to me? Yes, you should. Not because you have to believe any single thing that I say, but because you have to be pleased that there are people who have lived happy and complete lives, who feel that they can speak out of a full heart and full mind, all in the same frame.

1974

DR HENRY KISSINGER

I remember going to school in Germany and, in fact, I remember when somebody came into the classroom and said Hitler had been appointed Chancellor. It changed the lifestyle of my family completely. We were ostracised after that and one saw the Brownshirts in the streets. It was my first experience of totalitarianism. What it meant, for example, was that I had to go to a Jewish school. My father lost his position – he had been a teacher and he lost that position. Many of the friends of our family would no longer associate with us, so that brought it home rather dramatically. It was also permitted for children of my age and all children to attack Jews, and they would take advantage of it.

It was my first experience of the tenuousness of modern society, and how rapidly things can disintegrate and how, beneath the veneer of civilisation, rather elemental forces can break forth. I had an uncle who was immediately sent to a concentration camp, where he stayed for two years, and just disappeared. All of these things show you that modern civilised life has its limits and that one has an obligation to fight for freedom, or, at any rate, to try to vindicate it.

America seemed to my family to be the answer at the time; we lived in a simple district in New York. I was fifteen when I came to the United States, so for a year I went to high school and then I worked during the day in a shaving brush factory, in which my job was to squeeze acid out of the shaving brushes, which was a sort of mind-numbing exercise. If you do that for eight hours a day, it doesn't test your ingenuity greatly. I did that for a couple of years, then I worked as a delivery boy for another couple of years and then I was drafted into the army. When I was sent back to Germany, as a soldier, I felt that the vicious circle had to be broken somewhere. I felt that, if it was wrong for my family to be persecuted, it was wrong for me to persecute others simply because of their nationality. You know, I had no feeling of vengefulness, nor do I have it today, against Germans.

I think I had an understanding of what America represents to the world that the American-born Americans cannot fully have, but that maybe you in Britain can have from your memories of the Second World War better than people who have never suffered setbacks, who've never had to look potential disaster in the face. I have therefore always had to believe that America, with all its failings, represented a hope for free peoples in most parts of the world, and I could therefore never go along with those who saw in every American mistake or every American failing a justification to assault the fundamentals of American society.

Nelson Rockefeller invited me to join a group of scholars, who acted as advisers to him in 1954 or 1955. I had then just finished my Ph.D, or I was just finishing it, and I had no exposure to the world of affairs at all – I had been a total abstract scholar. Of course, with a man of such wealth and power, you can never totally dissociate his position from his personality, but then I later met many people of wealth and power, so that was not the principal reason why he influenced me so profoundly. Nelson Rockefeller was a man of great intuition, enormous courage. He was not verbally as precise and as articulate as some other American statesmen, but he had an artistic intuition. He could understand the essence of a problem, even when he couldn't articulate it very well, and he had a tremendous courage in then seeking to achieve what his instincts had taught him. I always thought he would have made a great President. There were a combination of complex circumstances that made him fail, partly because he was a Rockefeller so he always thought that he had to earn it in a very special way. He wouldn't do the things that others did to get delegates but, without those things, you can't become President. Over the years, we became very close friends, very. He had something that I liked – he had very good human insight. And I had something that perhaps he liked, which was a more formal, theoretical mind. He was unfulfilled, but, if he was sad, he never showed it. He suffered grievous disappointments and I do not recall that he ever complained or that he ever showed it to anybody. He tended to take the attitude that he was already so fortunate that he had no right to burden others with his problems. He was a remarkable personality, very strong, and he didn't quite succeed by a narrow margin.

I had absolutely no use for Nixon before he became President. My disdain was only matched by my ignorance of him. I didn't know anything about him except what the conventional wisdom was. I'd never met him. I'd met him once at a cocktail party and he was and is painfully shy with strangers, and I wasn't socially super-adept at that time, so we had the most stilted conversation that you can imagine for three minutes and we gratefully parted from each other, and that was the last I saw of him or any contact I had with him until after he was elected President of the United States.

His Appointments Secretary invited me to call on him when he was President-elect at the Hotel Pierre in New York, which was his transition headquarters. In the United States there's a three-month period between election and the time the new President takes over, and I had no idea what he wanted. One of Nixon's characteristics is that he's so afraid of being rebuffed that, when he has a proposition to make that he doesn't know will be accepted, he puts it forward in such an eliptical way that sometimes the recipient doesn't know he's made a proposition, which happened to me. I left him and I didn't know he'd offered me a job, so, two days later, his then associate, John Mitchell, who became Attorney General, called me up and said: 'Are you going to take the job?' I said I didn't know I'd been offered a job. He said, 'You'd better come down here. He's messed it up again', and so I came and saw him, and this time I knew I was offered a job. But I had so many doubts about Nixon that I had the unusual bad taste of telling the President-elect that all of my friends had thought so ill of him and as I couldn't perform my duties adequately unless I had the support of my friends, I wanted to have a week to consult them. This was, after all, the second or third most important job in the country, to be Security Adviser to the President. I must say, in retrospect, I think it was colossal impudence to do this, but he told me to take a week and I actually spent three days talking to friends until I got to Rockefeller. Rockefeller said I had a moral duty to take that job because, if anything went wrong in our foreign policy and I had been offered an opportunity to help and had refused, I could never forgive myself and he would never forgive me. So, after three days, I called up Nixon and said that I didn't need a week.

My image of Nixon, as a professor, was very condescending. All of the people that I knew thought that Nixon was morally inadequate, intellectually really below par. But I changed my mind about him. I think Nixon knew a great deal about foreign policy. He made very important decisions in foreign policy with great courage. He and I were never personally close. He's a man of enormous complexity so that it's very difficult to render him in a sentence or two or a paragraph or two. I think he was more drawn to people socially of a less intellectual background than mine – professors from Harvard were not his cup of tea. On the other hand, we had a very good professional relationship.

I don't think he was jealous of my intellectual capacity because we complemented each other very well. He had strengths that I didn't have and I had some attributes that he didn't have. He became jealous, as any President would, when I received such tremendous publicity after my secret trip to China. It was heightened by the fact – and he was right – that most of our Press tended to ascribe all the good things that happened to others (in this case me) and all the bad things that happened to him, so he was unusually sensitive when his associates received favourable publicity. I have to say that, while it's easy to cite examples that sound slightly paranoid in this respect, he was essentially right. The Press did give him a tough time.

Towards the end of his office, here is a man, who had all his life wanted three things: conspicuous success in foreign policy, a spectacular electoral success and a recognition as President of the United States. He achieved all of these three things within a three-month period, and he lost them all within a two-month period thereafter, so that had some of the elements of a Greek tragedy. He's not a natural politician, he is a very strange combination of characteristics: a man who really doesn't like people, who is a politician. He could do some things, which I think it is safe to say were tawdry, but he could also do things that were surprisingly gentle. He could drive you crazy in hesitating before he made a decision and then he could act with great decisiveness. He spent all his life becoming something he wasn't naturally and then, when he had it, threw it all away, which I think has its tragic aspects.

I think that to get into very high office in almost whatever system, you must be extremely egocentric and you must have the view somehow that your view is more valid than that of the general run of the mill, or you wouldn't make the effort. Secondly, when you have tough decisions to make, again in whatever system, what makes these decisions tough is that the pros and cons seem fairly evenly divided and therefore you must have considerable self-confidence, if you want to be successful in betting on your judgment. Those are qualities most of them have. I would also say a quality many leaders have is that, if they didn't have power, they wouldn't be all that interesting. There are very few of the top leaders that one has met that you would say that you would really enjoy talking to, apart from the exercise of that power.

In terms of intellect, I would have said Chou En Lai was the most impressive world leader that I have met. As for a man who could take over a room by walking into it, I would have said De Gaulle or Mao. It was something intangible. My children's generation speaks of vibes that rock musicians have, to which I am unfortunately immune, but they had that intangible quality and wherever they stood, there was the centre of attention. They didn't have to say anything; they seemed to radiate willpower, these two men.

Mrs Ghandi's a very tough lady, very ruthless, very self-centred, but I respected her. I cannot say that I would have travelled long distances to spend a social evening with her, but I respected her as a leader. Golda Meir was different. I would have travelled long distances to spend an evening with her. She was a tremendous character. She was incredibly tough, but she was a mother earth type, I mean, she was the mother of her people. You could feel that she suffered with them and my wife used to say that, when she and I disagreed, they were some of the most, greatest, dramatic performances she had ever witnessed, but it was fun to battle with her because you could see her repertory and, once you have convinced her that something had to be done, which was tough, she had enormous courage in carrying it out, so I was very fond of Golda Meir.

I'm actually more hopeful about the human race now than when I started out. Strange as this may seem, I had never conducted a negotiation in my life until then. I'd never held a press conference in my life. I'd never run large organisations, so I was really going into a void. At that time also, it seemed that we might face a major calamity in Indo-China with hundreds of thousands of American troops really begging for passage or negotiating about a passage home. We had no contact with China and no serious negotiations with the Soviet Union. Now at least we have seen that one can reverse these situations and the fundamental strength of the industrial democracies is there and now, I think, I have a sense of what can be done, and I have pessimistic predictions about the near-term future but I'm quite optimistic about the middle and long-term future.

I really have no plan for the future. I think, when you've been at the centre of events, you become quite fatalistic about what you cannot affect. It could happen that a conjunction of events makes it possible for me again to play a role, but, if that conjunction of events doesn't occur, I've had more of an opportunity than is given to almost any human being to make a contribution and I think I've been fortunate to have had this chance.

1979

ENOCH POWELL

I was a very bright child and I always won every-thing, except games which I hated! I was reading the encyclopaedia, not the Britannica, at the age of four when convalescent after measles and then at six I was transcribing medieval Latin manuscripts because I rather liked the language. There was a time when I was two years behind with my Greek and my mother brought me up level over one Christmas holiday! You see, she taught herself Greek as a girl. Towards the end of her life, she told me she had really only had one ambition for me, and that was that I should be a happy man, and I know this was true. I don't know what ambitions I have for my own children – they are so manifestly happy anyhow that I am not worried about it. I have not dedicated myself to my children's education in the same way that my mother did to mine. I was an only child and both my parents were teachers. These were the very narrow and confining years of the First World War with a certain amount of hardship, so it was very natural that we lived a closed life in which my mother was my first teacher and my best teacher. I suppose that with more than one child, there can never be quite that relationship. Also, I must admit, that having been a practising politician since before my children were born, I shall at the end be asking myself whether I shouldn't have done more for and with them. However, I must say that from the occasional attempts that I made at elementary mathematics with my elder daughter and classics with my younger daughter, I'm not sure that our relationship would have been improved had I pushed it further!

I don't remember being lonely or isolated as a child and I don't think that an only child brought up the way I was can be lonely because his parents are also his contemporaries. I do think that my life has been shaped by something in this background; I have never felt intellectual loneliness and when I find I hold an opinion, or have an intention in which I am isolated, I don't have the sense of having nobody around me to back me up. I know there is a danger to this and a bad side to it and perhaps there is a touch of arrogance about it as well. Still, just as you need a good head for mountaineering, you don't need to mind loneliness to practise politics!

I was a mischievous child and got up to a fair number of pranks. When I think of our days at King Edwards, Birmingham, where we travelled backwards and forwards to school on the Midland railway, the depredations which we committed on the rolling stock are such as to make me very restrained when I hear discussion of youthful vandalism today. I'm afraid we were bad, quite definitely bad, and I was as bad as anybody. But then I *am* as bad as anybody, it's original sin, and I got the full dose!

I know that C.P. Snow, who was a contemporary of mine at Cambridge, said of me that I was totally immersed in scholarship. I think that is hard; if that was said of my first year or two as an undergraduate then that would be true, for I had one of the disadvantages that a student from a grammar school can have of really not knowing what there is besides working. But by the time I was there as a Fellow, I had many interests outside of Greek, textual criticism and lexicography. In fact I remember that it was while I was writing a dictionary that there were days when I broke off doing my lexicography to write a poem and then I would go back with the next word in the dictionary. You shouldn't become interested in writing poetry, you should just *have* to; you should have no choice about it. It's not enjoyable, it's a most unpleasant experience to go through and the idea of volunteering for it is positively repulsive! The point is that when it takes you, you have to.

I was a Professor of Greek at Sydney University when war broke out and I came back here to enlist. I had been convinced since the early 1930s that another European war was inevitable, and basing one's notions on the end of the First War, one assumed that this was the end of all things. I never in adult life, until right at the end of the war, thought of a normal span of existence – marriage, manhood, old age – I assumed that for me and my generation that was out. I believed that Germany would win and that I would be killed. It was one evening in June in 1944, and a monsoon was breaking in northern India, I went out onto the verandah and just stood, got wet and loved it and suddenly said to myself: do you know, I could survive, I could have a whole lifetime, what shall I do with it? The answer was waiting there to come, and I think this is how it happens in life, and it said that I was going into politics. I had been intensely wrapped up with causes for which the war was fought, with the survival of the British Empire (forgive the old-fashioned expression) and with the survival of Britain and it suddenly came to me that if the war finished, it would go on in other terms.

I was writing poetry during these war years, particularly in India where I went in 1943 and I think most of the poems in the book called *Dancers End*, which is my book of war poems, were written in those latter years in India. The common thread through those was something which I suppose has its effect on those of us who were in the war and survived, and will have its effect on us until we die; at the back of our minds there is a tinge of shame that we came back and others didn't. That's one of those feelings that can present itself in a form in which it *demands* to be expressed:

> I dreamt I saw with waking eyes the scene
> So often in imagination wrought,
> The flame wall in the night at Alamein
> Before the attack. And I was glad and thought:
> My sorrow and despair was after all
> Some evil dream. It still is not too late,

My friends who passed before me through that wall
Not lost, nor I for ever separate
From them, condemned to live. I break tonight
As they did through the fire, and so again,
Knowing and known shall pass into their sight.
But then I woke, and recollection came
That I for ever and alone remain
On this side of the separating flame.

I don't think I'm the only one that feels we ought to have gone in on the other side with them.

I don't write poetry anymore. The professional poet has mastered the control of that side of the human imagination so that he can handle it as a continual form of expression. We amateurs are very much more at the whim of the muse – she comes and she goes, and I suppose there comes a time when she goes away for ever.

It wasn't until 1950 that I was elected as a Member of Parliament, and I had sought adoption in some twenty constituencies – perhaps they were wiser than they knew! It was a crucial year in my life because even though I am sure that no man who is really desperate to get into parliament ever failed to do so, I do think that the moment at which you go in can be determinate for the whole of your future life and even a year's difference can be quite decisive. A woman in the House of Commons is a contradiction in terms; I don't think any woman is ever fully at home in the House of Commons. Most of them, after however many years it may be, are still convinced that it is some sort of boys' game in the sixth form. As far as Mrs Thatcher is concerned, it's the sixth form she thinks she teaches! It is a man's environment, a man's institution and the word 'institution' is the key. The nature of the House of Commons, which no other assembly bearing a similar name anywhere else in the world can have, is that it is a corporation, it is a 'body corporate' and despite the strength of the tensions and animosities within it, when it is most characteristic it is behaving as a body and it is always conscious, however great the extremes are, of belonging together. Now I don't think that women have that kind of herd instinct, team spirit, regimental spirit or whatever you like to call it. I know I have been called a misogynist but it is just not true!

I have been in politics now for thirty years and have held office for five of them. This is not because I am a resigner, as is commonly supposed, because I only resigned once, although I did decline office two or three times.

I think there is a very big element of chance, as in all politics, which is one of the most uncertain aspects of human life, but I don't know that I regret it. On the back benches, much more than on the front benches, parliament becomes a home and parliament is the instrumentality through which you express what you feel you have to say to your fellow countrymen. I remember that after each occasion when I declined office, I walked into the House of Commons and had this sense of being embraced, of something closing its arms around me again. I felt I had come home and that that was the place to which I belonged. I don't regret the twenty-five years out of the thirty – unique perhaps for a Privy Councillor of high seniority to spend on the back benches.

When I stood for Leadership in 1965, I was doing what Wedgwood-Benn decided not to do – and the choice we both had was to leave our visiting card or not; to declare that you yourself, whatever anyone else may think, regard yourself as fit for the supreme position and to do so openly. I decided to leave my visiting card, and I suppose it is still there on an imaginary silver salver in the hall. You never know if anyone will ever pick it up! Knowing the uncertainties and the improbabilities and knowing that many men have had their finest hours after the age at which I have arrived, I exclude no possibility, as they say when answering parliamentary questions!

No man, I think, at the end of a life in parliament, not even the greatest, would say at the end 'I have achieved so and so.' Most of them would feel that when they left it, the world was a stranger place to them than the world into which they wandered, and that they don't really know what it is, if anything, that is different because they have been in it.

1980

LORD GEORGE-BROWN

Having been kicked out of 'the kitchen' ten and a half years ago, I don't miss them, but I think they miss me. I'm an Anglo-Catholic and believe in justice being meted out after a period in limbo and may I tell you that it has been meted out this year – Belper has been wiped off the electoral map and it serves the buggers right! Up until the last year or two I had no wish to get back in there, I had made a new career for myself, enjoyed myself, but recently when I've seen things going awfully, sadly wrong, I have wanted to go back. May I say publicly for the first time that if any of my friends, Mason, Sir Jenkins, Dr Owen, who I regard very highly indeed, are willing to start a new Labour Party of the school which we belonged to, I would be the first to join again. I feel I want to get back in there and restart a *real* Labour Party that believes in people, not theories and mechanisms.

Oddly enough, I have a quite civilised relationship with Harold Wilson, even now. We disagreed about almost everything, our methods of working were different, our ways of thinking were different. He has a tremendous mind but the strange thing about Harold is that he simply wouldn't know how to walk from A to B in a straight line. He's a terribly devious man, maybe because he comes from Yorkshire!

I don't rate Jim Callaghan in the same league – I don't know how he ever got to be leader. I never had a disagreement with Jim, whereas I had many with Harold and I retain a regard for Harold, but in that sense I have none at all for Jim. He's a man of terribly limited intellectual ability but he is also lazy.

As for Michael Foot, he is a charming, crazy character who writes the most beautiful prose, the great pamphleteer, but he is a one-eyed, one-legged leader of the Party.

Oddly enough I have quite a regard for Margaret Thatcher as a person. I think she's got it wrong, I think she's got her mechanics wrong. I don't think her aims were wrong and I don't know how she thinks you can go on with a situation where industry is being closed down and two, rising three million people are out of work. I don't think she'll last – I think they will dump her – the Priors, the Pyms, the Whitelaws. A year from now they will probably decide that they are getting too near the next election to keep her on.

1981

GEORGE MELLY

I was recently in Australia and had a thrilling time. I always had a totally wrong impression of Australia. I saw it either as people with corks all round their hats or aborigines flinging things at unfortunate marsupials or else as screeching harridans in the suburbs talking about their 'lounge-rooms'. And it wasn't like that. I thought I would be attacked as a whinging Pom; in fact the Australians were very nice. They were a little puzzled by my exotic dress to start with as we did actually go up to the mining areas on the edge of the tropics. When I heard we were going up there I thought I would be a bit like that famous caricature of Oscar Wilde with a lily in his hand, lecturing on Rossetti to the miners of Leadsville – I thought it was going to be pretty rough – but it wasn't. There was this amazing landscape with all these parrots hurling themselves about, shrieking, and lawns and cars and washing machines and all these very nice Australians clapping politely, laughing at jokes – charming people.

The difference between the early days and now is – money. I make more of it so we can stay in nicer places. We now stay in those fairly anonymous hotels which are nevertheless comfortable; I no longer have to stay in totally squalid digs. I stay in places that like using words like 'Euro' and 'Executive' a lot – you know what it means: black forest gâteau. The worst digs I ever stayed in were in Manchester, they weren't nasty but just squalid. The landlady was sweet but she wasn't very clean. Everything had a layer of grease on it. For breakfast we always had boiled eggs because we had seen the kitchen. There was this famous lampshade which for many years we thought was fur and one day somebody touched it and an enormous quantity of dust fell down into their cornflakes and watered milk. There was a burnt sofa in the back yard – burnt, and the lady said 'Aye, we had a waiter here once, he was a lovely fella, but he was a drunk, he set himself on fire on that sofa' – that was probably the pits.

There was this lovely girl called 'Mucky Alice' – she came from Bradford. She was a scrubber. She is now a respectable girl living in Canada. In those days she was a scrubber which is the old-fashioned word for a groupie. They used to wait for bands to come up and then they would sleep with members of the band – very cosy.

Well, Mucky Alice once came to see me. She dressed in an outré way; she wore sort of split tights with cross-gartering and that sort of thing and she brought with her a friend and I said 'Alice' not 'Mucky Alice' because she wasn't dirty, it was another girl who said, 'I don't know how you can go with that mucky Alice' – meaning 'immoral'. She came in with this other girl, a respectable lady rather older than herself, and she said: 'Don't say anything in front of her – she doesn't like a bit of fun' – but by God, Alice did!

Cole Porter is one of my favourite songwriters because as a sophisticated writer he is almost without parallel. He rhymes so well, he takes so much trouble with his rhymes which makes them very difficult to remember especially at the end of the evening! There was one occasion (when I was legless on stage) in the early days when we had just gone professional. We were still doing our day jobs so we could afford to go legless because it didn't matter if we were never employed again as we always had something to fall back on. It was at Ronnie Scott's – the first season we ever did there and I actually slid slowly under the piano and John Chiltern said to the audience: 'I'm afraid the Captain is no longer in charge of the ship!'

1982

BARRY HUMPHRIES

Acting started really by accident. I was given parts in some school plays and invariably I played the eccentric parts or housewives. It seemed that I was very early on cast in the role of the housewife. In school plays, for example, which were about miners being trapped, I was always at the pithead with a bundle, and then once I was the *femme fatale* in the Ghost Train at Melbourne Grammar School, but I always felt uncomfortable in those old clothes of my mother's, as a matter of fact, because they never fitted very well. Later I went to university, where I studied philosophy and law. It was decided that I should be a lawyer, but it was in those years that I started creating theatrical happenings. I think I realised that I was a frustrated performer.

From university I drifted into amateur university theatre and then into professional theatre. That is to say, they paid £5 a week, and I toured in a production of *Twelfth Night*. On the bus trips between one town and another every member of the cast had a party turn. Someone sang a song, someone recited a poem. I used to sit in the back seat of the bus and impersonate the lady mayoress of the next town because everywhere we went there was always a party after the show and the lady mayoress would always stand up and say what a wonderful thing it was that these people were bringing Shakespeare to the Australian bush, and then she'd get the name of the play wrong. So I had this falsetto, which I'd learnt from school plays and that kind of thing and I would sit in the back seat and do this voice, which amused everyone greatly, so that, at Christmas time, when we had to do the pantomime, the producer asked me why I didn't do that character and I said I could do it in the wings. I could do the funny voice and one of the actresses could impersonate this person, whom we'd christened 'Edna' because it was probably the dullest name we could possibly think if. I'm sorry Mrs Healey. So I was Edna and I wrote a sketch for Edna and I borrowed appropriate female attire – I resembled a pantomime dame more than anything else, but the character was born. It seemed suddenly that I'd hit upon a vein of humour that no one had tried before, certainly not in Australia, so, on and off, in the years that followed, interrupting a pretty busy life as a professional actor, I did the character of Edna.

Sir Les was created because we have in Australia as you have here, clubs, and the clubs have a big audience, and the people who go to the clubs don't really always go to the theatre and a friend of mine said: 'You haven't really got to the real Australian audience, if you haven't done the clubs,' so I was persuaded to do one of the biggest in Sydney and I had to invent someone to warm up the audience. I thought I can't just go on there cold, so I invented Les Patterson. I made Les Patterson the entertainments officer for the club. I made him very drunk, and he staggered on and – it hadn't occurred to me – he exactly resembled the real secretary of the club. I hadn't consciously based him on anyone but apparently he was absolutely identical and everyone listened very sympathetically to his apology. He was actually apologising to the audience that they didn't have an overseas act, saying: sorry, Sammy Davis can't be here this year – because in fact they do pay these stars big money to go out there – as you well know, Michael! So he just happened like that, and again he caught on. It was a surprise to me, just like the success of Edna because people liked the reality of the character. They liked the fact that although it was a bit over the top, the person could exist and basically the person was warm-hearted. I think it's because these characters are a bit sympathetic that people enjoy them, and I like to think, too, that in devising these and some of my other people I've brought Australia just a bit closer to the home counties.

For a very long time, Australia was a very peculiar and remote place to the British public, and I perhaps flatter myself in thinking that I may have been instrumental in towing it, if not as close as the Isle of Wight, almost as close, so that we feel more sympathy perhaps with Australia than we do with Canada or even that wonderful place, New Zealand – because at any rate I wanted to demonstrate that Australia is a funny place. Australians weren't so sympathetic when I did the Barry Mackenzie films, however. We were given a government grant to make the first one and the official, who'd given us the money, rushed across the tarmac as we flew off to London to make it, and his final words to me were: 'By the way Barry, I hope there won't be too many *colloquialisms* in the film' – because there was still this image of the Australian as a genteel person. I think most of us have grown out of that now.

SIR LES PATTERSON

What is the image that I am bloody successful in projecting? That of Australia as a thinking organism. It's bloody fantastic the publicity we're getting, and largely due to the efforts of my good self. You know, it wasn't many moons ago that they thought we were a bunch of rough diamonds down under, but you know we've got more culture than a penicillin factory. No worries.

I was very much instrumental in getting movies off the ground in Australia. They've been going along a long time with Chips Rafferty and that fraternity, but they needed to be dragged kicking and screaming into the twentieth century and I'm very proud of the role that I played there. You know, the trouble with the fillum industry as it is with the yartz in general today, is the 'poofter' element. Don't get me wrong, I don't mind what people do in the privacy of their own homes. Don't get me wrong on that score, ladies and gentlemen. You know, I see eye to eye with old Ken Livingstone, but what I'd like to say is the industry needs a fair bit of *weeding out* and you know, it's rife with the poofters in Australia, as it is here. I had a lovely idea for a fillum a few years ago. It was about a football team going to the bush. It was called 'Piss Up on Hanging Rock' and by the time the poof-mafia, or the *Poofia* as I call them, got onto that they turned them all into Sheilas drifting around in the nursery curtains and getting eaten by the Abos . . .

I know a lot of actresses, personally. I had this little lassie, she was a star of one of my fillums and I was showing her the sights around London, you know, Buckwinster Castle, St Paul's Abbey, Trafalgar Circus, and we were driving around and we got to her destination and the driver says: that'll be so and so, you know, and he says: how are you going to pay me? and she said . . . I'm sorry I can't say it, but she did an Erica*. She did an Erica, but not the top part. She flashed the map of Tasmania, ladies and gentlemen. For those of you who aren't too crash hot on the geography, Tasmania is a triangular continent a bit on the bushy side . . . To cut a long story short, the driver said: haven't you got anything smaller? The cockney wit you know, you can't beat it and I think we've inherited it in Australia.

I don't talk much about Lady Gwen. I don't talk much about my wife either. I hardly ever think about her as a matter of fact. But now you've reminded me, she's sitting back there in Australia – she's a bit of a grass widow, as a matter of fact. She keeps a very low profile, one of the lowest profiles I've ever seen. I don't see the little woman as much as I'd like to, but in a way that's cemented our relationship, but I don't know – I'd like Mary, little Mary Parky in on this because she'd have her own tale to tell!

DAME EDNA EVERAGE

It's extraordinary really but, when I stand on the stage, as of course I'm going to do at the old spooky Theatre Royal, Drury Lane, I'll look down. There'll be senior citizens. There'll be infirm people, because a lot of people are hoping to be cured by me. I'm not saying I can. I don't want to be a second Lourdes. But I will say that when I touch little nooks and crannies of the human anatomy you'd be surprised what springs to life. You would be, and you know my tax lawyer rang me the other day from Switzerland and he said 'What are you doing?' and I said 'I'm going on the Parkie Show' and he said 'What are you doing it for, you don't need the money?' I said, 'Well, money's hardly involved!' But he said 'Why are you doing another season? It's putting you in a bracket you don't need', and I said 'I'm sorry, I have to give, I've got such a lot to share,' and it's something in me and Dame Nature and I'm sure the studio audience and all

*Erica (Rowe): a celebrated 'streaker' of the eighth decade of the twentieth century.

of you will realise that I've given something. Old Dame Nature, when I was born many moons ago, gave me a little something and it's a precious thing, I think, the ability to share with others and if I don't give it away, I don't keep it. Do you know what I mean by that? I give it away to keep it. Do you follow me there? It's a bit metaphysical that concept.

You know I am powerful but I never wield it. I never us it for ill. As far as I'm concerned I'm still an ordinary Melbourne housewife. I'm still in a spiritual way up to my wrists in the kitchen sink but I've given a lot of hope to women. There are a lot of women watching me and they think if old Edna can pull herself up by the boot-straps and get up there and be on the Parkie show, it's possible for us, and I suppose I'm a crusader. I'm a bit of a feminist, in the nice way, you know, I'm not one of those old bra-burners, not one of those spooky looking people. Some of them do look a little bit mannish. I think I'm the acceptable face of feminism. I'm the feminine face of feminism if you like.

Do you know what I did this morning? I was in Park Lane Street, which is outside where I live and I saw a little dog that had lost its mother or something and it had its little paw hurt and – do you know what I was doing most of the day locked in my toilet? I was looking after this little creature – I was looking after a dumb animal, and I do that kind of thing and I don't do it for publicity. Another woman in my position like Meryl Strich, you know, if she did a thing like that, she'd have the media there, wouldn't she? I mean this nicely, Meryl, but I mean she'd have cameras and all the papers. But I don't want publicity for the nice things I do, and if the animal kingdom could thank me for the good turns I've given them we wouldn't be able to hear each other think for the moos and the barks, and the grateful little hissings and things of that kind.

I have had the odd fling but I've never gone the whole way. Aren't you used to honesty on this programme? This is an honest programme and I can feel the closeup homing in on me. I have them you know, when I'm staying in luxury hotels, sometimes I hear a little tap on the door in the small hours of the morning, but I don't you know. I might ask them in for a cup of tea but no more than that. I never play hospitals with them. That's what you wanted to know and that's what I've told you. I'm sorry because it could reach Norm. It could. It would have an effect on every little nook and cranny of that man's anatomy and he's passing through a stage and my daughter Valmai is giving me a lot of worry. She's back in Australia and again with your mother a megastar it's not easy. Now this is not a thing that my audience can identify with very easily, but just imagine for a second that your mother was a megastar. You can't but . . . Valmai has had a little shoplifting experience. Oh yes, and of course she modelled herself a little bit on Patty Hearst too. She held up a bank the other day in Australia. It wasn't in the news here. I had Margaret stop it as a matter of fact. Here's me blurting it out on TV but it's over and done with now. She held up a sperm bank as a matter of fact. There were secret cameras. She wants to be a one-parent family. The secret cameras got her. Can you imagine looking at the paper one morning and seeing your own daughter with a little rifle and sawn-off shotgun and people throwing test-tubes at her. I don't know who she was looking for but there was rumour Warren Beatty had made a deposit. Now you see we shouldn't laugh at this. This is something that can be aired on the Parkie show – you've got little Barry Humphries going about this and that, and I saw a human side to him frankly I hadn't noticed before. Can I say that? Yes, I can. I can say whatever I like. But I'll say this now. When you are in my position – and this is more so than for you, Michael Parkinson, your life is a bit of an open book. Your family are open to the public scrutiny.

My son, Kenny, was lost the other day now. He was lost – a bit like Mark Thatcher*. It was spooky the way it was so parallel. He's got a flatmate called Clifford Smail. He and Cliff were doing a bit of snorkelling, and they were up at the barrier reef, which is beautiful coral, up near Australia. It's a bit like a beautiful bit of costume jewellery pinned on the bodice of Australia, and they were swimming around there looking for coral. They make coral jewellery. This jewellery was made by them. This is the rare black coral of Queensland and a little fashion tip for you ladies, and they were snorkelling and my son was lost, and Norm couldn't go out to him like old Denis because of his machine. It would sink straight to the bottom. Really, there is no provision on a prostate governor for a snorkel. I'm sorry, but there isn't, or Norm would have been down there with the sharks and the jellyfish looking for Kenny. He vanished off the face of the earth. I gave him a good old smack as I advised Margaret to give Mark, and she has.

You see, I don't divulge things. I can say that much about what VIPs and royalty say to me – and *they're* watching incidentally. They rang to tell me they were. Now what other guest of yours has been phoned just before the show by the Royal Family to say they're watching? I don't have a message for them now – we communicate in a different way altogether. We do, and this is why they like me, because they know their privacy is inviolate with me.

1982

---

*A celebrated mystery of the eighth decade of the twentieth century.

'Down under . . . we've got more
culture than a penicillin factory'
Sir Les Patterson

'I've had the odd fling but
I've never gone the whole way
. . . I might ask them in
for a cup of tea
. . . but I never play hospitals
with them'
Dame Edna Everage

'In school plays invariably
I played the eccentric parts
or housewives'
Barry Humphries

CLIVE JAMES

'The thinking woman's crumpet' – that's a terrible term, and I don't know how it got attached to me of all people. One thing that constantly impresses me about my own career is that what I am doing now has no connection with my childhood or even early adulthood. The extent to which sheer accident plays a part in one's life is absolutely staggering so that I don't like even to think about it.

I grew up just outside Sydney in a suburb which is on Botany Bay, just about where the first convicts landed. Australia is one of Britain's most successful exports because Australia began by Britain sending out its prisoners. My family were rich in personality – they weren't rich in any other ways. It was a very low income area but in Australia that is different from being low income in Britain. The standard of living is very high. Everyone had steak three times a day and that kind of thing! The toughest thing I had to talk about in my book *Unreliable Memoirs* was the loss of my father. I didn't realise how important it was to me until I sat down to write and I'm forty years old now. I never knew him (he died on his way back from being a prisoner of war), and I must have been a hell of a handful to bring up for my mother. Looking back on it now I realise that she must have had a hard time and I tried to put that in my book. But she was a great coper – she coped.

During the war we went to live in the bush because my father thought the Japanese would bomb the city. The house was full of characters – my aunt and my grandfather. Our loo was outside and it was unsewered. Every week the man would come to take away the full pan and bring another one and he was called the 'dunny-man'. The dunny-man arrived on the dunny-cart which came down the street – clank-bong, clank-bong and the idea was that you drew your blinds and didn't look because it was generally accepted that it wasn't discussed how the lavatory pan was changed every week. It wasn't a subject for gentlemen. Actually you could hear the dunny-man running down the side of the house and you could hear the clank-bong-clang as he picked up the full pan which after a week was bad news. He'd clip a lid on it – you could hear all this through the walls – and he'd run down the side of the house with the full pan on his shoulder. And he never, never missed his footing. But at Christmas you acknowledged the dunny-man's presence by leaving a bottle of beer in the dunny and by the time he got to us he must have sampled a lot of beer. I heard him come down the side of the house and then running back up the side but I'd left my bicycle there which he must have hurdled over on the way down, but on the way back he must have forgotten. I heard this terrific noise exactly like a man who is carrying a full dunny-can on his shoulder, tripping over a twenty-six inch frame bicycle. Then there was the even more sinister sound of the lid springing off – it made a boing, ping sound. I looked at my mother who had her hand over her eyes, she still wasn't acknowledging his existence. So I went out and I took a look down the side of the house and there he was and you know, well . . . the stunning thing was that none of it had missed him.

Australia is quite toxic. In England there are only adders but Australia is full of things that want to bite and sting you. There are two different kinds of completely lethal spiders – the funnel-web and the trapdoor. The funnel-web spider builds a sort of hole in the ground and lines it with silk and emerges from this tunnel at a high velocity and reveals itself to be a sort of ping-pong ball in a fox-fur coat. It can leap an incredible distance and sink its mandibles in you and you've had it. Now the trapdoor spider is the same only it puts a trapdoor over it so you can't see it.

It made a profound difference going to do National Service because it got me away from home and I quite liked home but a lot of humiliating things had happened there. For someone who has been craving order in his life the army is a very reassuring thing. Army discipline is a great gift because it tells you what to do every minute of the day. I quite liked that aspect. The single most impressive man in the army was the man in charge of the whole regiment called Ronald MacDonald. He was known throughout the army as 'Ronnie the One' and he was the single most terrifying man I've ever met in my life. His voice sounded like a train coming. His appearance was almost inconceivably unpleasant – a pig born looking like him would have demanded plastic surgery. We had someone in the army who should never have been there – he was called Peebles. I think the doctor who passed him as medically fit must have been having a joke on the army. He arrived in sections. He was so unco-ordinated, his fork missed his mouth when he ate and everything. The great thing about having a guy like that was that he was the lightning rod – he attracted all the aggravation.

Australia has changed so much since I left it twenty years ago. I went back and it now has got so much confidence. It's also so warm. The sheer heat and richness of the food and the colours and the brilliant light and everything. You can just lie around like a lizard which is why I don't think I could go back there because I am fundamentally a lazy character and there is a terrific temptation out there to work on your suntan. Going back there made me realise a few things and one of them was that I really value my privacy, like every other Englishman. For example I've got used to the idea that people don't immediately address you by your first name in Britain and it is a sign of friendship when you finally do, a declaration of intimacy. Well, in Australia you get on first name terms immediately and this leaves the language of intimacy nowhere to go. I mean you're friends from the first second. I find that rather bland and rather shocking which is a measure of how much I've changed because before I would never have noticed it.

Australians' attitude to Britain has changed profoundly – but this happened about the time Britain entered the Common Market. I think it was then that they woke up and realised that they weren't that close to Britain anymore and should find another place in the world. They found their own identity. It's a weird thing to leave your own country for a long time and then to go back and find it altered.

Sex was very funny stuff in Australia in the 1950s – there wasn't any. You thought about it all day and all night but nowadays I think the kids do what we thought about and we thought about nothing else which is of course the difference. It's the big reason for sexual liberation in that it moved sex off the front page as a subject. In the fifties everything we did was geared to this one concept, this forbidden activity. There was no way of doing anything about it but you thought and talked about women all the time. The thing is, you didn't talk to women while they were there though, because in Australia that wasn't done. They used to have a dance every Saturday which was called a 'church social' – the only reason you went to church was so that you could go to the church social. The social took place in the church hall and the music struck up, and all the men went up to one end of the hall and all the women went down to the other. And that's the way it stayed for three hours and nothing happened. I think the one advantage of not actually being able to engage in these activities was that you learned the language of inhibition and I think a lot of humour springs from that – I think our generation will probably be funnier about sex than the current generation which is just another aspect of life.

I was concerned with my appearance from daylight to dusk, usually about strange things which didn't really matter such as I was very worried when I was young about the back of my head which I thought stuck out too far and I used to spend a lot of time with two mirrors to see whether it stuck out. I wanted the back of my head to go in and my chin to go out. The first thing I was worried about was just pure size. I was very small before I matured and of course girls mature earlier anyway which is very, very daunting if you're a midget in these terrible shorts. All you want is a pair of long pants which you're not allowed until you're fourteen, or have got an adam's apple or something. I wanted pimples – other boys had pimples and I didn't – where were mine?

I suddenly found that I could answer the questions in the English classes. I had a good subject; I was good at spelling and I was good at words and as soon as you are good at something it gives you a role and it is very important to have a role. I had a permanent identity crisis which is still continuing now. I was very self-conscious and when I found I could answer the questions it made me a smart ass.

I'm not one of those people gifted by nature with wisdom – I have to learn everything by experience. This means that it has taken years to learn elementary things. I was painfully slow at school.

1980 and 1981

JONATHAN MILLER

The filming of the thirteen week series *The Body in Question* was enormous fun. It took me to a lot of places which I had always wanted to go to. There is a very extraordinary magic carpet feeling about writing anything for the BBC – you find yourself writing a line about some place and suddenly you're there and it's almost like the Midas touch – be careful because you find yourself writing about places which you normally wouldn't wish to go to, and you suddenly find yourself conveyed there whether you want to or not, you're bound and gagged and deposited in the middle of Africa or somewhere so in that sense it has been extraordinary.

There are passages of filming that are very hard and difficult, the worst aspect of the filming is something which no person ought to be exposed to. If anyone wanted to break the mentality of someone the best way to do it is the business of being exposed to one's own 'rushes' every night. People talk about white noise and having black bags over the head, but if you really want to break a person's personality in a short time, just expose him to endless versions of himself speaking lines which he has written and after a while he will give everything away!

I won't see the series – I usually go to the top of the house and pretend it's not happening and look out elsewhere. I can't bear to see myself on the screen especially having seen it three thousand times on the editing machine. It would be an absolute nightmare.

We went to Africa – Nairobi – by an ordinary civil airline and then we had to hang around and hire a small light aircraft to fly from Kenya to the southern Sudan. We were going to film a small tribe who an English anthropologist called Pritchard went to investigate in the 1920s. I was very interested in the reports that the anthropologist had brought back about the way in which the tribe regarded illness and misfortune. All serious illness was the result of the malice of others – either produced by witchcraft or sorcery. In the West, we think illness is the result of some physical cause and we expect to diagnose it by examining the body, whereas they have no interest in the body at all and they look for culprits rather than causes and their diagnostic machines, their oracles, are used to identify the person who did it. It's a 'who did it?' rather than a 'what did it?' They investigate and try to find the person who brought about this misfortune. In the old days if someone was proved to be a witch she could have been killed. A witch for them was not quite as it is for us, for them it is someone who has a congenital defect, a cyst under the liver which heats up and broadcasts some malignant influence which produces illness or misfortune, which can cause a granary to fall down or a crop failure.

I wanted to show by going there how the different views of cause and effect are regarded in connection with illness. For them their medicine is really a branch of law, for them it is a civil action, because it cures grudges in their community. In this way it isn't an accident that the word 'remedy' is used in both law and medicine.

It is interesting to ask why people in this country do seek their solutions outside conventional medicine, now that conventional medicine is comparatively successful in comparison with fifty years ago when you could have removed doctors from the scene and it would have made no difference. In the 1830s if you had removed them the population would have gone up slightly because they bled people and purged them so vigorously that they actually killed them. But the reason why I think people seek some sort of redress outside medicine now is because there are awful illnesses which a doctor cannot do anything about – often not the serious ones, but the chronic ones such as backaches and colds. But there is a much more important reason now and that is that there is a dread and a fear of modern science, a feeling that science is inhuman, that it neglects all the warmth and spirituality of human beings and that therefore we should look elsewhere for some sort of medical practice which acknowledges what we feel to be our humanity. I think that this is a gross simplification. It wasn't until we got scientific medicine that we could treat people as machines and put things back in them and therefore improve them as human beings.

Until the turn of this century a doctor had nothing of practical importance to offer anyway. Therefore he had to swathe himself in mystery in order to continue his medical practice. In addition to the skill and expert knowledge which a doctor brings to bear on the body, the patient can nevertheless withhold his recovery if the patient is not in a relationship with the doctor as a person – not mystical – purely personal. Unless he has confidence, warmth and affection the patient can almost vengefully withhold his improvement. What we call the charismatic element of medicine is very important.

The 'pantomime of complaint' is something which is vanishing from a lot of medical training – which is the attention to the diction and the style and the stance of a patient as he tells you his or her story. A patient is giving an account of their situation as they complain – this is not merely an account of the illness but also a short story about themselves. By hearing the patient talk and by watching what they do with their hands in describing themselves, you are actually hearing a portrait painted of the personality. The doctor must watch everything while the story is being told and this skill is perhaps becoming underplayed now, partly because doctors, if they are sloppy, can rely too much on the machinery and think they can get the answer simply by the biochemistry.

What is happening today is not that people are living longer but that more people are being allowed to live the biblical span of life, and are being allowed to complete the course because we have removed the main hazards of illness in the first six months of life which is where the main chances of death were, and so more people are allowed to reach seventy but whether we extend this is a debatable point – probably not. The important thing is not to ask for immortality but to ask for a better life within mortality which is something modern medicine has given. But we must also recognise that the improvements in life are nothing to do with medicine at all.

1978

CHRISTIAAN BARNARD

I have just finished editing a book called *The Body Machine*. In many ways, certain parts of the body can be compared with man-made machines. It is never possible to compare the whole body with machines made by human beings because you must remember the human body has evolved as a result of millions and millions of years of experience and experimentation so it's much more complex than any machine that man can make. The book was actually written at the request of hundreds of thousands of people all over the world. As I travelled along I found that lay people wanted to know more about their bodies – how the various systems work, what they can do to maintain adequate function and what to do if something goes wrong. The book first describes the systems of the body: the cardiovascular system, respiratory system, digestive system and nervous system, and then it goes on to the maintenance of those systems.

After all, everybody takes their car to a garage after so many miles for a service, but we don't think about our bodies. If you hear a noise in your car, then you take it to the garage because you want to know what the noise is all about, but if you hear a noise inside your body and things are wrong, you just take it for granted – the 'it will never happen to me' attitude. For instance, extra beats of your heart, excess noises of the stomach rumbling could be very important, the start of an obstruction in the bowel which may be a cancer. You can feel if something is going wrong inside the body machine, but you do nothing about it.

When this book first came out people immediately asked me if a little knowledge wasn't a dangerous thing. My reply to that is that was a little knowledge may be a dangerous thing but *no* knowledge is even more dangerous and I think it is important to know something about your body.

I still think that the most important goal in medicine is to improve the quality of life, to give the individual a better life – not so much a longer life. If you withdraw something from an individual with the purpose of giving him a longer life, but this makes him completely miserable, then I think that's wrong. I think that one should first see that individual is happy about what he is doing. I am not somebody that encourages smoking – in fact I ask most of my patients to stop smoking – but you sometimes find that an individual becomes really miserable when they stop smoking. Under those circumstances I would say that if they were to cut down to about five cigarettes a day, then I don't see how that can be so very wrong. For the same reason, I also say in the book that fat people should not worry themselves about dieting – they become so miserable that it's not worth it.

I also deal with the process of ageing in the book. I would have no hesitation in having a facelift, although I haven't so far. I think that in many ways plastic surgery is more important than heart surgery because if you have a hole in the heart, nobody sees the hole, but if you have wrinkles and bags under your eyes, everybody can see this. If you look better, you enjoy life more. I'm not a plastic surgeon – I don't know how to do a facelift, but I think what usually happens is that even though the end result is not perfect – you can see that the skin is stretched – it is better than before the facelift.

It will be a tragedy if we do reach the point where we can prolong life indefinitely. Death is essential to life because it is only through death that you can get a new life and it is only through death that you can get a different life. If there was no death there would never have been any evolution because evolution occurred by the old species dying out and better species being born. So death is absolutely essential and we should never try to eliminate it. What we could try and do is not make people live longer lives, but better lives. Life span has never changed since man was created because it is genetically determined by evolution and every species has a predetermined life span. Each species must live long enough to adapt to environmental changes and to reproduce – that is all that we are here for really. Some living organisms need eight hours to do that – man needs one hundred years. Now life expectancy has changed because of control of disease and we frequently live under optimal environmental conditions. There would be no sense in increasing life expectancy if it does not go hand in hand with a more enjoyable life.

I support euthanasia and I actually carried it out on my own mother. She was terminally ill – she had had many strokes and was paralysed, and she developed pneumonia. We could have treated the pneumonia with antibiotics, but what would have been the sense? To prolong her existence for another month or two? There is no sense in that. Once we have exhausted all medical means of maintaining an acceptable quality of life, it is our duty as doctors to terminate that treatment. It is only if a doctor actively terminates life that he can be charged with murder – that is called active euthanasia. Unfortunately, active euthanasia in the world today is murder so I have never practised active euthanasia, but there is a real need for it in medicine. To me it is very hypocritical really that I can actively turn off a respirator to allow a patient to die but if, instead of turning the respirator off, I gave the patient an overdose of a drug, that is murder – and there is very little difference between the two actions. The thing that always amuses me when we talk about active euthanasia is that when you ask the right to end the existence of a terminally ill patient, the world is horrified but we take lives all the time – we send people to war, in some countries there is capital punishment and we accept this. In England you even accept abortions, but that is taking a life – you are denying life to that child. But when you see an individual with no quality of life anymore, and where all medical methods to help that person have been exhausted, people say you cannot terminate that existence.

The heart is such a simple organ that if there is anything we can make mechanically, it is the heart. It has one function: it is a pump, and we can make pumps so there is a great possibility that one day people will be walking around with mechanical hearts. There are still some problems, but I do believe that in the very near future mechanical hearts will be used – as temporary devices, not permanent. I think we are very far away from the 'bionic' man. There are many things we can replace today, but I don't think we could ever make a computer that would match the human brain.

I once tried acupuncture in an effort to cure my arthritis and the doctor put many needles into my hands, legs and behind my ears and the next day I had the worst attack of arthritis I have ever had. James Coburn told me that he was completely cured of the same thing by drinking only water for about three weeks. I think that some of those treatments are like the man who sat banging his head against a wall because he felt so much better when he stopped. I am not ruling out fringe medicine at all – I think it plays a very important part in psychosomatic disorders, but there is no sort of fancy medicine that can correct a leaking heart valve.

1981

DESMOND MORRIS

As a student of human behaviour I was attracted to the game of football. When I was in Malta, I took my five year old son to a game of football and it ended in a complete riot because they decided to kill the referee and the poor man had to flee, literally for his life, and he flew into the bit of grandstand beneath us. I was studying human aggression at the time so it was a field day for me and I was observing the colour change when people fight – some go red, others go white and it was all fascinating.

When we came back to England my son had become a football fanatic so I took him to see the local team. While he was wrapped up in the tactics and strategy of the game, I was much more interested in the crowd and by the intensity of the passion that was being aroused. It was like something of an ancient ritual – a tribal gathering. The faces weren't faces that were being entertained, they weren't relaxed. I could see anger, apprehension, anxiety and occasionally ecstasy on the faces. This led me eventually into my book *The Soccer Tribe*, the tribal warriors being the players and the witch doctors being the managers. I had to get to know the fans, players, directors and supporters. There is a myth about players – that they are thick – but it simply isn't true. If you give them an intelligence test which depends on quick thinking, but that doesn't require bookish skills, then you find that they are extremely bright. Their intelligence is geared to muscular movement more than to verbal action and it is only those who can translate that quickness of reaction into words who become the great managers, and they are full of the most wonderful phrasing and quick response.

As far as all this embracing between players on the field is concerned, FIFA have just issued an edict stating that embracing after the scoring of a goal is to be prohibited because it is unmanly, effeminate, which is ludicrous of course. In this country and in most of north western Europe, we have a long tradition of holding back – we don't embrace male friends when we meet. In Mediterranean countries it is a perfectly natural thing to do and it *is* a perfectly natural thing to do. It's got nothing to do with sex, it's just an act of love and joy. As Denis Law once said: 'When you've scored a goal you feel like a bit of a kiss.' There is nothing sexual about kissing.

Following this through, I find Eammon Andrews' programme *This is your Life* absolutely fascinating because it's real human behaviour from real people who aren't used to being in that situation. If you watch the introductions in this programme, when you have a male 'victim' and a male guest arrives and they haven't seen each other for thirty years, the 'victim' gets up and as they meet, on numerous occasions, the natural thing is for them to embrace. But because of our cultural inhibitions you see the movement towards it and then it freezes and they go into a handshake or something else. The natural urge to make contact is held back. It's a curiously British thing and it's all down to the Victorian period when there was suppression of everything with all sorts of restrictions put upon us.

It's about fifteen years since I've worked with animals as I've been working on our own species, and I must confess I'm thinking about returning again to animals – I'm getting very nostalgic about them. I miss the depth of involvement I had with animals, especially when I think back to the last wild animal I had a strong relationship with – a Chinese Water Deer which had been hand-reared in the bedroom by my wife. Eventually it actually escaped and got onto the London underground and if you've ever tried to catch a deer with a ten foot butterfly net on the London underground, you'll realise that I do miss my animal days!

I've now been asked to go off on an animal safari around the world and I must say I am looking forward to that because waking up in Africa and opening your door and finding fifteen zebra standing outside is magical. I want to try and get some of that magic into people's sitting-rooms if I can.

1981

DAVID BELLAMY

I don't really think I had any early ambitions at all. Mum and dad wanted me to be a medic and I thought it would be rather fun to be a doctor, but I don't think I would have ever had the right bedside manner – you can't wear welly boots for a start, except in the operating theatre. I drifted through school and enjoyed it enormously, or at any rate I enjoyed the sports and chasing the girls from the school next door. Consequently I left school with very little to go on and had a variety of jobs. Then, at the age of twenty-two, I met two guys who told me that I had something between my ears and that it really was fun to learn, and I think that was the turning point for me. They were both biologists, so I suddenly went into biology and botany. Had I not met those two guys, I'm not sure what would have become of me; the one thing I had always wanted to do was to go into the ballet, but when I was fourteen and a half stone at the age of fourteen I knew it was impossible!

I think there are the Albert Einsteins in this world, and thank goodness there aren't too many of them because too many theories of relativity would turn us all off. But then there are the rest of us – this wonderful block of humanity – and I don't think there is all that much difference in the level of ability once you have found the thing you are able in. These days there are so many children being forced through our educational system, I think a lot of them really do miss out, and are very often educated totally irrelevantly. I don't think that children at school have ever been exposed to the full spectrum of life, living and relevance of learning. Also television goes about its educational programmes the wrong way. For example, you have the poor old Open University with a budget of say £600 to make a programme on the nation's architecture and at the same time you have one of the other channels spending a quarter of a million on making exactly the same thing. One goes out as 'education' and the other goes out as 'entertainment'. I think there could be an enormous balancing up there. Children should be exposed to exciting things on television as education, rather than exciting things say that, for example, David Bellamy happens to be doing on television. None of what I do on television is 'show business', I don't put an act on.

Teaching is just an extension of acting and I think that every teacher really should go to RADA or somewhere similar – it would do us all a lot of good. You have to project yourself, it's no good going behind the lecture bench and being all wishy-washy and reading your lecture notes. You have got to prepare it and you have got to get butterflies in your stomach before you walk out there and do it. I know that if I don't get butterflies before giving a lecture it will be a bad one. I think I am labelled as somewhat of an eccentric because of my extrovert manner, but I can ride that one.

I have been around the world three times in the past two years and been exposed to people from the most developed to the least developed, and I have found that everywhere there is a sense of wonder. Once you have that sense of wonder and once you understand, you want to pass that understanding on to other people. I think that the energy crisis which now faces the whole world is now pushing us back to the importance of local communities and they are beginning to work again. I think that the next decade could be one of the most exciting times for really revolutionary social change within the developed countries of the world. Not just the alternative technology thing, but the refinding of what people and local communities are all about. I think we could emerge the noble savage again.

1979

CHRIS BONINGTON

When I went to visit the people whose adventures are described in my book *Quest for Adventure* I felt immediately that we had something in common. We relaxed into a friendship in the first few minutes of actually sitting down and talking and it wasn't just a one way thing. The motives for adventure are the same whatever the adventure might be – it might be mountaineering, it might be someone who wants to fly across the Atlantic in a balloon, it might be a sailor. Firstly there is a tremendous questing drive of curiosity, of wanting to know what is round the next corner in a valley, what's over the horizon on the seas, and also a curiosity about yourself – wanting to delve down into yourself and then stretch yourself each time to further limits. Involved with this is also a feeling of the risk and this is what I think all adventurers have to different degrees.

Climbing is not actually doing something dangerous, dangerously; the elation comes from being in what seems an extremely dangerous situation when literally your life is in your hands. The elation is having mastery of that situation, feeling completely relaxed in that situation and when you have done a series of really difficult moves and there is almost a kind of poetry in that movement and in the perfection of those moves – it must be like acting.

I wondered at first what I would have in common with the American astronauts who are the end product of technology. When I went out there to talk to them I started out with a prejudice against them and thought: they are not the same as I am – they are mostly service people who have risen through their organisation – they are little puppets being manipulated by computers. I went to see Neil Armstrong; he has retired as an astronaut and is the chairman of a big company. I got into his big office and he has a huge desk and there he was in his dark suit and I thought: I wonder what I've got in common with him? We started talking and at first it was really stilted. Then he started talking about his flying, before he became an astronaut, and he was talking about taking his plane to the absolute outer threshold of its limits and I suddenly realised he was using exactly the same language and he was just as cool as the climber. The climber isn't romantic in his climbing – the climber is dead cool – he was dead cool about taking himself to this threshold and I suddenly realised 'we are the same people' and it really pleased me and it meant that I could write a chapter about the astronauts with a perception which I couldn't possibly have done otherwise.

I would be dead scared of cave diving which I think is the creepiest, most extreme form of all the adventures that I looked at. The cave diver is diving into a cave that is completely waterlogged. Visibility is practically nil because there is a lot of sediment on the ground so there is just the narrow pool of yellow light that is lit by his lamps as he swims or crawls – of course he has his aqualung strapped to him – that to me is further than the other side of the moon.

I have always climbed but unfortunately no one will actually pay you just to climb so one has to have a living too, and my living happens to be writing and taking photographs. I am going to Everest next year because I have never been to the top and I would like to go there. It's absolutely true that if you want to climb Everest that you have to book – in fact it's booked until 1992 but we managed to get to the front end of the queue to go in from China, and we will be following the route taken by the pre-war British expedition. It means that you are almost a part of history. But we are going to try a somewhat different route; we are going to try the East/North East ridge.

I suppose I have been near to death climbing about eight or nine times in different ways – sometimes nearly stepping into a crevasse. I think the worst was years ago when I had just started to climb and I was with a friend of mine who was a great solo climber. We were climbing a new route in Skye and he had gone up first; we were climbing without a rope and were about five or six hundred feet above the deck and I'd taken the rock for granted as he had been up before me and the rock just wasn't there. I swung and was just hanging on by one hand and I could feel my hand going off. Fortunately I have very slow reactions and my instincts therefore kept me in balance and kept me cool and I got back into balance and got back onto the rock again and managed to get to the top.

I climb for the fun of it which could be called irresponsible if one is a father and a husband but it is something I desperately need to do – my wife Wendy accepted it. It is an indulgence but I hope that these adventures give something back to society. I think they have, because you have to go to society to get finance for them; society gets something back, primarily from the story we are able to give to people. It's not just the vicarious thrill. I think it's the sharing of a precarious adventure that perhaps they dream of doing although they might never do it. I think this is the serious contribution that the adventurer gives and the other thing is that unless people have got this, perhaps, irrational desire for adventure I don't think the world would ever go on – I think you need this for the development of the world – this irrational, restless urge and this is what I hope we've got.

1981

ALAN WHICKER

I hate being interviewed. If your best side is the back of the head, as it is with me, I'd be much happier sitting here asking *you* questions. For example, I had a very nice Scots corporal during the War who turned up afterwards in Fleet Street, and one day rang me and said, 'Look, you've got a Series coming up, could I come and do a story about you?' and I said, 'No, I don't want to be interviewed – I'd much rather not.' '*Please* do it, you lead such an interesting life . . .' He went on and on, so finally and reluctantly I said OK. He came along and I struggled to make an effort, tried to produce some interesting stories for him. He took notes for an hour or two and when he got up to go he said: 'Well, Alan, it's good to see you again and you're still quite a pleasant chap but, let's face it, you *are* a bit full of yourself.' You can't win.

Interviewing styles are different: your style is a long way from mine. I get conversations on film, and let people relax in their own surroundings, whereas you're interviewing here in a television studio. They're coming in and putting on a show for you – they're doing a performance. You keep them waiting behind here, getting all nervous and tense – so you're trying to get them on edge, whereas I'm trying to relax them, to keep them natural.

I don't think I'm blasé about the amount of travelling I do. If you enjoy travel, as I do, as soon as you board a plane you want a window seat, you want to see, you're excited, you want to get moving. When I was writing *Within Whicker's World* this year, it was the first time for goodness knows how long that I'd not been on the move – so now I'm absolutely ready to set off again. In fact I'm going to Leeds tomorrow. *There*'s exotic travel for you!

At the age of twelve, I think it was, I got my first typewriter. I wanted to travel and I wanted to write and, of course, I've never stopped doing both – so I've been most fortunate. I think what started it all for me were the beaches in those travel brochures – the silver sands, the waving palms. As I sat in Suffolk and Middlesex at the age of fourteen and looked at those I thought: these are the places I must get to.

The only time I ever contemplated changing the direction of my life was once during the War when I could have had so much money that I would never have had to lift a finger again. I was about nineteen and in Italy. I was then in the Army Film Unit, directing cameramen in battle. The army was about its business and I was on my own in a car with my driver – and I captured Milan! I arrived ahead of the troops and got to the Piazza del Duomo when a lot of partisans came up and said that the Germans who were occupying the city would not surrender to them, but only to an Allied officer – and I was the only one around! So I went to this hotel where there were armed SS men at every window and behind barricades. The SS general saluted and handed me his revolver and explained that he *would* surrender to a British officer – although he was a little distressed at my lowly rank. Then his adjutant said to me: 'On top of everything else, Captain, there's this trunk.' This he regarded as very important. When I opened it, it was stuffed with money, the pay for the German army in Italy, the SS treasure chest – money of every possible currency. Millions! What I *could* have done was to tell my driver just to slip it into the car, when I would have driven back to my Italian friends in Florence, buried it, and gone back a few years later to claim it – and never worked again!

I've been lucky all my life. As a War Correspondent in Korea I was reported dead, because one day as I was about to fly back to Tokyo to file a story, I went up in an artillery spotter plane to help the pilot by working out map references of enemy positions, and a second plane that was in the next valley was shot down. It was reported in the papers that I'd been killed – an embarrassingly small story, I noticed – so that was *another* life gone . . .

Perhaps the most frightening interview I've done was the Papa Doc in Haiti. He very rarely came out of his palace but with a bit of Whicker's luck, the very day we reached Haiti he was going to inaugurate a new building. We got to it early and the men with machine guns, the Tontons Macoute, moved aside when confronted by me saying: 'Excuse me, clear a path, British television,' like a school prefect, which was the last thing they were expecting. We got alongside Papa Doc quickly when he arrived, as we'd been told that once we were seen *talking* to President Duvalier, we would not be killed. He asked us to go to the palace to see him next day, and became flattered by being filmed, and invited me to tour Port au Prince with him in his bullet-proof Mercedes. He would drive along and in order to gather the crowds and prove his popularity, every now and then would throw money out of the window. Then when he got out of the car, he'd peel notes from an enormous wad and just hand them out to people. That was the man who used to go down to the dungeons beneath his palace and watch prisoners being tortured.

I think my basic philosophy about reporting is telling it like it is, going into every programme straight down the middle and trying to find out what's happening – not going into a situation committed before you start.

Do you remember the woman in Palm Beach who had her breasts fixed and said if she died she wanted to be buried topless – as having *had* them done, she wanted someone to see them? Then there was the plastic surgeon and his wife I interviewed in Los Angeles. He, in fact, had completely remodelled his wife, and to them it was a very serious business. She told me then that her husband would never have to divorce her as he could always change her. He had already operated on her eyes, ears, chin and her breasts – which was her 'favourite operation' as she had previously worn two or three falsies on each side and was liable to bounce off her partner at dances, if held too close! She chose the medium size as the extra large are very heavy, she said – about a pound on each side! It seemed that appearing on television with me really validated her life. Often in America people don't believe they exist until they see their picture in the paper, and to appear on television is the ultimate validation.

Years ago on the BBC we were doing a programme about people in trouble and one chap I remember was a male prostitute, a homosexual transvestite junkie. You think *you've* got problems? He told me that our interview was the first time he had had a serious conversation with anyone for years, because he was living in some doss-house with a prostitute and used to get up at midday and go to a news theatre where he'd spend the whole day before coming out at night to turn a trick. He developed a sort of fixation upon us because we treated him as a normal person and tried to look after him, tried to care for him. Then about six weeks later he was found dead, in a telephone box.

Spending a month filming with the police in San Francisco was also an insight and once again, we're back to this validation thing, because I remember one run we had was to a man who had been almost murdered in a flea-bag hotel. We went screaming through the streets at a hundred miles an hour and when we arrived, there were about twenty people in the lobby of the hotel, watching television. We went upstairs and behind a locked door was a drug dealer and somebody had taken a tyre-iron to him and bashed one side of his head in. I raced downstairs and radioed for an ambulance, and when it arrived, the stretcher came up through the lobby and the bandaged man was put on to it and carried down – and all the time these people kept on watching 'Spiderman', while behind them was this man who was almost dead, police, television crew, ambulance men . . . To those people – and this is typical in many strata of America – 'Spiderman' was more real than the drama going on behind them.

As far as Press speculation about my private life is concerned, I find it all rather boring. I don't believe that *anybody*, apart from the Press, finds my private life interesting. I don't want to talk about it. I think if you live as we do, you have to keep something back for your friends – not go pouring everything out to any reporter who asks. I try to be a private person and I would like the Press to treat me as I treat other people.

I started travelling in my teens and I've never stopped, so if you are forever wandering, you do miss a lot. Careerwise it's very satisfying, but once you've lived like this for years it's hard to stop and settle for domesticity. I think I've got the best job in the world, and I always set off with joy and excitement.

1982

BARBARA WOODHOUSE

I am absolutely amazed at the success of my series on dog training. I've really been doing it for thirty years and nobody has paid the slightest attention to me except the dogs and suddenly it seems to have become a sort of 'joke' show. The owners catch it pretty hot sometimes, but they like it you know. There was one poor lady who really got ticked off all the time because she did everything wrong and at the end of it she wrote me a most charming letter saying that she had never enjoyed anything so much in her life!

Now that I have become 'famous', people do recognise me when I go out. I certainly have a different relationship now with my butcher who thinks I'm better than Les Dawson! As long as I am amusing people as well as entertaining them and training people to train their dogs, that's fine. The lack of training in this country is terrible – people let their dogs behave very badly and they can't control them. It is only lack of instruction so I hoped my series would teach them in a simple way – if it is hilarious, all well and good – to get their dogs to be really obedient because it is so much more fun to have a dog that everybody loves instead of everybody hating it.

I use this very special choke chain – it's got rather big links and people think it's heavy but it is very light and a little dachshund came to me once who would not go in the show ring – she was terrified. So I put a choke chain on her and told her owner to take her into the ring like that. As she was going in, a great, big, fat woman with five dachshunds said to her: 'Fancy going into the ring with a great big chain like that – my goat wears a smaller one than that.' Anyway as luck would have it, my little pupil took the first prize and as the owner came out of the ring she turned to this great fat woman and said 'Bring your goat next time!'

When I am training a dog, there is always a doubt in my mind that I may not be able to do it, but I have tremendous confidence that the dogs can pick it up by telepathy and I believe that telepathy is everything. I get onto the dog's wavelength and if the owner keeps chattering, I can't do it. They cross my wavelength like interference on a radio, but if they leave me entirely alone for two or three minutes, and I reckon basically to train a dog in six minutes. I can pick that dog up and it will obey me and instantaneously be fairly obedient – it will sit and walk to heel and stay until I call it when it should come and sit in front of me.

I've been bitten very badly by dogs, but always by a 'mental' dog. I was bitten by a schizophrenic dog – I had been kissing it all day, heaven help me, and then it was free in the field with a lot of other dogs and it attacked me. I had sixty two stitches in all from trying to prise a bulldog off my arm. Ten minutes later that dog was lovely again – it's awfully sad. We have a lot of schizophrenic dogs these days – they will suddenly attack babies in prams or their owners and I think it is because they are overfed. They are getting too much protein, too much meat and too many unnatural things, and probably not getting enough exercise. They are also under stress as people go to work and leave their dogs all day long and they tear up the furniture. One person left their dog in a car and there was nothing left of it when she came back – it had even eaten the seat belt!

I think it is revolting that pavements are so fouled in London, but you can't blame the dogs, it's the owners who are at fault. People should train their dogs to perform on command. I give the command 'quickie' for puddling and 'hurry up' for the other function. There is a true story about a little boy who went to his mother the other day and told her he had been watching my programme and that I talked about 'puddling' and 'the other function'. Then he said: 'Don't ask me to go to the loo, simply tell me to go and do "the other function".' It is perfectly simple to teach a dog to perform on command from the age of eight weeks on, and you have to choose a nice spot that won't offend people. If you can't, then you must carry a small spade and plastic gloves in your shopping basket. There are impossible people though; I was walking through our village the other day and I saw an Alsatian puppy on a lead and it was about to misbehave on the pavement. So I automatically grabbed it and dragged it into the kerb where it performed. Out got a furious woman from her car and said: 'How dare you let your filthy dog mess near my car!'

My own dogs were trained from six weeks old and they knew at least two hundred and fifty words and commands. I believe that dogs have tremendous brains if you develop them. One day, my husband told our Great Dane to go and fetch her feeding bowl and our other little dog's bowl. So she went off and she thought it would save her legs if she put them inside each other. She picked the two round bowls up, put them inside each other and brought them. So we thought we would test her out and we put a square dish and a round one down and she looked at them for a few seconds and then she put them side by side and picked them up by the two edges, side by side. People just don't realise how clever their dogs are and just don't develop their brains. Because my dog Junior worked in films I used to think of new tricks for her to do all the time. She could open windows, ring the gong, hoover the floor, strip the beds and put the dirty linen in the basket, water the garden with the hosepipe – and she answered the telephone by taking the receiver off and putting it on the floor and fetching me!

I don't prefer animals to humans – I love humans, but they have to obey me! I'm afraid I treat them rather as dogs sometimes but it is true to say that dogs are ten times quicker at picking things up at training sessions than their owners. This is what is so funny, and what makes the series hilarious.

1980

ROD HULL & EMU

I was doing a show in Australia and somebody sent me a large emu's egg. I put it on the radiator and it grew steadily until one day there was this knocking sound and it hatched, and that's where I got the idea for my emu from. I have an extraordinary relationship with Emu and he does things which I secretly want to do, but I'm a bit of a coward. All the things I would love to do with people, Emu does for me, because who is going to punch an emu? Like going into a supermarket – haven't you ever wanted to go in and knock over all the piles of tins and toilet rolls? Well, I did it with Emu and it was ever so good!

I really don't see how Emu can be frightening for children at all – I think that is an adult conception. Some kids are a little wary of him but I make sure that when I am with them I don't take Emu over to the frightened kids, but I can guarantee that within three or four minutes those kids have come over to Emu.

Emu is very happy here in the studio – I'm not sure why he is looking at you like that. He is really very friendly, but he does have to get your scent first. He really isn't at all aggressive – once you get to know him!

1976

Listed below are the names of the guests
Michael Parkinson interviewed during the
361 editions of 'Parkinson', broadcast over
eleven years:

Larry Adler
Jenny Agutter
Anouk Aimée
Alan Alda
Muhammad Ali
Chesney Allen
Dave Allen
Peter Alliss
Kenneth Allsop
Anthony Andrews
Eamonn Andrews
Julie Andrews
John Arlott
Lord Arran
Arthur Ashe
Arthur Askey
Michael Aspel
Fred Astaire
Rowan Atkinson
David Attenborough
W.H. Auden
George Axelrod
Pam Ayres
Charles Aznavour

Lauren Bacall
Barbara Bach
Sir Douglas Bader
Ronnie Barker
Isabel Barnett
Christiaan Barnard
Blaster Bates
The Bee Gees
David Bellamy
Ray Bellisario
Tony Benn
Alan Bennett
Tony Bennett
Jack Benny
Michael Bentine
Ingrid Bergman
George Best
Sir John Betjeman
Jacqueline Bisset
James Blades
Danny Blanchflower
Lt Col John Blashford-Snell
Claire Bloom
Miss Bluebell

Dirk Bogarde
Chris Bonington
Lord Boothby
Victor Borge
Ernest Borgnine
Borra
Reginald Bosanquet
Max Boyce
Geoffrey Boycott
Katie Boyle
Bernard Braden
Commissioner Catherine
    Bramwell-Booth
Chris Brasher
Julian Bream
Bricktop
Leslie Bricusse
Dr Jacob Bronowski
Elkie Brooks
Mel Brooks
Yul Brynner
Dee Brown
Faith Brown
Georgia Brown
Janet Brown
Isobel Buchanan
Art Buchwald
Peter Bull
Anthony Burgess
James Burke
George Burns
Raymond Burr
Richard Burton
Sir Matt Busby
Max Bygraves
Douglas Byng

Earl of Caernarvon
James Cagney
Sammy Cahn
Marti Caine
Michael Caine
James Cameron
Glen Campbell
Patrick Campbell
Chan Canasta
Cannon and Ball
Al Capp
Charlie Carioli

Lesley Caron
Georges Carpentier
Lord Carrington
Willie Carson
Lynda Carter
Mike Carter
Barbara Cartland
Barbara Castle
Roy Castle
Peter Cavanagh
Jackie Charlton
Carol Channing
Graham Chapman
Lorraine Chase
Kyung-Wha Chung
Petula Clark
John Cleese
Brian Clough
James Coburn

Norman Collier
Joan Collins
Perry Como
Denis Compton
Billy Connolly
William Conrad
John Conteh
Tom Conti
Peter Cook
Alistair Cooke
Henry Cooper
Tommy Cooper
Ronnie Corbett
Robin Cousins
Jacques Cousteau
Fanny Cradock
Elizabeth Craig
Quentin Crisp
Gemma Craven
Michael Crawford
Bing Crosby
Andrew Cruickshank
John Curry
Tony Curtis
René Cutforth

Roald Dahl
John Dankworth
Paul Daniels

Jim Davidson
Windsor Davies
Bette Davis
Sammy Davis Jnr
Les Dawson
Sir Robin Day
Blossom Dearie
Frank Delaney
Paco de Lucia
Jack Dempsey
Robert de Niro
Florence Desmond
Angie Dickinson
Barbara Dickson
Richard Digance
Phyllis Diller
Sacha Distel
Ken Dodd
Basil D'Oliveira
Placido Domingo
Val Doonican
Diana Dors
Kirk Douglas
Phil Drabble
Nell Dunn
Gerald Durrell
Lawrence Durrell
Ian Dury

Billy Eckstine
Blake Edwards
Jimmy Edwards
Percy Edwards
Britt Ekland
Duke Ellington
Dick Emery
Rowland Emett
David Essex
Dick Evans
Dame Edith Evans
Sir Geraint Evans
Harold Evans
Kenny Everett

Douglas Fairbanks Jnr
Adam Faith
Georgie Fame
Vic Feather
Marty Feldman
José Feliciano
Fenella Fielding
Gracie Fields
Jack Fingleton
Chris Finnegan
Cyril Fletcher

Henry Fonda
Peter Fonda
Dame Margot Fonteyn
Michael Foot
Bryan Forbes
Bruce Forsyth
Frederick Forsyth
Edward Fox
Clare Francis
David Frost

J.K. Galbraith
James Galway
Bob Geldof
Lord George-Brown
Sir John Gielgud
Lillian Gish
Brian Glover
Tito Gobbi
Joe Gormley
Elliott Gould
Dr Billy Graham
Stewart Grainger
Stephane Grappelli
Larry Grayson
Juliette Greco
Benny Green
Hughie Green
Joyce Grenfell
Joel Grey
Kenneth Griffith
Sir Alec Guinness

General Sir John Hackett
Lord Hailsham
Adelaide Hall
Marvin Hamlisch
Susan Hampshire
Sheila Hancock
Richard Harris
Rolf Harris
Rex Harrison
Mike Harding
Russell Harty
Goldie Hawn
Helen Hayes
Helene Hayman
Denis Healey
Edward Heath
Tippi Hedren
Sir Robert Helpman
David Hemmings
Dickie Henderson
Woody Herman
Charlton Heston

Thor Heyerdhal
Henry Higgins
Graham Hill
Jimmy Hill
Sir Edmund Hillary
Thora Hird
Sheila Hocken
Dustin Hoffman
Stanley Holloway
Celeste Holm
Bob Hope
Anthony Hopkins
Antony Hopkins
Trevor Howard
Frankie Howerd
Roy Hudd
Peter Hudson
Rod Hull and Emu
Engelbert Humperdinck
Barry Humphries
James Hunt
Rita Hunter
John Huston
Wilfred Hyde-White

Eric Idle
Brian Inglis

Tony Jacklin
Glenda Jackson
David Jacobs
Clive James
Olga James
Ricky Jay
Lionel Jefferies
Clive Jenkins
Elton John
Olivia Newton-John
Glynis Johns
Brian Johnston
Jack Jones

Kiri Te Kanawa
Fred Kaps
Robert Kee
Kevin Keegan
Penelope Keith
Barbara Kelly
Gene Kelly
Felicity Kendall
Deborah Kerr
Barney Kessel
Lord Kilbracken
Alan King
Jonathan King
The King Singers

Pat Kirkwood
Dr Henry Kissinger
Eartha Kitt
David Kossoff

Cleo Laine
Eric Laithwaite
Laurie Lee
Michel Legrand
Tom Lehrer
Jack Lemmon
John and Yoko Lennon
Alan Jay Lerner
Bernard Levin
Revd Don Lewis
Liberace
Patrick Lichfield
Maureen Lipman
Jeannie Little
Little and Large
Jeremy Lloyd
Jimmy Logan
Gina Lollobrigida
Anita Loos
Harry Lorayne
Jacques Loussier
Lulu
Joanna Lumley
Dame Vera Lynn
Ben Lyon
Humphrey Lyttleton
Shirley MacLaine
Dame Fiona MacLeod
Michael MacLiammoir
Walter McCorrisken
Alec McCowen
Donald McCullin
Roger McGough
Don McLean
Laurie McMenemy
Ralph McTell
Magnus Magnusson
Norman Mailer
Henry Mancini
Manhattan Transfer
Barry Manilow
Bernard Manning
Marcel Marceau
Sir Robert Mark
Dame Alicia Markova
Alfred Marks
Arthur Marshall
Mary Martin
Steve Martin
Lee Marvin

James Mason
Walter Matthau
Jessie Matthews
Johnny Mathis
Michael Medved
Michael Medwin
George Melly
Yehudi Menuhin
Johnny Mercer
Ethel Merman
Bette Midler
Jonathan Miller
Lord Bernard Miles
Sarah Miles
Spike Milligan
Hayley Mills
Sir John Mills
Helen Mirren
Warren Mitchell
Cliff Mitchelmore
Robert Mitchum
Albert Modley
Monty Modlyn
Bob Monkhouse
Kelly Monteith
Marion Montgomery
Ron Moody
Dudley Moore
Patrick Moore
Roger Moore
Kenneth More
Eric Morecambe
Cliff Morgan
Robert Morley
Sheridan Morley
Desmond Morris
Johnny Morris
Harry Mortimer
John Mortimer
Ted Moult
Malcolm Muggeridge
Frank Muir
Arthur Mullard
The Muppets
Pete Murray

Vivien Neves
Anthony Newley
Nanette Newman
Derek Nimmo
Nina
David Niven
Denis Norden
Kim Novak
Trevor Nunn

Rudolf Nureyev

Edna O'Brien
Pat O'Brien
Des O'Connor
Mary O'Hara
Earl Okin
Tessie O'Shea
Peter O'Toole

Elaine Paige
Michael Palin
Lilli Palmer
Sir Peter Parker
Dolly Parton
Joe Pass
Luciano Pavarotti
Tom Paxton
Paco Pena
Itzhak Perlman
Valerie Perrine
Jon Pertwee
Oscar Peterson
Julian Pettifer
Sian Phillips
Ron Pickering
Harold Pinter
Erin Pizzey
Pat Phoenix
Paul Phoenix
Pointer Sisters
Enoch Powell
Robert Powell
Sandy Powell
Otto Preminger
André Previn
Alan Price
Vincent Price
Magnus Pyke

Suzi Quatro
Anthony Quinn

Anna Raeburn
Alan Randall
Esther Rantzen
Robin Ray
Claire Rayner
Ray Reardon
Al Read
Helen Reddy
Robert Redford
Chief Red Fox
Oliver Reed
Christopher Reeve

Beryl Reid
Jimmy Reid
Lee Remick
Zandra Rhodes
Tim Rice
Buddy Rich
Cliff Richard
Sir Ralph Richardson
Richiardi
Diana Rigg
Angela Rippon
Rachel Roberts
Fyfe Robertson
Harold Robbins
John Romer
Mickey Rooney
Annie Ross
Diana Ross
Rossie Ross
Demis Roussos
Dr A.L. Rowse
Arthur Rubinstein
Dr Robert Runcie
Willie Rushton

Andrew Sachs
Mort Sahl
Pierre Salinger
Telly Savalas
Jimmy Savile
Leo Sayer
Arthur Scargill
Arthur Schwartz
Sir Peter Scott
Ronnie Scott
Sir Harry Secombe
Peter Sellers
Lynn Seymour
Omar Sharif
William Shatner
Robert Shaw
George Shearing
Barry Sheene
Revd David Sheppard
Lord Shinwell
Phil Silvers
Paul Simon
Posy Simmonds
Donald Sinden
Peter Skellern

Wayne Sleep
Maggie Smith
Mel Smith
Harvey Smith
Jon Snow
Lord Snowdon
Lord Soper
Soraya
Johnny Speight
Mickey Spillane
Dame Freya Stark
Freddie Starr
Ringo Starr
Isla St Clair
Martin St James
Norman St John Stevas
Tommy Steele
Rod Steiger
Pamela Stephenson
Isaac Stern
Jackie Stewart
James Stewart
Richard Stilgoe
Meryl Streep
Elaine Stritch
Harry Stoneham
Lt Col George Styles
Eric Sykes
Donald Sutherland
Janet Suzman
Gloria Swanson

Jimmy Tarbuck
Jacques Tati
A.J.P. Taylor
Shirley Temple Black
Gwyn Thomas
Leslie Thomas
Terry-Thomas
Jeremy Thorpe
Christopher Timothy
Lily Tomlin
Barry Took
Mel Tormé
Pete Townsend
Polly Toynbee
Ben Travers
Lee Trevino
Tommy Trinder
Fred Trueman

Twiggy
Kenneth Tynan

Stanley Unwin
Peter Ustinov

Roger Vadim
Chad Varah
Frankie Vaughan
Robert Vaughan
Wynford Vaughan-Thomas
Ben Vereen
Gore Vidal
Eva von Rueber Staier

Max Wall
Ian Wallace
Marjorie Wallace
Wall Street Crash
Jack Warner
Dennis Waterman
Lyall Watson
John Wayne
Martie Webb
Andrew Lloyd Webber
Julian Lloyd Webber
Racquel Welch
Orson Welles
Sir Huw Wheldon
Alan Whicker
Toyah Wilcox
Andy Williams
Dorian Williams
Emlyn Williams
John Williams
Kenneth Williams
Shirley Williams
Michael Winner
Harold Wilson
Shelley Winters
Ernie Wise
Terry Wogan
Barbara Woodhouse
Joanne Woodward
Bill Wyman
Tammy Wynette

Mike Yarwood
Michael York
Jimmy Young

Mai Zetterling

ACKNOWLEDGEMENTS

The illustrations appear by kind permission of the following:

Godfrey Argent: Michael Parkinson photographs appearing on pages ii, 18, 37, 59, 81, 102, 146, 147, 169. *BBC Photographs*: Bette Midler 18, Robert Redford 19, Fred Astaire 36, Gene Kelly 36, Dame Margot Fonteyn 36, Twiggy 37, Muhammad Ali 59, Sir Alec Guinness 81, Ben Travers 81, Spike Milligan 124, Dr Henry Kissinger 147, Jonathan Miller 169. *Sten Rosenlund (Rex Features)*: John Cleese 18, Billy Connolly 18, James Cagney 19, Robert de Niro 19, Rudolf Nureyev 36, Michael Caine 37, Ingrid Bergman 58, Lilli Palmer 58, Sammy Davis Jnr 80, Mel Brooks 80, Warren Mitchell 80, Sir Ralph Richardson 81, Meryl Streep 102, Goldie Hawn 103, Bob Hope 124, Ken Dodd 124, Bernard Levin 125, Placido Domingo 125, Tim Rice 125, Anthony Burgess 146, Adam Faith 146, Dave Allen 146, Enoch Powell 147, Sir Les Patterson 168, Dame Edna Everage 168, Barry Humphries 168, George Melly 169, Clive James 169, Michael Parkinson 187. *David Edwards*: David Niven 37, Lauren Bacall 58, Dirk Bogarde 58, James Stewart 59, Trevor Howard 59, John Arlott 59, Peter Ustinov 80, Alistair Cook 102, Sir John Betjeman 102, Diana Rigg 103, Penelope Keith 103, Jimmy Tarbuck 124, Lord George-Brown 147. *International Artistes Representation*: Emu 187.